Pub 40°

~~2250~~

~~£12.95~~

(E)

£7 50

AR 100

The Recovery of the Modern

Architectural Review 1980–1995: Key Text and Critique

Butterworth Architecture
An imprint of Butterworth-Heinemann
Linacre House, Jordan Hill, Oxford OX2 8DP

A division of Reed Educational and Professional Publishing Ltd

A member of the Reed Elsevier plc Group
Oxford Boston Johannesburg
Melbourne New Delhi Singapore

First published 1996

© Emap Construct and Michael Spens 1996

Designed by Borja Goyarrola

British Library Cataloguing in Publication Data. A catalogue record for this book is available
from the British Library.

ISBN 0 7506 27891

Library of Congress Cataloguing in Publication Data. A catalogue record for this book is
available from the Library of Congress.

Printed and bound in Great Britain by The Bath Press, Bath

Butterworth
Architecture

Summerson Stirling Jencks Curtis Johnson
Van Eyck Graves Moore Bofill Terry Botta
Farrelly Price Kaplicky Cook Tschumi Hollein
Coop Himmelblau Baller Banham Rogers Best
Foster Spence Leplastrier St John Wilson
Leiviska Davey Hopkins Pawley Horden
Simpson Farrell Frampton Folonis Outram
Pallasmaa Gehry Ellis Nouvel Anderton
Gough Herron Dethier Craterre Blundell Jones
Behnisch Venturi Scott Brown Moore Buchanan
Aalto Piano Cruickshank Richter Ghirardo
Eisenman Anderson Koch McGuire YRM
Slessor Noero Davies Alsop Summerson
Stirling Jencks Curtis Van Eyck Farrelly Price

AR 100

The Recovery of the Modern

Architectural Review 1980–1995: Key Text and Critique

Edited by Michael Spens

The Recovery of the Modern

CONTENTS

Ron Herron, canopy over Imagination building, London 1989

The Death of Modernism.

By John Betjeman.

A SERIOUS comment on architecture must always be in the nature of a sermon. Today it is impossible to get away from buildings. Their importance increases with the disappearance of rural scenery. Rapidly every inhabitable part of the world is becoming industrialized, and communities which formerly possessed a creative art of their own, by coming into contact with the rest of the world, imbibe another culture—the culture of industrialization. Nor should we despair that there is no longer a city which is unexplored, no longer a country replete with eighteenth-century towns of mellow houses and spacious streets, nor even an island of medieval towers and fortresses that is not strung across with wires and scarred with tarmac roads. Only the swamps and thick tropical forests remain and on them it is impossible to build. We have prepared and planned the world beyond recognition, and can hardly be blamed for not turning our attention to the rubbish heap.

In England, with a brave pathos, many, though not all, of the older architects and speculative builders have followed only the mannerisms instead of the spirit of tradition and created an architecture like stage scenery. In the middle of this country of pylons, telegraph poles, factories and water towers, of moving vehicles whose shapes, never devised before, play as important a part in civic life as the stationary objects, they have deluded themselves that the link with tradition is the reproduction of the mere façade of the past. Hardly a villa rises without its half-timber, hardly a front door without its stained glass to hide the world. Hardly a monumental building is erected which is not masking some honest English face behind. On the ground floor the show is given away, for the feet of the honest person peep through. Palpably it would be impossible for that large acreage of shop window thinly divided by pilasters to support the weight of so many storeys of cosmopolitan masonry above, if the building were indeed the stone palace it pretends to be. No amount of skill will disguise the fact that it is a man in fancy dress; no bronze or mahogany devices increase the solidity of that ground floor and the thin pilasters. The truth will out, even when rustications are suspicious. This is a needless break with traditional architecture, as unnatural as it is pedantic, as superficial as the plaster work on Strawberry Hill. These architects and builders have bravely tried to keep to forms of the past, although their plans and materials demanded other proportions.

The revolting phrase " The Battle of the Styles," wherein architecture is now considered a fighting ground between old gentlemen who imitate the Parthenon and brilliant young men who create abstract designs, can only have been coined by the stupid extremists of either side. There is no battle for the intelligent artist. The older men gradually discard superfluities. The younger men do not ignore the necessary devices of the past. Both sides find their way slowly to the middle of the maze, whose magic centre is tradition.

What conflict there is, exists only between the principles of Gothic architecture and of the Renaissance. In the former the design is influenced by the construction; in the latter, the façade is designed and the rooms are fitted in behind it. It is therefore a Gothic revival to which the more sensible are tending.

In an extraordinary article which appeared in the October issue of THE ARCHITECTURAL REVIEW Mr. C. F. A. Voysey, one of the oldest of living architects, used an old-fashioned word " Gothic." He has probably been misunderstood by those whose minds are not yet rid of " period " taste. They will have taken him to mean by " Gothic," machicolations, and crockets, pierced hearts and artiness, which are but the trappings of medievalism.

Voysey means by Gothic the architecture of necessity. The Crystal Palace is Gothic, far more Gothic than the St. Pancras Hotel. " We must remember," he writes, " that this revolt against styleism and pursuit of utilitarianism was in the womb years before, and was the child of Science and the Prince Consort." The influence of Voysey has been felt all over the Continent and is just being noticed in England, while the more prolific Gilbert Scott has faded out of existence.

Gothic, in the sense that Voysey used it, was even put into practice in the early days of Strawberry Hill Gothic. Those silent country boxes, with their decent fittings and well-planned interiors, expressed the needs of the aristocratic eighteenth century. Inside and out they had become traditional, shorn of the gaudier eccentricities of contemporary architecture abroad. Later, when the pseudo-Gothic of the late nineteenth century was reasoned out of existence, traditional English domestic architecture, by Voysey, and, in a lesser degree, Lutyens, Dawber, and Baillie Scott, again emerged. From the present sightless mass of Greek, Roman, Tudor and Cubist, we are waiting for some monumental architecture to appear that will be fit to house our numberless offices and flats. It is an architecture for artists and not for scholars. There are new materials, a new social order, new proportions to be commanded, and the possibility of creating a new beauty which this generation must not be too stultified to see.

The word " modern " is becoming old-fashioned. It is used by one writer to describe the latest effort of the oldest old stager, by another, some building of Corbusier. Perhaps it were better to do away with it altogether and to discriminate traditional from what poses as such. And traditional architecture, while conscious of the claims of humanism, draws its vitality from the needs inherent in construction. This is the Gothic characteristic, and it is leading to the true Gothic Revival.

November 1931

AR Critique 1980 – 1995

INTRODUCTION

Michael Spens
March 1996

The Architectural Review *(AR) was founded on a committed Arts and Crafts podium, in November 1896, designated 'a magazine for the Architect, Archaeologist, Designer and Craftsman'. In the first issue, an article on the relative strengths of beams and pillars sits uneasily amongst material of a predominantly aesthetic nature. The cover price was 6d, Queen Victoria was on the throne and architects could survive without difficulty on a thousand pounds a year income. The editor, Henry Wilson, drew the cover himself, an Arts and Crafts man to the core.*

But, this inauspicious beginning could not disguise a certain lack of focus: the journal's wide-ranging premise could not disguise this weakness in a decade of issues. Such editorial looseness was not redeemed for many years, although the intelligent layman, essential in a viable readership, could be reassured that an early leader firmly defined Architecture as an applied art, as opposed to a fine art. There was strong competition in this respect from the Studio *magazine, founded just three years earlier and already holding a largely prosperous,* fin-de-siècle *readership in its thrall, not only in Britain but throughout northern and central Europe.*

C.F.A. Voysey, The Pastures, Rutland 1901

Has architecture gone mad in Germany? The determination of the new school of architects in Germany to turn their backs upon all the good work done in past ages and strike out a new line of advance for themselves is producing results so extraordinary as to call for some words of protest.
Volume 8, July 1900

Such was a typical attitude from the island fortress, expressed by the editor. By contrast, in the pages of the Studio, *concurrently, the work of Charles Rennie Macintosh and I.M. Baillie Scott was beginning to link up with just such European developments. From 1900, Wasmuth's famous journal,* The Architecture of the Twentieth Century, *published in three languages in the period to 1910 (German only 1910–1914), assiduously documented the new tendencies. From this journal, not the AR, Frank Lloyd Wright became aware of such developments and was inspired to make his first visit to Europe. In the post-war decade after 1918, there was no significant change with the AR but, during this same period, the* Studio *magazine sank into a regrettable decline. Even the influential and scholarly work of Hermann Muthesius in 1905,* Das Englische Haus *(The English House), and the subsequent recognition overseas that a significant architecture of this time was emergent in Britain in the hands of the English Free School of Philip Webb, George Devey, went unheeded in subsequent years.*

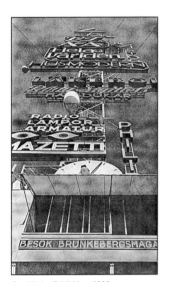

Stockholm Exhibition, 1930

P. Morton Shand's AR issue on the Stockholm Exhibition (1930) demonstrated that the new decade represented a profound change of emphasis for the AR and this effectively marked the basis for the AR as we recognise it today. This was acknowledged, subtly if perversely, in a remarkable article written by John Betjeman, entitled (as if to shock) 'The Death of Modernism' (November 1931). This was itself a response to the article by C.F.A. Voysey in the preceding issue and, indeed, may have been triggered by Shand's article on Behrens (September 1930) and the presence in the pages in July 1930 of Raymond McGrath's work. As Betjeman said, 'the word modern is becoming old fashioned'. There was evident confusion amongst the readership as to what to approve or not to approve.

DETAILS OF RUSSIAN TASTE

Michael Spens

11

Speer, family house, Heidelberg 1932

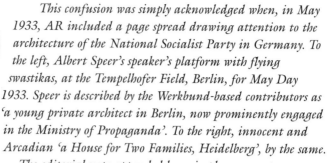

This confusion was simply acknowledged when, in May 1933, AR included a page spread drawing attention to the architecture of the National Socialist Party in Germany. To the left, Albert Speer's speaker's platform with flying swastikas, at the Tempelhofer Field, Berlin, for May Day 1933. Speer is described by the Werkbund-based contributors as 'a young private architect in Berlin, now prominently engaged in the Ministry of Propaganda'. To the right, innocent and Arcadian 'a House for Two Families, Heidelberg', by the same. The editorial note appended here simply comments:

We offer no comment on the pictures that follow. They are presented as information, merely. Some readers of the AR will greet them with delight, others will regret them. Both kinds must judge for themselves. We have heard it said that the Nazi school of architects are setting up our current English architecture as an example. That is probably true.

J.M. Richards, editor of AR 1937–72

Hubert de Cronin Hastings was the driving force behind the improvement in AR from the end of the 1920s and had a keen journalistic sensibility, as well as a healthy scepticism about AR's readership. Percy Hastings, his father, had helped to found the AR in 1896 as chairman of the Architectural Press. When J.M. Richards joined the firm in 1933, he was surprised to find that Hubert de Cronin Hastings was not, in fact, editing the flagship AR. This post was occupied then by Christian Barman. Richards became assistant editor to Hastings on the Architects Journal, *AR's stablemate. Barman soon left and Hastings took over both magazines. John Betjeman had been AR's assistant editor and, only when he also left in 1935, did Richards join the AR as assistant editor. Two years later, he was editor.*

Throughout the 1930s, change was rapid and exhilarating with the AR. The contributions of P. Morton Shand, such as that on the new Viipuri Library in Finland, by Alvar Aalto, were impor-

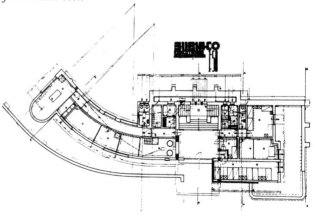

Pilichuwski, SUBIACO ground floor plan, Kremsmünster 1931

tant; here was a milestone in the shift of modernist sensibilities away from the mechanistic standpoint advocated by CIAM and Le Corbusier at the time, towards a more natural design philosophy. Shand had been quick to spot this.

But, there was a wide range of coverage, names to become famous and names once glimpsed and now all but forgotten. The work of Pilichuwski in Austria is forgotten, however talented, while that of Connell Ward and Lucas in England is barely secure. By the end of the 1930s, AR's reputation was established as the leading English language architec-

tural review, with subscribers and readers world-wide. Clearly, the initial Arts and Crafts standpoint of the founding magazine had laid the basis for a sustained commitment to the 'new' for the next half century.

In the post-war years, Hastings and Richards assumed unassailable control and the magazine's reputation for scholarship grew. Pevsner's contributions were now joined by those of the young Colin Rowe, who in 1947 made his historic debut with The Mathematics of the Ideal Villa. *The comparison of Palladio's Villa Foscari* (The Malcontenta) *of 1550–60, with the 1927 villa at Garches by Le Corbusier, extended the historical*

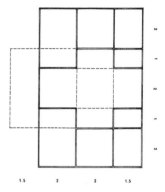

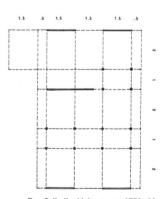

Top: Palladio, Malcontenta, 1550–60
Bottom: Le Corbusier, Garches 1927

meaning of Modernism, showing that the proportional systems were similar. Subsequent Rowe articles, such as 'Mannerism and Modern Architecture' (1950) and 'Chicago Frame' (1956), further enlarged the scope of contemporary research deeper into the background issues confronting many architects in the firing line. P. Reyner Banham contributed soon after and James Stirling published (1956) 'Ronchamp: Le Corbusier's Chapel and the Crisis of Rationalism'. Rowe, Banham and Stirling opened up new perspectives for AR readers at this time, exploring aspects of developing Modernism that touched upon the mannerist traditions of the late Renaissance as transmuted into the preoccupations and solutions of contemporary designers. Such depth of analysis broke out for a whole generation of students. Banham's article on the New Brutalism was a further milestone. Inside an architectural avant-garde, *Banham was able to clarify the essential thinking behind such buildings as the Hunstanton School by Peter and Alison Smithson and the University of Leicester Engineering Laboratory by James*

Gordon Cullen, 1951

Stirling and James Gowan. In 1961, Colin Rowe returned to contribute what has been probably his most brilliant single-building critique, 'Dominican Monastery of La Tourette, Eveux-sur-Arbresle, Lyon'.

Le Corbusier's late masterpiece is set into an ingenious framework of critical analysis, which demonstrates that in a master's hands, a block is not, manifestly not, a block as we have come to expect but a unity of opposing values normally kept apart.

Following close on the heels of Philip Johnson's review of the Smithsons' Hunstanton School (disavowed by the architects), AR had established new levels of critique unsurpassed in any other architectural magazine. Such prowess was by now accompanied by Gordon Cullen's highly innovative urban design articles, illustrated by his superb draughtsmanship, which altered the whole manner in which the composition of the built environment was viewed.

By the late 1970s, however, the pace had slowed. Economic factors played a significant part in the battle for subscriptions. In February 1979, AR was steered by a triumvirate of editors, Lance Wright, Colin Boyne and J.C.G. Hastings. There were notable high points, such as the juxtaposition of John Winter's review of Utzon's Bagsvaerd church with the Riola chapel in Italy by Aalto, review by Peter Hoffer (March 1979). Colin St John Wilson wrote on Scharoun (April 1979), Judi Loach on Da Carlo at Urbino (April 1979) and Peter Blundell Jones on Scharoun's State Library, Berlin (June 1979). In July 1979, that author, now a long-standing contributor, produced a perceptive report of Wilson's lecture at

14

Jorn Utzon, Bagsvaerd church, Copenhagen 1976

the Alvar Aalto Symposium, Jyväskyla, describing the existence of 'the Other Tradition of Modernism'. The key representatives recognised in this re-appraisal of pre-war developments were listed as Aalto, Scharoun, Haring, Duiker and Melnikov. History was already under revision. Here, in November 1979, J.M. Richards edited his swan song, a magisterial Special Issue on the 1930s.

At this key juncture, significantly in retrospect, Peter Davey joined the masthead as Executive Editor (Buildings). Presumably, it was 'hands-off' anything that did not quite fall into that category. The issue was Davey's perfect cue, however. The triumvirate of editors withdrew gratefully and elegantly to the wings. Not before time, a new mood emerged in the corridors and by the copying machine in Queen Anne's Gate. And this was true in the country as a whole. Uncertainties remained widespread but new arbiters of style and creativity were 'on the wing'. Old economic uncertainties had been binned by the party in power and a new generation at last had its moment. In truth, the changes ran back a few months. In AR, however, the messengers of PostModernism were challenged from the beginning to prove their argument. Certain alternative architectural journals lost their way at this time, misconstruing a cultural shift of mood for an historic turning point, which it was not, as subsequent events have proved. In Queen Anne's Gate, they sat tight but threw open the windows.

Into the 1980s

This compilation of selected texts from AR over the past fifteen years could, if history had turned out otherwise, have proffered intimations of an architecture reflecting the condition of a world on the brink of disaster, the product of a new anschluss from East to West, perhaps, or even one where civilisation had to all intents and purposes collapsed, where cryptic texts, tapes or disks would circulate amongst the few survivors inhabiting catacombs below the urban wasteland. Or, alternatively, consumerism had so conflated society that these contributors would collectively amuse cult audiences in a lament for a lost and distant Modernism. For, over this period, dwarfing the cultural emissions of the PostModernist cultural gurus, the contemporary zeitgeist had, in any case, been transformed by momentous and historic changes, from Perestroika on to Glasnost; inferring, perhaps, 'the end of history and the last man', as the advocates of a continuous and uninterrupted development of conventional liberal democracy would have us believe. And, we have been more than fortunate, not that this apparent festschrift can in any way be seen as part of the preliminaries to a new golden age. For to look back from the mid-1990s now is to recognise the extent to which, in surviving postmodern cultures, traditional criteria in architectural critique were found not less but more in demand, in an age of confusion. An inherent paradox within PostModernist criticism was the

Michael Spens

The Bride of Denmark

*survival of an unwarranted determinism;
having abandoned dialectical discourse,
the prophets, forecasting the demise of
modern architecture, professed the
nihilism of a thousand free choices, yet
excluded the continuity of principles.*

*Paradoxically too, in this late mil-
lennial second 'dissolution of the monas-
teries', the centres of learning and critique
and related organs that
have survived have been those which have sustained their
editorial freedom. In the 1980s, economic growth had
seemed an inevitable and continuous programme, conglom-
erate expansion in the free space of international capital.
Knowledge is power, as an epithet, could then have been
reversed to mean power is knowledge or, at least, its control.
Prestige being the vanity of power, organs of knowledge
began to boost the balance sheet. Survival for AR meant
adaptation to new economic systems, embracing new information technologies and exploiting these for greater circulation benefits. How did AR achieve this, operating to a
disadvantage within a highly conservative national cultural enclave? And, not only to survive in this radical change
of mode but also sustain the level of critique at the same
time as improving the quality of colour origination, for
more accurate building exposition; while sustaining too the
essential line drawings to scale (abandoned for the most
part by others)?*

Reyner Banham in the '60s

*In 1980, in Queen Anne's Gate, as has been observed
above, change had come lately. The long-standing and venerable Architectural Press book list was soon to be separated
from its journals and sold off by new, if temporary, owners
and has since, of course, continued to prosper as before. The
distinguished proprietor and enthusiast, H. de C. Hastings,
had gone by 1985 and the Bride of Denmark was soon to be
bailed up (the celebrated below-stairs watering hole that,
like a deep well, had sustained generations of architects and critics in a
lubricated cocoon of generic cultural memory). After this change of proprietor, there came a general air of insecurity, as if an ancient family seat
was forced to take on paying guests or, worse still, to be pillaged by guest
workers. And, soon enough, by 1986, that proprietorship was over. Peter
Davey had taken over as editor in full in 1983. This volume is, of course, a
resumé of one saga in the set of wider circumstances over the past twenty*

years that led to the survival and recovery of Modernism, as a continuity of culture whereby the 'new' is considered to be more of a preoccupation creatively than what had already been. Modernism has never denied the presence and value of the past. As Peter Reyner Banham said (Memoirs of a Survivor: The New Brutalism *p. 135*):

> From the time of Berlage and even before that, the idea of morality of design has been one of the main motives for serious innovation in modern architecture.

H. de C. Hastings

It is indeed the concept that architecture takes account of morality that has continually recharged modern design. This principle was not abandoned by Davey in the hubris of the early 1980s. The close relationship with the Architects Journal, *AR's weekly stablemate, always ensured that the AR team remained close to the logistics and mechanics of actual building construction. They have remained totally distinctive and separate from each other, however. Two members of the same family, their particular relationship has continued after the present proprietors took over in 1992 to be vital to each. This volume is a* festschrift *of the good ship AR and all who have sailed in her, not least of the skipper* per se, *who steered her away from the rocks of the archipelago of uncertain values in the early 1980s. A clear course could be plotted, since by good luck and good fortune, there was no evident tendency by the proprietors to create, in the 1980s, a publisher-driven, commercially-ephemeral advertising vessel. There was a similar approach with the new ownership in 1990, backed up by an infusion of new technology with improved origination, web-press printing and the further flexibility which that permits.*

Such is the background against which editorial policies have been free to develop during the years 1980 to 1995, through three separate owner-ships, under one principal editor.

Arguably, the celebration of a centenary of publication should comprise a resumé of the full century. In the case of AR, it is rather more relevant, given the particular history of the journal and also the broader development of architecture in this century,

Stirling and Gowan, engineering laboratory, Leicester University 1963

17

to examine the story's key feature, that of survival and regeneration over the past decade and a half. It has seemed more relevant to offer key examples from this period of the exceptional and sustained level of critique displayed by AR's contributors during the latest editorship: in such a way that this is recognisable as more than just ephemeral but of cultural significance to the overall historical and theoretical development of architecture through a tempestuous, insidious and, potentially, debilitating period of global culture.

It was evident that AR was a critical force that could turn events in the early 1980s, as will be shown here. But, it has taken a full decade since for it to be clear that PostModernism, in the peculiarly regressive architectural variant, fell short of the cultural achievement the PostModern period has revealed in other fields, such as music, literature, painting or, for that matter, land art. PoMo, as the architectural variant was soon dubbed, was, in architecture, a debased currency. AR, thus, had chosen its ground carefully in the early 1980s on the basis of enquiry, scholarship and a healthy internationalism.

At this point, one has to glance upwards to the bridge of the good ship and catch the skipper's quizzical eye between the sideburns. (In fact, pursuing the marine analogy, it is more a case of looking down the conning tower of a submarine). The AR profile has been low-drawn, there has been no anxious pursuit of national press promotions or media slots. Davey has submerged and surfaced at any one of three dozen locations around the globe. He keeps readers guessing as to which theme next. Running low and running quiet, he is there when and where no one expects. That is why emphatically this most British of journals is also the most obviously international of its European rivals in global and cultural reach.

In part, of course, this quality is the result of improved information technology. But, this could only work if Davey, as editor, was prepared to move around the hemispheres himself. The period of Richards' editorship, for example, was one of great success for AR but international ambitions and affiliations were inevitably inhibited and curtailed by slow travel, creating a certain fixity of critical gaze, which would be wholly anachronistic in the 1990s. AR in the past decade has thus emerged, by contrast, as a genuinely planetary organ of architectural description and critique. This is not the spurious ersatz *internationalism of airline, cookery or travel magazines. It is the gradually grown revision of text and pictures, as critique, over a decade and a half, across the world, on a basis of sound scholarship by means of both traditional and contemporary criteria.*

The underlying principle governing the future survival of AR then was, clearly, Davey's decision to stay the Modernist course, believing that the canon of this already substantial historical tradition, half a century later, was still capable of sound future growth. It cannot be said that this went unprompted but a more ephemeral spirit would have opted for the blandishments of PoMo, as happened elsewhere. The publishers are to be credited too, in each appropriate period, for resisting the short-term appeal of design and fashion trends and their ephemeral economic appeal.

A second key principle emerged, best defined here as range and elevation. Davey's specific policy of fostering and developing new regional–global contacts, exploring new work far afield, recognising regional differences, as well as parallels, began to pay off soon in terms of breadth of readership interest, as well as providing new 'modernisms', as opposed to the cloning of PostModernist historical references. Buildings were never viewed for their superficialities, their gestures or rhetoric alone; before this, the consistency of syntax and technique was always appraised in plan, elevation and sectional range. Inevitably, a growing diversity of buildings came to be displayed in the AR pages. The flipside, International PoMo, a derivative architectural vocabulary, claimed its legitimacy from a small group of critics and offered a debased vernacular historicism, a trendy and jokey permissiveness, which denied the actuality of technology, claiming to replace 'mechanistic' modernism as the spirit of the age. The age, it is true, was postmodern and still is. But, unlike music, literature or film, architecture's variant, PoMo, differed. There was no recognisable body of inherently evolved theory, purely a useful (if in a jam) Thesaurus of usable and replaceable visual quotations.

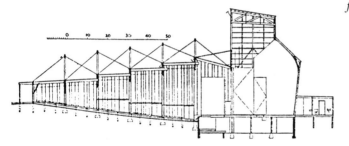

Saarinen, Swanson and Saarinen, Stockbridge Opera House, Massachusetts c1955

Over a decade or more, AR's regionalism has flourished. From India to Spain, from Australia to Finland. Halfway through a teaching programme at two Australian universities, I myself had direct experience of Davey's mobility. On an invited research trip to Finland, I realised that AR was simultaneously recording the dramatic new developments in Sydney and Melbourne (1986), while at the same time covering the 'New Spirit' in Finland. Davey had been to both places first and got it right. AR's awareness that in Finland a particularly sophisticated continuation of the Modernist canon (the work of Pallasmaa, Leiviska and of Gullichsen) had outflanked a lively provincial variant of PoMo was timely and astute. Likewise, AR's explorations of East Coast, Middle and West Coast US tendencies could form a valuable historical documentation of its own.

Michael Spens

The third strain in AR's direction has been less obvious, more diffuse, yet is possibly the more original venture. A growing interest in landscape and ecology as related to architecture. This has been subtly mixed with a traditionally English awareness of the provenance of the suburb, as both a home-grown phenomenon, stemming from Ebenezer Howard and the Garden City movement, as well as a world-wide development of car-borne society as transformed from agrarian roots. It is against the vast canvas as a concept such as that of Raymond Williams in 'The City and the Country' (1984), where global divisions are so definable, that Davey's preoccupation gains significance. There is revealed a certain, separate, specific focusing on such subjects, running through the 200 issues of this period like a green filament. Such articles as E.M. Farrelly's survey of Geoffrey Jellicoe, or Charles Jencks' intimate and poetic description of a Californian sanctuary (p34), or Davey's summary of Peter Aldington's housing and garden infill at Turn End as garden landscape, or Caroline Constant's study of Le Corbusier's landscape designs at Chandigarh, are typical of this. The latter is a timeless classic in landscape critique, comparable in power and clarity of perception to Colin Rowe's 'La Tourette'.

AR is, of course, implicitly a review of built works, as well as projects for construction. For that reason, a balance has hopefully been struck

20

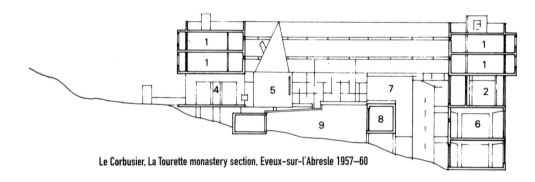

Le Corbusier, La Tourette monastery section, Eveux-sur-l'Abresle 1957–60

in this survey between building critique and historical, theoretical or polemical texts. In Davey's book, they are wholly complementary. The building reviews form a primary structure, so as to say, in the grid. Such critique by Peter Buchanan (Deputy Editor through the main years) is typified by his review of the Essen Opera House by Alvar Aalto (p202), by Peter Blundell Jones (eg. Hysolar by Behnisch), by Martin Pawley in his review of the Imagination Building by Ron Herron (p158), by Colin St John Wilson (buildings by Leiviska and Gullichsen on p90), by William Curtis (AT&T building), as well as those by Davey himself (Lords Cricket Stand by Michael Hopkins) are normative of a wide and distinguished

*range. These are balanced here by a selection of the shorter, no less percep-
tive, reviews, such as of Eisenman (Ghirardo), Alsop at Marseilles (Colin
Davies (p249)), Rick Le Plastrier in Sydney (Rory Spence (p84)). Architects are often best judged by their peers, in Davey's view. Such is a small
selection from the steady flow of edited texts.*

*There have, at certain key stages in the period, been certain care-
fully planned, major theme issues. These appear to have been generated by
a perceived external necessity for a re-appraisal or a shift of direction.
After all, Davey made his debut in just such an event, Richards' 30s issue
(1979), which was a confident recall of Modernist achievement, being
Richards' own swan song. The New Spirit by Farrelly was just such a
major intervention. This was a remarkably enlightened, prescient and
immaculately timed (1986) compilation of articles, which sought to define
a point in time, when the mood of the 1980s turned in architecture, with
lasting effects. Davey stood aside and the issue appeared in August, when
advertising space is less in demand. The new generation broke cover, with
electric effect. Prominent in this famous issue was an early review of the
work of Coop Himmelblau (a Viennese group notoriously hard to pin
down), which was accompanied by contributions from Günther Domenig
and Itsuko Hasegawa. If AR had not taken the initiative at this point in
time, the confusion of PoMo would not have been spiked until possibly a
decade later. To the wizards of High-Tech, PoMo advocates had no answer.
Yet, Davey seemed effectively to use High-Tech itself (the works of Rogers,
Foster and Hopkins) as a stalking-horse for the recovery of Modernism, the
architecture of the new, now revised and reborn. All was gift-wrapped in
an evocative and perceptive resumé of source material by Peter Cook
('Architecture is on the Wing Again'). The correspondence columns
buzzed excitedly with the news in the next issue... except for 'disgusted' of
Johannesburg. Adequate confirmation had gone into circulation that the
New Spirit was not just a phantom but a* Zeitgeist *in the making.*

*In August 1986, AR visibly exuded an increasingly confident note
editorially and this equated well with the achievements by British architects at the time. The Hong Kong Shanghai Bank by Foster had been celebrated with a special issue in April. And then, in October, Rogers' Lloyds
building in the City of London got the full treatment again.*

*1986 was also the year when Robert Venturi and Denise Scott-
Brown won the competition for the extension of the National Gallery, London, relegating the entry of Stirling and Wilford. This was a setback for
advocates of the New Spirit. The attitude was admirably summed up in
the consummate perspective drawing submitted in Piranesian style by Stirling and Wilford. The site was presented as an abandoned plateau, complete with the precipitate rear half of an equestrian statue.*

Michael Spens

If the New Spirit was a carefully aimed Exocet missile at the PoMo lines, Philip Johnson's AT&T Building in New York had already become, in critical terms, a 'Towering Inferno'. Reviewed critically in August 1984, it was effectively satirised and dismantled in theory by Peter Reyner Banham and William Curtis. The late 1980s now saw a well-organised distribution of scholarship and technical expertise in AR; a new series of issues exhibited an evenly-balanced dispersal of building critique, with case studies set out on a raft of important and searching theoretical texts. Martin Pawley's article 'Technology Transfer' (p102), Juhani Pallasmaa's 'Tradition and Modernity' (p132) and Peter Blundell Jones' findings on 'Aperspective Space' (p174) are noteworthy. This theoretical argument and discourse was further founded upon a solid base of in-depth historical studies, such as Kenneth Frampton on the Usonian Legacy (p118), Slapeta on the elusive but vital Czech Organic and Lebherz on Schinkel.

This positivism in Davey's hands remained open ended, however. It was possible to celebrate the a priori brilliance of John Outram's graphic presentation of the environment of St Paul's as it might be (p127), without begging any value judgement as to its buildability.

From 1990

The new decade of 1990 began with Martin Pawley's review of Ron Herron's Imagination masterpiece in Central London. An important editorial 'Public Face and Public Place', analysed the legacy of the arguments of the 60s and 70s and the degree to which these were now redundant. The atavistic Classicism, propounded with great charm both by Leon and Robert Krier and Aldo Rossi, was now itself of the past. In November 1982, AR had blazoned, as a case in point at the time, Michael Graves' Portland building, which seemed to show that architecture as advertising could work. Economic simplicism was set up to prove its viability as a useful product in the PostModern age. Davey lambasted the inherent pastiche anew, this time with no holds barred. The debilitating effects of all this fun and games were then presented in terms of the now completed National Gallery extension.

Rowan Moore's devastating critique of the National Gallery extension did the rest. Venturi was parodied as 'transfixed, like a rabbit in a headlight, by respect for architectural history'. This was a satire on snapshot tourism. And, the building was to emerge from the scaffolding, in effect, as a series of witty (or embarrassing) architectural snaps. The significance here of this editorial of 1990 and its adjacent building critique is a telling example of the constructive deployment by an editor of negative critique. This is a practice very rarely applied by Davey in the decade and a half of his editorship. Here, as with AT&T, it was used to positive effect.

When a giant of contemporary architecture died accidentally, AR demonstrated a sense of history, as well as sharing with the architectural community world-wide a profound sense of loss. The special issue in memory of Sir James Stirling provided a standpoint from which to test the lesser achievements of the past decade. Stirling inevitably was an eminence that figured occasionally, yet powerfully, in the background of time, occasionally demonstrating his genius in the works illustrated in AR over the years. The best writers had been enlisted to do justice to his works, initially, Summerson and Colquhoun; Baker and Wilson, Maxwell, plus Davey himself.

A journal in the best hands develops a community of common interest in discourse. AR has never been exclusive, apart from the necessity of grammar, and today it shows a confident approach to the new architecture it presents. The context is essentially post-conflict. Modernism as a canon was not destroyed and exists again in recurring pluralities. If this was the mission of P. Morton Shand and J.M. Richards in the 1930s, through Davey it has been sustained and enriched as never before.

The story is of one mission accomplished in the past fifteen years, namely the Recovery of the Modern and the revitalisation of contemporary architecture; and of one now underway, for an architectural discourse of benign relativism within a truly world-wide constituency, running well into the XXI century. Without the solid foundation of critique now established, that would be harder. At least it looks now achievable.

The criteria employed in the selection of these 33 articles over fifteen years have been normative in essence —to seek out those texts which overall indicate the normal expectation per issue of a highly selective readership. At the same time it was necessary to encapsulate something of the progression of issues, controversies and ideas burgeoning forward in these pages in the most accurate and relevant way. Obviously certain issues stand higher than others but in each one published there was always something memorable. It is such memory traces that history tends to eliminate. AR's centenary year is best celebrated for posterity by delaying that inevitable process, in providing briefly here, in simple format, this palimpsest of key text and critique, which by the written word collectively represents an important enterprise tried and won, – the recovery of the Modern – the progress of a revision which continues as today, unabated.

M. S. June 1996

Michael Spens

What is it that Stirling has brought to architecture and released to loud and prolonged applause, into what seems to have been an aching void?

Is it that Venice greatest Renaissance architect, Mauro Coducci, 'belonged to the Modern Movement (to use... most to the... Posts, ... or Pests?

Is Modernist maxim 'Less is more' too restrictive, and might be replaced by the PostModern proverb 'a few things are enough'. The result of looking at PostModernism is that it makes you hate the real thing If architecture is the true quality of modernity, does the client? The repressive thing... AT&T encapsulates the glibness of... architectural style... some precedent

1980

What is it that Stirling has brought to architecture and released to loud and prolonged applause, into what seems to have been an aching void?

Is it that Venice greatest Renaissance architect, Mauro Coducci, 'belonged to the Modern Movement (to use... and most to the... ats, Posts, and other Pests

Perhaps the Modernist maxim 'Less is More' is too restrictive, and might be replaced by the PostModern proverb 'a few things are enough' The result of looking at PostModernism is that it makes you hate the real thing If architecture is the true quality of modernity, does the client? What is it that Stirling has brought

1986

released to loud and prolonged applause, into what seems to have been

Is it that Venice greatest Renaissance architect, Mauro Coducci, 'bel

Vitruvius Ludens

THEORY

John Summerson

March 1983

Of James Stirling's originality there is no doubt, nor of his fame. His fame, at 56, is especially remarkable when we consider that not more than three or four of his executed buildings (not one of them a cathedral or a vice-regal palace) is likely to be familiar to more than a tiny section of the population. I have seen only three. There are photographs galore, published designs for unbuilt projects, many thousands of descriptive words and, more significantly, the architect's own idiosyncratic drawings, exhibited and published. On this evidence, assessments of a sort can, I hope, be made and an answer attempted to the question: what is it Stirling has brought to architecture and released, to loud and prolonged applause, into what seems to have been an aching void?

The answer must depend on how we view the architectural history of the past 30 or 40 years. Looking through my old lecture files I find that in 1945 or thereabouts I wrote this: 'In 1957, one rather weary generation will be building as it would like to have built in 1927–37, but desire always rides ahead of practice and the springing thought of 1957 will be different.' I went on to predict that a new generation would have 'to study the overtones of architecture and the geometrical discipline of space as space; to learn not only to use space but to play with space'. The important word is 'play'. Before 1957 'modern' architecture has a dogged seriousness of aim inherited from the '20s. At the back of the architec-

Siemens AG, Munich 1979 (model)

tural mind was progress towards architecture rather than the making of architecture. Around 1960 that seriousness began to crumble. Brutalism was its last bastion. By 1970 it had gone to dust. Permissiveness had mined it; reaction swept up the ideological debris with haughty disgust. The Modern Movement was dead and we were left with its ghost. Or so it was said. But it was not true. The real change in the '60s was not so much the dilapidation of the Modern but its transfiguration. If the living movement had become a bore, the movement vanishing into limbo became subtly, irresistibly attractive—it was becoming historic.

Taste for vanished styles has always been the grand elixir of architecture, and, in our accelerating century, the more recent the style's recession the more exciting the new thing to be made of it. Such is the state of affairs at the moment, and I see Stirling as the architect who, more than any other in this country, or perhaps anywhere, has identified himself with this transfiguration, turned the old seriousness back to front and re-engaged it as play. He is essentially a great player – even something of a gambler – and architect cast more distinctly than most in the role of *homo ludens*.

Architecture as play is a familiar idea. There have been the classic Lutyens 'high game' and Le Corbusier's *'jeu savant, correct et magnifique'*, etc. But I would not compare Stirling's game with either. A more seductive analogue is Richard Norman Shaw, the Shaw of New Zealand chambers and Lowther Lodge, where he turned the moralising, moribund church-bound Gothic Revival inside out and shockingly recreated it as monstrously ingenious 'Queen Anne' play. Blomfield said of New Zealand Chambers that ten years after it was built, people were still wondering whether it was a work of genius. People still wonder about Stirling's Cambridge History Library, built in 1966, and for the same reasons.

My first experience of Stirling was a fleeting visit to his and Gowan's engineering building at Leicester in 1968. I took against it because I saw it as old-style functionalism grossly overdone. The jutting Melnikov-style lecture theatres exposing their tilted bottoms, the exaggerated articulation of everything, and the vanity of trying to make positives out of things intrinsically negative. I was, however, wrong. I was judging something as exhibitionism which was really the acting-out of a deeply felt and studied thesis. Revisiting Leicester, I found the 'play' idea always coming uppermost. Here was an architect declaiming, fashioning a 'one off' rhetoric out of material anything but rhetorical; it was brilliant, arrogant play.

The Cambridge History Library, first seen in 1972, made a different impact. Here was the same rational articulation but 'over-play' had been censored and the energy behind it diverted into a redoubtable, daunting monument; enigmatic (which way round is it?); a crystal fort with a shiny brick rampart (a touch of Sant' Elia here); something of a factory, something of a conservatory. The reading room,

Florey building, Queen's College, Oxford 1966–71

John Summerson

Arcade, Derby Town Centre, 1970

sheltered under a monster technological awning in the angle of the two wings, whose inner flanks the awning cruelly deface, I found difficult to take. I still do. But the building as a whole strikes me with something like awe.

Much more recently I saw that disturbing object, the Florey building of Queen's College, Oxford; different again and perhaps something of a turning point, as I shall suggest later. But before we go any further let me try to be a little more explicit about what I think is going on in those designs. I find this impossible to express without dragging back the word 'functionalism'. Stirling is a functionalist; and let me qualify this by adding that he is a *deep* functionalist. 'Functionalism' I take to have two quite separate meanings. There is technological functionalism and there is social functionalism. Stirling involves himself deeply with both and has brought them together in various ways. But they are different. Technological functionalism signifies the intrusion into architecture of materials, methods and prepared artefacts more commonly associated with industrial than with architectural practice. The criterion is performance and a building wholly conceived in such terms is engineering or, is modulated with a consistent sensibility, 'High-Tech'. Social functionalism is another thing and the one real and imperishable legacy of the Modern Movement. Social functionalism works at various levels. At its least profound it signifies the extraction from the programme of its categorical requirements and their reinterpretation in a continuously harmonious self-expressive totality. The result may be more adequate or less, more eloquent or less, within any given typological classification. But social functionalism can have deeper implications. It can mean not only the mastery of the brief in rational terms and its sensitive projection as a structure but a fusing of those terms into a monogramatic complex which is a unique symbol of the building's function in its particular time and place. This is *deep* functionalism. It has passed the point where the image of appropriateness has crystallised in the architect's mind: the tables are turned against the functional quest and from 'image' we pass to 'imagery'. The rational test no longer holds.

'Imagery' is a word more often used in the discussion of works of literature than those of architecture but is a word we can hardly do without in discussing Stirling's work from 1970 onwards. The stuff of his imagery is, in part, what one must call his 'personal style', of which the following are the more obvious symptoms: a predilection for slanting glass surfaces, splayed brickwork; hard-bent curves (like bending a poker) but also free undulations round rigid elements; platforms or podia. All these are explicitly exposed in Stirling's axonometric projections of his designs (often, following Choisy, from under the building, a mole's eye view), drawings which have something of the character of abstract graphic art, even a faintly mesmeric effect, like *objets trouvés*. They are often taken as the quintessential Stirling and, in a limited sense, they are.

Absorbing and overriding these personal insignia are the larger images which in his most recent work carry associational and metaphoric meaning. It is impossible to generalise about these because they come different every time, which I am inclined to take as

Engineering School, Leicester University, 1959–63

confirmation of their 'poetic' integrity. The Florey building at Oxford (1966–71) was, I think, the first in which imagery was concentrated in one emphatic formal statement; the glazed embrasure leaning on its concrete trestles, a mocking but not unkind metaphor for contemplative academical enclosure. There are harsh and uncomfortable elements in Florey but it is a powerful piece of 'deep' functionalism.

After Florey we find Stirling's imagery beginning to absorb Neo-Classical ideas. The Neo-Classical has been the 'natural' alternative to the Modern ever since Gropius stated the converse in his Werkbund building of 1914. The Modern Movement sprang from Neo-Classical soil and to the soil it is always liable to return, and return it does in Stirling's work, though less as a recessional than an inspirational act. Some of his most striking imagery brings the Neo-Classical into play. The housing at Runcorn has a Gandhi-like primitivism; Ledoux's industrial Utopia is invoked in the huge Siemens AG design (1969) and in 1970 comes the astonishing Derby Town Centre project, where a Burlington Arcade, more than twice natural height, wraps itself round the end of a Roman amphitheatre to create an urban symbol as dramatic as John Wood's performances at Bath. The museum projects for Düsseldorf and Cologne marry deep functional analysis to topography and history; the designs are like relief maps of ancient sites. The Bayer AG centre at Monheim (1978) is laid out to a radical plan of defiantly Beaux-Arts provenance, but with an administrative tower-block shooting up from the U-shape for which Stirling seems to have a special reference. With the building of the Clore Wing of the Tate Gallery, Stirling will at last come before the British public on a conspicuous and prestigious metropolitan site. What is he to say? The design is, once again, hard to relate to any of the others—a new gamble of Stirling the player. The play here is as much with styles as with forms: bare-bone frame *versus* coursed ashlar, Bauhaus

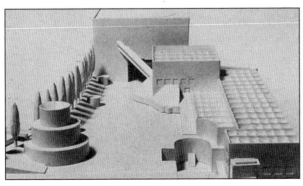

Wallraf-Richartz Museum, Cologne 1975

John Summerson

versus Neo-Classical, with a trick or two from Art Deco, all tied up with a cornice borrowed from the old building and then illuminated by a blinding flash of surrealism (Look! no pediment) in the spirit of Magritte. It is exciting in a fashionable art-conscious way—a deliberate comment, I suspect, on the function of an art gallery, and somebody is sure to say that. Stirling here is making a concession to the New Thing. I doubt that. The deep slot of space in which the stair climbs is provocative in the true Stirling fashion and if the design as a whole seems less powerful than Leicester or Cambridge or Oxford; it promises to be a fairly devastating interpretation of the programme. Stirling is a player—an architect who takes what seem to be uncalculated risks. He has, as Norman Shaw had, a marvellous streak of comic inventiveness which has to be rigorously (and inventively) corrected. That above all is what, I suspect, makes him the magnetic figure he is in the contemporary scene.

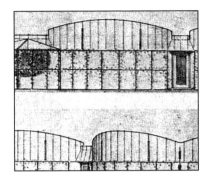

New Amsterdam School

BUILDING CRITIQUE
Church, Doventer
Communal facilities building, Noordwijkke

by Aldo Van Eyck

Aldo Van Eyck

June 1984

Moluccan Church

The site is the usual kind of space-residue planners tend to leave between suburban row houses. Since one can't really build in non-space or next to the kind of architecture that generally goes with it, I imagine this unfortunate space-residue to be solidified and the required built spaces scooped out of the solid.

Since the traditional church going ceremony begins at home some time before the actual service as an intimate family affair, getting to the church – the way there – is regarded as a formal prelude to entry (extended entry).

With the kind of negative – or inverted – space notion in mind, I did away, so to speak, with all exterior walls by having roses grow up thin trellis work screens right round the church (and looping out and over the entrance porches) —30 cm away from the walls. Roses with a similar colour will also feature in the surrounding garden linking it to the building.

Inside the exterior perimeter walls will be adorned all over with traditional Moluccan (pre-Christian) motifs adapted in the flat from decorated bamboo

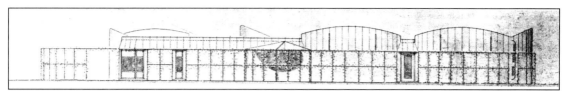

Moluccan Church, elevation

tubes. These motifs are distinctly vegetative. So with ample light from above, the church interior should echo the exterior. Both sides will be 'outside' with the difference all the more marked by the partial congruity. By thus 'veiling' the walls on both sides they will be subdued – partially annihilated – which is what planned non-space asks for.

A propos the interior: I did not want one single point of focus (pulpit) to hold people's attention involuntarily fixed, but, instead, preferred to allow it to shift (wander) away and back. Hence multi-directional axiality and symmetry (multiple symmetry rather than asymmetry).

Why, oh why is it that Venice's greatest Renaissance architect – Mauro Coducci – 'belongs' to the Modern Movement (to us) and not to the Rats, posts and other Pests? If I were to build Santa Marie Formosa again, and I would love to, I'd be an innovator, but not an eclectic! It was in my mind all the time (not that there is any direct comparison): that entry from the side; that postponed, at no point frozen, fluid symmetry—a balance gracefully sustained. The space breathes evenly; spreads out and away; whilst beautifully contained, it opens up all the time, because one's attention is kept agreeably on the move in various directions—especially diagonally across. This brings about a sense of articulated depth—a view beyond and transparency. It is in fact a multi-directional central space with a wonderfully subdued axis and, although wide and clear and open, it still eludes definition. Mauro's touch. There's an architect for you.

ESTEC Noordwijk

Since the present ESTEC building complex has no recognisable 'core', the idea of locating the new facilities, all of which have a more or less communal function, half way down the main internal traffic artery on the ground and first floor above it, seemed to be the right one. The

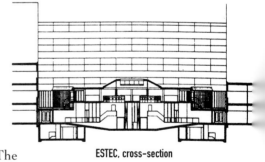

ESTEC, cross-section

curvilinear interior and exterior walls made a compact linear organisation possible, whilst sustaining a fluent spatial development and easy movement from place to place along the stem. The formal contrast *vis à vis* the existing structure is, of course international.

As to construction and materials, only the two large conference meeting spaces will have walls of masonry within a concrete structural frame. The entire rest of the building, i.e. restaurant, kitchen and reading room-library superstructure, will be of steel painted white with natural-colour timber window and door frames. The curved hollow walls – also of plywood – will be given a different rather active colour on the inside.

From the restaurant doors open into glass-covered exterior terraces and gardens. Inside, it will provide a considerable variety of places from which to choose. Some are oriented towards the outside others are more introvert. Curved screens will articulate the length of the restaurant and coffee-bar corners.

The roof is the new building's most exposed feature. It holds the sequence of spaces together; transmits light from above; collects and channels rainwater; and, seen from the upper doors of the existing building, will represent from the outside what occurs below it. Thus the roofing material should be aesthetically pleasing as well as durable (against a sea wind). Hence we propose copper sheet.

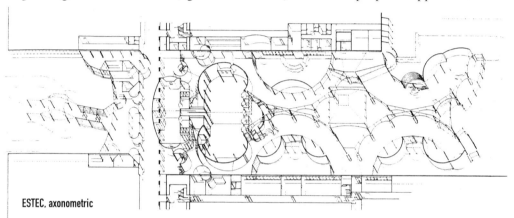

ESTEC, axonometric

33

In general, representational extravagance has been avoided. It is the construction, the proportions and the straightforward unadorned use of a small number of sound materials that will convey what we believe to be the right atmosphere. Elegance without unnecessary luxury.

An Endecagonic Proposal

The circular columns down the centre of the restaurant are made up of 11 steel tubes in a ring between two steel discs. The columns are squat: height 1.90 m, diameter 0.80 m, the distance between them 6.80 m. Inside they will contain heating and ventilation ducts. The hollow panels between the tubes are of thin plywood bent into position.

Endecagons have angles which correspond to those of the building's principal construction. Moreover, like pentagons and heptagons they have sides opposite corners, so that in the case of the columns, there is always a corner tube to terminate and hold a partition or wall.

We like our endecagons; they keep telling us that relevant – accurate – solutions often hide in what is less obvious or still unusual, but is waiting to become straightforward through application.

Fewer quotes, but rather more endecagonic enquiry will indeed be useful!

House of Elements in Rustic Canyon

BUILDING CRITIQUE
Private Gardens, Los Angeles
by Charles Jencks and Maggie Keswick

Charles Jencks
June 1984

Rustic Canyon, on the edge of Los Angeles, is something of a magical area, where myth has been confirmed by reality. It has everything one would associate with its name: ranches, Indian remains going back 3000 years, a rushing stream and waterfall. It also has the closest 'jungle' to downtown Los Angeles and the most extraordinary collection of eucalyptus trees in America. These were planted by a tobacco millionaire Abbott Kinney who, in establishing the nation's first experimental forestry station here in the 1890s, wanted to discover what would grow well and fast; nearly everything did, including 72 species of eucalyptus. Today the tip of the lower mesa in Rustic Canyon, the site of this house, is full of towering specimens: eucalyptus, acacia and pine trees, many over 100 ft tall.

To build a house in such a contrived wilderness is necessarily to enter into the myth. Some houses in the area exaggerate their rusticity with a proliferation

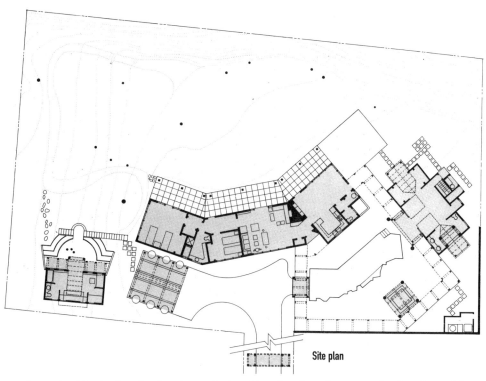

Site plan

of rough shingle that looks almost hairy, like thatch; others emphasise the quirky woodbutcher's aesthetic. Only Modernist designers such as Richard Neutra and Harwell Hamilton Hart have designed in an International Style, oblivious to the rusticity, and even they dramatise the step slope and view. The *genius loci* is so strong that it overpowers everything—including our own desire to develop a symbolic architecture.

Our answer, when we decided to add to the existing 1950 ranch house, was to compose a series of various-sized but basically simple pavilions over the site. Together they add up to the 'Elemental House', its four main pavilions based on the four Classical elements – Earth, Air, Water and Fire – as well as a series of elemental themes. All of these are intended to give an iconographic meaning to architecture – significance before aesthetics – since one of the problems with modern architecture is its mindless elegance.

The most obvious architectural theme is the rustic elemental style suggested by the ranch: wood framing, two-by-fours, telephone poles and vertical wood sliding, stained (not painted) in 8 or 10 different colours. Played against this background are the growing vines and trees, sculpture, painting, lettering, ornament and an 'Order' of repeated columns and walls. It's not the Tuscan or Doric Order, although it's close in spirit. Rather it's the fundamental 'LA Order' which one sees on builder's sheds all over Los Angeles. Happily, its Y-shape also forms part of the letters of L and A, by a stretch of the imagination, if you turn your head and see the top tilted to the right. This motif is taken up in much of the stripe ornament and made obvious on the two columns inside what was designated as the 'Air' pavilion.

Charles Jencks

The Y-shape Order has become fashionable in architectural circles today: one sees it in the work of Leon Krier and Michael Graves, but it really has a very old provenance going back to the Renaissance, Cesare Cesariano and much earlier. Yet it is a direct expression in wood of elemental structural forces. For such reasons it became the ordering motif for the 'corral', the pergola which surrounds the active area around the swimming pool.

Another aspect of the elemental style is in the plans of the individual pavilions. A Greek cross is used for the Air pavilion, a Latin one for what became known as the Hermitage. Working with the architect Robert Yudell we first produced a design in two main parts; it proved too expensive and

The Terra Gate

since we were often in England during the building process, we wanted forms that could be constructed without difficulty. The two simple cross plans are both economic and symbolic, intended to signify a primitive sacral quality, the idea that house and church share a common sheltering ritualistic role. This has been analysed by John Summerson in his essay 'Heavenly Mansions'. Here in Rustic Canyon, what Summerson calls the 'aedicule' or 'little house' has become the repeated motif all the site: as well as the main pavilions there are entrance aediculae, little houses over the bath tubs and jacuzzi, and over each gate and face of the additions.

The idea is to be elemental and obvious, even dumb; in an archetypal sense. We wanted to build the most primitive, rustic idea possible: the four square aediculae canonised by Vitruvius and Abbè Laugier. They termed it the primitive hut – the fundamental building block of architecture – and for that reason it's eminently suited to Rustic Canyon.

The six aediculae and the old ranch house make up a 'village' on the site. This relates to another idea which currently interests architects as far apart as Philip Johnson and Frank Gehry: that a village layout is excellent for breaking down large buildings, and that it affords variety and surprise. Here each of the six aediculae could be conceived of as an independent chapel or temple: disposed informally, but internally geometric and rigorous.

The notion that there are only four basic elements (instead of the current 104) is as anachronistic as the Greek idea of the atom: that unit of matter which is not subdividable. In the case of the elemental House, the four elements are used dramatically to create a game of Hunt the Symbol. The abstract Greek signs first appear (very small) in the gatehouse pavilion; although perhaps only an ancient Greek would recognise their meaning. After parking in the open garage, one walks through the second gateway, now explicitly identified with its own symbol, the words 'Terra Terra Terra' and the image of a mountain eroded and split in half. For in California there is no 'Terra Firma': the San Andreas fault gives the earth a meaning which is the opposite of stable, its traditional quality. And if here in California Earth portends earthquake, what of the remaining three elements? clearly 'Aqua', Water, has its mud slides; Fire, 'Ignis', its canyon fires, and 'Aer' its pollution. Thus the four Californian elements of the elemental house reverse their traditional meanings.

As images, however, they were partly based on engravings from an eighteenth-century version of Ripa's 'Iconology'. These images, along with descriptions, were sent to the architect Charles Moore, the sculptor Timothy Woodman and the painter Sidney Hurwitz who have all transformed Ripa's imagery to suit the situation. Charles Moore layered his representation of 'Aqua' to fit within that already layered aedicule of the Water pavilion and Timothy Woodman changed the colour of Ripa's description of 'Aer': instead of having white, cloud-like robes, she has a green and multi-coloured costume because this dress suits the greens and oranges and terracottas of Tina Beebe's colour-scheme for the whole corral. In each case a traditional programme is being reinterpreted, not followed strictly as an eighteenth-century artist might have done. And yet these par-

tial limitations have perhaps helped their work. The artist, like the architect, may have his freedom actually increased by conventional programmes: whereas modern architecture has failed to provide either the perennial subjects of building – nature, the human image, social realism – or the traditional code within which to represent them.

The four, or 104, elements may not be quite the most signifi-

The LA columns

cant cosmic code which architecture can represent, but they have a modest role here that, I believe, is marginally more interesting than representing the flange of an I-beam—which is how Mies van der Rohe is reputed to have spent his last 20 years. They also share a fundamental geometric principle which is fundamental to architecture: the concept of 'fourness'. Almost every room we inhabit has four walls, and the omnipresence of four in nature, and culture, is represented in many examples as the tetramorph, from the four Evangelists to the Four Seasons.

In the 'Aer' pavilion Sidney Hurwitz's watercolours of the Four Elements accentuate the four corners of the room, just as the four light sconces set up these divisions. They are also related geometrically to the decorative stencilling of the

Four Elements on the walls, and thus constitute an overall syntactic system, or Order. Taken together with the sliding doors they point up the cross-axis, the Classical symmetry, indeed the Greek cross plan, and help prepare one for the final understanding of the code. This is reached, finally, in the bathroom where according to a literary convention, all is meant to become explicit. Here stencilled on the window shade and spelled out in rustic lettering are the signs and words together: those who have played Hunt the Symbol, from the first gate, are ultimately rewarded.

Of all the organising themes that are represented, the most obvious concerns California. It is pictured in different ways including the images of the tree. Probably the

The Aer Pavilion

most archetypal tree of California is the palm, and fortunately for our purpose a perfectly proportioned one exists in the back garden. It has a strong vertical stem which culminates in a nice bushy fountain of palm leaves. This form is stylised as an arch above symmetrical steps and used in different guises throughout the house—first on the 'Terra' gate.

The arch/step motif itself, like the 'Serliona' or Palladian window, is very flexible as an image and a functional shape. It can stretch both horizontally and vertically to encompass a variety of openings, while symbolically it looks not only like a palm but also like a face. There is a suggestion of eyes just below the curved arch, or 'forehead'. I have modestly called this the 'Jencksiana' since using it and developing it several years ago, believing that, like Sourly, no architectural critic should ever die before naming a motif after himself. In the Elemental House the motif is used as an organising element in nine different transformations, so that one keeps returning to the same, but different, form: first it's the palm tree, then a gate window that frames the swimming pool. After that one on the 'Aer' pavilion it becomes the overall façade, or face of 'Aer' itself. While inside it is used as the void in the dresser drawers. Then it is turned into lighting sconce and, in the old house, transformed onto the surround for a chair and the base for a table and light. Finally, in the Hermitage pavilion it's used in the floor plan of the terrace. There were probably more uses of the form, but typically, after doing a motif to death, one loses count.

Originally, in the first designs, it played an organising role. One was to enter the face of the 'Aer' pavilion, walk upstairs, cross a bridge, open the balcony door, open a balcony gate, then step onto the 'tongue' of the face – a diving board – and plunge into the pool. What a clear, Californian idea! alas it has been confounded by a Californian reality, the necessity for earthquake reinforcement around the pavilion. And this has meant the tongue, and route, do not exist.

But the pool exists and it is in the shape of California. Red pool lights carefully identify Los Angeles and Eureka, blue lights signify San Diego and San Francisco. Death valley is a white light, Sacramento is a black hole in the middle of the pool. California is also symbolised quite elaborately in the furniture designed for the old house. The main side table has a thick round log cut to show rings. These represent quite naturally the sun's glow as well as each year's growth. Further signs of California in the silhouette of the table include a strawberry and a palm tree, but there are also conflicting, or multiple cues, which provide another set of readings which it would take too long to enumerate.

The living room of the old house really is the centre of California images, summarised in the paintings of Roland Coate. They portray archetypal notions of life in 'Kuruvunga', a strange name given to the area by the Indians several centuries ago. It means the 'place where we are in the sun'. Coate captures this sun in his paintings: clear, sharp light, the bleaching purity of the whites, blues and sand colours.

The final organising idea which we sought sort to represent, and which pulls all of this together, is of a controlled walk through the sequence of two poems by John Milton: 'L'Allegro' and 'Il Penseroso'. These two poems were suggested by Maggie Keswick as a natural response to the site and its duality. As one can see from the air, to the planting plan , the site off the road is a kind of oasis located on the tip of a mesa overlooking the stream 200 ft below. The drama of the place is obvious. You enter into a semi-public area, paved with brick – the active side of the house where swimming and playing children make noise, and then you move through to the contemplative side – the tree-shaded natural side. Here is a archetypal-Californian-staggering-view, especially at sunset, when the eucalyptus throw long shadows across the lawn. In the distance are cliffs opposite. From this 180 degree panorama, one has a view over the noisy stream, at full rush in the Spring and occasional buildings below, including those by Frank Gehry. In the evening there is the incessant burping of bull frogs, broken by the occasional barking of the Canyon's Canine Security System. Except for this, all is seclusion, peace, relaxation—a true oasis, a secluded wilderness as far from downtown Los Angeles as you can get.

The two Milton poems give form to the active ('L'Allegro') and passive ('Il Penseroso') sides of the old house, and a route follows line by line, verse by verse, flower by flower through the site, travelling back and forth in several loops. It's quite true that all of the proper flowers and trees have not yet been planted, and some lines of Milton haven't quite grown to full maturity, but in at least two parts the gardens are somewhat complete.

Charles Jencks

Just in front of the 'Terra' gate can be seen the lines 11–16 of 'L'Allegro':

'But come, thou goddess fair and free,
In Heaven yclept Euphrosyne,
And by men heart-easing Mirth;
Whom lovely Venus, at a birth,
With two sister Graces more,
To ivy-crowned Bacchus bore:'

In California, the Three Graces must obviously be the three Californian fruit trees – lemon, orange and tangerine – and just as clearly, the most exotic of these, the tangerine, is the subject of 'L'Allegro': Mirth. West of the old house lies the over-abundant nature of Il Penseroso, where the Tibouchina plant's purple petals and velvet leaves stand for the positive side of Melancholy. In his portrait of her, David Remfrey painted a trail of these petals on the ground behind Melancholy as she walks, a painting that brings the poem 'Il Penseroso' to an end in the guest-house 'Hermitage' (lines 155–160).

This is where Milton imagined himself retiring

'To walk the studios cloister's pale,
And love the high embowered roof,
With antique pillars massy-proof,
And storied windows richly dight,
Casting a dim religious light.'

His 'peaceful hermitage' is indeed isolated and restful in our garden. However, although the light may be described as 'religious', falling as it does through 'gothic' windows, it is hardly 'dim'. Bright light streams all over the tiny bedroom through the giant skylight directly above the bed. It forms a kind of aedicule, or baldachino, above his bed, whose religious meanings are further underlined by its shape and decoration. The bedstead's ornament, as elsewhere, consists of the Y-shape motif incised with silver-grey tape, and voids that set up axes and cross axes. Throughout this small pavilion sacred themes are used – the three dimensional window cross over the door, the tabernacle window, the 'cathedral chair' – but they are formed in a domestic manner to once again emphasise the relation to the house to the church.

In Milton's poem the 'peaceful hermitage' is characteristic as a 'mossy cell' where the poet can enjoy the 'pleasures' of 'Melancholy' — that is the enjoyment of contemplation rather than depressions. In a sense these have two views of Melancholy: the positive creative force of the poet and the dark, saturnine side.

A symbolic bathroom

It is this last which starts the first poem, 'L'Allegro':

'Hence, loathed Melancholy,
Of Cerberus and blackest Midnight born
In Stygian cave forlorn,
Mongst horrid shapes, and shrieks and
sights unholy!'

Clearly all this blackness had to be represented, along with the 'shrieks', and where better than in the garage? It is finally the temple-garage, with its green-black cylinders, that connects the two ends of the poems and the two aspects of Melancholy. Here rustic lettering spells out the message, again a mixed message of an ideal realm – the temple with round chapels – and the practical space which every Los Angeles house must have—storage for garbage, automobiles and tools ('horrid shapes... and sights unholy'). A great deal of time was spent designing the Mid-Tech Order of green and black bolts, the black in various shades to symbolise all those qualities of depression which Milton enumerates and then finally banishes in the two poems.

Although the Elemental House and garden are still not complete, and will take many years to fill out, it has taught us the pleasures of following a few ideas as the basis for design. The most successful parts were those where architecture, art and symbol come together—the 'Aqua' Pavilion. The most disappointing occurred when we couldn't follow the programme. It seems to me that in a symbolic architecture, or allegorical design, one must be parsimonious with themes, and stick to them in spirit, if not in letter. Otherwise design becomes riotous, the game of architecture too permissive. Perhaps the Modernist maxim 'less is more' is too restrictive and might be replaced by the PostModern proverb—'a few themes are enough'. In any case, as the scheme grows, ages, changes hands in the future, different owners may enjoy sticking to the rules that have been established: they give more freedom than restriction.

Charles Jencks

On Appearing to be Classical

THEORY

William Curtis

August 1984

Macaronic Classicism

The difference between authentic synthesis and superficial pastiche seems pertinent to PostModern Classicism about which so much has been said and written in recent years. Charles Jencks, the chief salesman of the movement (some would say its fabricator), has argued that it offers a new *'lingua franca'* – he dare not say 'International Style'[1] – but every effort is also made to show how sensitive the style is to particular regions and urban settings. Social concern is addressed through the device of 'double-coding' so that ordinary people as well as architectural elites can relish the displays of wit. Ornament is valued for its decorative potential and because it allows 'representation': there is even the suggestion that buildings covered in references must mean more than those *not* so covered. PostModern Classicism does not single out any particular moment in the Classical tradition for revival; on the contrary it revels in the promiscuous possibilities offered by modern air travel and coloured slides: all periods are game and a technique of bricolage is often used to stick the references together. This is

Arata Isozaki, Fujimi Country Club, 1976

sometimes discussed in terms of social pluralism, but the result often smacks of a merely academic formalism. An observation made by Viollet le Duc over a century ago might well apply:

'… A certain school has lately arisen based upon the principle of composing a new architecture out of all the good features of these former styles; a dangerous error because a macaronic style cannot be a new style. It may indicate some knowledge and a certain amount of skill and spirit… but it can never be the manifestation of a principle or an idea.'[2]

PostModern Classicists contrast present-day *savoir faire* and inclusiveness to the supposed mundaneness and univalence of Modernism. It is against their rules to illustrate anything done since 1914 unless it be a monstrous housing scheme or skyscraper which everyone agrees is horrible. But comparative bits and pieces of Mannerist and Baroque Italy are highly prized as if they were talismans which could somehow transfer their qualities to the present. The implication is that lost arts are being refound after a dark age. But there is a limit to the number of times that works can be justified for having overthrown recent taboos. If a design claims special status because of a new orientation towards tradition let

Philip Johnson, AT&T skyscraper, New York 1979 (model)

it be judged in the long perspective of tradition rather than via the myopia of fashion. If a kind of Classicism is intended, let it be judged alongside past Classicism, including those outstanding buildings of the past few decades that have rested in part on Classical principles: Le Corbusier as well as Ledoux should stand witness.

Columns and Skyscrapers

Recent American attempts at an overt Classicism search for rhetoric. Rightly or wrongly, the reductivism of modern architecture is blamed for lack of meaning. The mission is to save the American city from an excess of industrial standardisation and the abstract glassbox. The Prognosis is in the use of metaphors and historical associations: the Italian past is regarded as a repository of architectural and urbanistic answers. Classicism has a clean pedigree in America: there are no Fascist stains. The lineage contains the civic efforts of the Beaux Arts as well as Thomas Jefferson's belief that Rome and France in the right mixture were apt for the new republic. Classicism, reduced to a commercial veneer, or a Pop sign, can somehow be absorbed by these lofty credentials.

Since so much fuss was made about Philip Johnson's AT&T when the model was first revealed and since it is now on the point of completion, the building is an appropriate starting point. Five years ago the model was discussed as a rejection of the monolithic slab formula that had begun to dominate every American skyline. Johnson's critique included reassertion of entrance, base, middle and top. Of course Mies and Johnson had both attempted to endow the Seagram building and plaza with latent Classical qualities of symmetry, repose and nobility, but this was within the steel and glass vocabulary. Johnson now sought a less mute and less subtle Classicism including the Serliana reference at the base, and the 'Tallboy' pediment at the top. The building was clad in a restrained veneer of stone and its vertical piers were adjusted towards the boundaries to reinforce the corners. Much of this was well within the bounds of Johnson's personal stylistic evolution in the previous 20 years, but the media (with a little help from the architect) jumped onto the piece as a complete break with Modernism. Actually the building was more reasonable than revolutionary, being a blend of Sullivan's late nineteenth century definition of the skyscraper as essentially tripartite, an idea of both Classical and natural inspiration (base, shaft, capital; feet, body, head; roots, trunk, branches)[3]; and of the handling of vertical piers in such 1920s Neo-Gothic schemes as the Chicago Tribune Building by Hood & Howells. Thus AT&T took its place with a lineage of skyscrapers emphasising verticality as a primary feature of the type.

Ironically Johnson has remained too restricted by his own version of the Modernist straitjacket, and is not Classical enough. A difficulty of skyscraper design is maintaining unity and human scale when seen close to or far away. Mouldings and protrusions have their uses to introduce multiple rhythms and a certain relief and texture. The base of the new building has presence at the street level, but from the avenue the top just fades away without sufficient termination of the sort that some species of cornice might have provided. The middle level has a deadness and blandness of character traceable to the feeble distinction between horizontal and vertical planes. Sullivan handled this area with distinction in the Wainwright Building (1895) with the help of vertical brick beading and terracotta ornament; these were not used extraneously but as means to accentuate the visual forces of the design and to give unified expression to the building's idea. The Sullivan solution possesses that sense of repose, proportion and tactile strength that one associates with the harmonious resolution of visual load and support in the truly Classical work; a harmony that works within each storey or for the façade as a whole (eg the Coliseum, the Palazzo Rucellai). It is what Geoffrey Scott had in mind when he discussed 'coherence' and stated: 'Architecture studies not structure in itself but the effect of structure on the human spirit'[4]. At AT&T the lower piers on either side of the arch have an uncomfortable thinness, while in the building as a whole there seems to be hesitation between the notion of sculpting voids from a block and the notion of accentuating a frame; there is an overriding flatness.

Well-groomed in granite but shallow in expression, AT&T is like an upwardly mobile executive who has picked up a veneer of patrician pretension.

There is a sniff of vulgarity that some might associate with the rather obvious show of prestige and others might designate 'High Camp'. Johnson has proclaimed that there are no rules, that one must take everything from everybody; that there are no faiths worth entertaining, only 'currents in the air'[5]. So an agnostic indulgence in the 'freedom' of fashion is proposed. But chic historical reference lacks symbolic substance —and without depth of content a work of true formal power becomes impossible. The pose of the dandy aesthete is linked to cynicism; moral convictions are regarded as tiresome, pointless or impossible. But one lesson that the history of Classicism has to teach is that the peaks of expression have occurred when significant content is given a significant form. It can at least be said that the expressive thinness of AT&T encapsulates the glibness of Johnson's amoral stance with some precision.

Michael Graves, Portland Public Services Building, 1979–1982

The Decorated Box

Michael Graves' Public Services Building in Portland (1979–83), another protagonist in tilting matches of opinion, has been promoted for reasserting the façade as a public, rhetorical device, referring to some very ordinary Classical buildings nearby, and invoking the tripartite order. Opponents have compared it to a jukebox and an oversized Christmas parcel. Despite the contextualist rhetoric they say that it sticks out like a sore thumb. The 'Classicism' is obviously highly idiosyncratic. It values the clash of scales and fragmented devices: the giant wedge of the keystone, the vertical 'fluting' and horizontal 'rustication', the highly abstracted pediments and aedicules are handled with a dissonance that one hopes was deliberate. It is no surprise that the term 'Mannerism' has been used, except that Mannerism requires some preexisting and appreciated norms and rules of appropriateness if the distortions are to achieve their point. Profound Mannerist works like the Palazzo del Tè by Romano possess an armature of harmony and unity of theme over which the naughty play with Classical grammar occurrs; a courtly and knowledgeable élite was assumed as an audience. But these days nobody cares much whether you drop a keystone or two. If this precocity has an audience, it is certainly not in the streets of Portland, but in the magazine section of the library at Princeton, Harvard or Yale. The populist pitch of PostModern is surely a masquerade.

Venturi & Rauch, 'Ironic Column', Allen Art Museum, Oberlin 1973–76

Graves' acquisition of Ledoux's *architecture parlante*, of Pompeiian wall paintings, of Schinkelisms and even of Rossiisms over the past few years has had a painful self-consciousness about it. What has emerged is a bizarre personal style which courts the grotesque and the primitive. The sensibility is perhaps at its most effective in drawings and paintings because there one can perceive the various transformations and permutations of private themes occurring. But seen in real light Graves' buildings have a flat, lifeless, unrelieved character, like billboards that have been dolled up with cultural graffiti. They remind one that the new Classicism has still to establish its craft if architectural ideas are to find an appropriate life in the society of building materials.

John Soane, Dulwich Art Gallery, 1811, entrance

Pop Mannerism

The Piazza d'Italia in New Orleans (1976–1983 approx) by Charles Moore, has been set up as an exemplum of PostModern Classicism on the grounds that it rests on 'three basic justifications for choosing a style; or mixing them, as the case may be: the context that the building fits into, the character of the particular functions which must be enhanced by style and the taste culture of the inhabitants'.[6] The approach from Poydras Street is heralded by a vaguely temple-like portico with crude concrete columns surmounted by a metal truss system masquerading as a pediment. This dreary and off-hand piece of Classical slang is the preamble to a sequence of gaudily-clad architectural one-liners: the map of Italy built up in relief with Sicily at the heart of the bull's eye; the rows of screens with their ill-proportioned arches and Pop Art capitals; the death masks of Charles Moore spraying water; and, at the other end, the Lafayette Arch, a top heavy concoction combining tubular fluting, a bulky reminiscence of a Florentine masonry arch, and Italian flag stripes about where there might be an entablature. Just what it is about the urban setting that is being respected remains unclear after a number of visits day and night and in all weathers, especially since the most worthwhile neighbours – the row of façades on Lafayette Street – are violently bullied by the heavy-handed bulk of the Lafayette Arch in a way recalling the illmannered urbanistic behaviour of various Brutalist creations of the 1960s. The celebration of 'Italianness' implied by the map, the flag details and the pile-up of columns reeks of the sort of jovial sneering that might conceivably make a polystyrene water melon patch to celebrate the 'taste culture' of Southern rural blacks.[7]

Through a Longer Historical Lens

Perhaps there is more to cultural interpretation in architecture than the embroidery of ethnic stereotypes.

This is to assess the Piazza d' Italia by criteria custom-made to fit it. Scrutinising Moore's jolly Falstaffian Classicism through a longer historical lens it is the lack of a controlling order that is most striking. Because the columns and arches are so feeble, the jokes never achieve the status of true wit (such as in Michelangelo, or Vanbrugh, or Lutyens or Le Corbusier). Much recent Pop Mannerism in the USA has used cute games with imagery to mask the lack of any real content. Lutyens' stricture never seemed more relevant:

'You cannot play originality with the Orders. They have to be so well digested that there is nothing but essence left. When right they are curiously lovely...unalterable as plant forms. The perfection of the Order is far nearer Nature than anything produced on impulse or accident wise.'[8]

Columns for the People

Overt use of Classical Orders encounters more political, moral and aesthetic taboos in Europe than in America. Some still think of storm troopers when they see columns. Tight economic conditions do not encourage whimsy, unless it is on paper or in the odd TV studio. Besides, the past is longer and weightier than in America; the antique Classical inheritance is present in fact as well as in imagination. The prospect of trying to compete with Palladio, or Ledoux, or Hawksmoor on their own territory is daunting. You do not put up a Piazza d' Italia when the Trevi fountain is just down the road. But the Venice Biennale of 1980, under the banner 'The Presence of the Past', suggested that the overt exploration of Classicism was not exclusively American property.

Hans Hollein has shown himself capable of a suave and glitzy historicism of some wit and control; Ricardo Bofill has pre-empted international attention with grandiose gestures close to Paris; and James Stirling has continued to straddle trans-Atlantic fashions with cunning, skill and the occasional pediment. Among the most interesting probes into the Classical tradition have been those attempted by Ungers, the Kriers, Rossi and the Ticinese group, notably Botta: architects who have been concerned with the abstraction of traditional lessons in bold, simple forms.

Bofill and the Taller de Arquitectura had already begun to explore a vocabulary suggesting an eerie monumentality in their housing schemes of 10 years ago. In Les Arcades du Lac and at Marne la Vallée an attempt has been made to evoke the Classical language in plan (grand axes, dominant symmetries, circles, squares) in typologies (viaducts, theatres, circuses, triumphal arches, palaces) and in the façades through the gigantic mimicry in concrete of columns, pilasters, rusticated bases, triglyphs, pediments, attics and mouldings. Bofill could claim an honorable pedigree in providing a Baroque Palace for the people in Fourier's Phalanstere which had also inspired Le Corbusier's *Unité* and *á redent* housing. Bofill like Le Corbusier argues that the individual example should be seen as a *démonstration-type* portending a desirable form of city for the future. The full implications of this are a little hard to grasp as one comes across the huge bulk of the 'Theatre' and 'Palacio de Abraxas' stranded together in a half-formed and vacuous overflow district off an autoroute to the east of Paris. Evidently the inward-turned configuration of the Theatre is supposed to supply an iconic public place ('public realm' in buzz terminology) linked to the evermore private areas further up the buildings by vestibules and streets in the air. To dissuade you from thinking that you are dealing with Team Ten street decks there are symmetrical

Ricardo Bofill, 'Palacio', Marne la Valée

stairs linking upper street levels, Pompeiian-red rusticated concrete surfaces and little plastic notices bearing the names and dates of such luminaries of the Classical tradition as Ledoux and Boullée. Evidently Marne la Vallée is yet another critique of the free-standing tower block in the open park; the park is back inside the block. Much of the ingenuity of the scheme lies in the interlocking together of a variety of standard apartment types within the rather rigid edges that the architect has set himself. The building as a whole does have the support of an ethos of habitation:

'The exercise showed us that it was possible to build symbols (theatres, temples, triumphal arches, etc) which in the future could be transformed into habitable communal spaces... that it was important to be able to use the vocabulary and elements or architecture of the past and to bring these within the reach of the whole society...' [9]

How easy symbolism has become. You want a symbol? Open up a history book and find one and if you need a little functional justification then 'typology' can come to the rescue: communal space equals theatre: grand public residence equals palace. Some people toss around keystones; others prefer Colossea.

Rather than symbols this facile approach to typology manipulates signs — signs that give only the longest distant echo of a previous meaning and which are only lightly re-charged with content. The danger is skin deep instant history very close to 'kitsch' in which appropriateness is superseded by a facile replication of type. Both Wood at Bath and Aalto at Otaniemi used Classical theatre architecture as an inspiration but they transformed their prototypes to infuse them with new meanings appropriate to site programme and culture. Marne La Vallée would be more convincing if it were an appetising and well-scaled environment. As it is, the worthy-sounding intentions are expressed in a Fellini-esque stage-set of oppressive monumentality gratuitously clad in mockeries of the Classical grammar. The place conveys the impression of a smart marketing trick designed to lure prospective inhabitants away from the true city into a suburban commuter silo. Alongside it the Marseilles Unité d'Habitation looks positively delicate!

Bofill, like Johnson, is much less of a Classicist than perhaps he would like to be: mouldings, profiles and columns have a lifeless and wooden character quite at odds with the fluidity, grace and unity achieved in many a Château façade within 30 miles of Paris. Some difficulties perhaps stem from technique: joints in the concrete of primary volumes set in motion an 'ornamental' system that speaks a different language from that of the intended ornament; mouldings, capitals and rustication are extremely blunt. The architect has fallen between the stools of a language he controlled well but did not like and a language that he may admire but cannot control.

Ironical, Representational and Ambiguous

Some argue that arbitrariness of signs is inescapable in an electronic age in which the manipulation of images for persuasion leaves no relationship between form and content inviolate and in which the barriers between the natural and the ersatz become extremely confused. Japanese architects of the past decade have explored the bizarre confrontations offered by a highly urbanised and commercialised culture with more than a slight schizophrenia between old and new, East and West. This milieu helps to explain Arata Isozaki's attempts at colliding sometimes fusing motifs from various traditions over an armature of primary geometries. In the Fujimi Country Club the snaking vault form is a counterpoint to the surrounding countryside and provides a dominant image which seems somewhat forced on the complexities of the programme. The vault lacks the haunting Antique *gravitas* of Kahn's solution at the Kimbell Museum, nevertheless a resonance with Classicism was intended. This becomes overt at the sliced-off end over the entrance with its teasing though bland overtures towards the Villa Poiana by Palladio. The unease generated by the wide placement of columns that feel too thin is exacerbated by the upturned planter walls which acknowledge where a pier or pilaster might have been were this a masonry building. In this instance the 'Maniera' of the solution does at least grow from witty control of ambiguities offered by constructional logic. In the Tsukuba Civic Centre by contrast arbitrariness sets in: the quotation of Michelangelo's Capitoline piazza is that and nothing more.

Montage – the confrontation of two or more images – allows the development of a theme which may be more than just the sum of the references. When the confrontation is weak you have an empty pose; when it is strong a Surrealist tension can be created which

Ricardo Bofill, 'Le Theatre', Marne la Valée

49

William Curtis

recalls the best of Cubist collage: identities become suspended, things are, and are not what they seem. One guesses that a procedure similar to this may have been at work in Stirling's buildings and projects of recent years. Visual explorations of ambiguity and irony balancing belief and scepticism might almost be seen as illustrating the puckish cynicism of Stirling's main intellectual mentor Colin Rowe; it is a perspec-

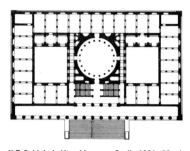

K.F. Schinkel, Altes Museum, Berlin 1824–28, plan

tive on Modern architecture which combincs admiration for past conviction with a disbelief in the possibility of a similar utopian fervor for the present time.[10]

In truth Stirling's work has long possessed something of this flavour of collage and commentary. The Leicester Engineering Building could be seen as an eclectic assembly of partially disjointed fragments lifted from industrial archeology, nautical engineering, and the luke-warm remains of the 'Heroic' period of Modern architecture: Constructivism spliced together with Le Corbusier, Futurism with Wright. In recent years the pallette has widened historically, but the personal style has maintained some of the same procedures and patterns.

Stirling's recently completed Staatsgalerie, Stuttgart, is dominated by the clear conception of a symmetrically placed monumental doughnut flanked by rectangular strips, two of which act as wings; this controlling form is cut through by a zig-zag path clearly signalled by diagonal ramps and curved planes. The placement of a circular form towards the heart of a vaguely Neo-Classical armature inevitably recalls the plan of the Altes Museum, Berlin, by Schinkel, or one of Durand's museum plans. The family has other members too: if one were to slice out a chunk of façade and portico from the British Museum and then dramatise the Panopticon Library as a cylinder the result almost gives Stirling's diagram. The Parliament Building in Chandigarh is another cousin. Part of the richness of the Stuttgart building lies in the synthesis of axiality of form and asymmetrical expressions of movement. Simply the Cubist flanges inviting the flow of the city into the building have been mated with a type-form for the civic monument; an ideal type has been eroded and deformed to meet a particular context.

Basic polarities spelt out in the plan idea are continued in some of the smaller parts of the building. The free form curves in glass and

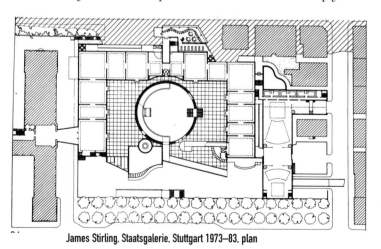

James Stirling, Staatsgalerie, Stuttgart 1973–83, plan

'modern' materials elide – and collide – with masonry and ornamented walls; free plan areas enmesh with areas of strong enclosure; High-Tech details confront Egyptoid columns or cornices. The side wing masses controlled in bulk to match nearby structures and define the street also echo some of the surrounding colours and textures. At this point the contextualism becomes too fussy and, along with all the other fragments and elements that are in ironical 'quotation marks', threatens the unity of the building. The feeblest aspect of the design is the High-Tech costume jewellery. The little pedimented portico does not have sufficient power and stance to do its rhetorical job. A tight matching of details, material surfaces and underlying formal intentions has never been a strong Stirling point and here again a showy cosmeticism afflicts the handling. Stirling does not yet seem to have found a way of orchestrating theme, form and detail in a way that embeds 'realist' historical references into an overall *gestalt*. Artists need a prodigious power of abstraction to pull everything together; they also need an ordering 'grammar'. As Wright put it: ' "Grammar"... is the shape relationship between the various elements that enter into the constitution of the thing... its manifest articulation of all its parts. This will be the 'speech' it uses... Everything has a related articulation in relation to the whole and all belongs together: looks well together because all together are speaking the same language. If one part of your (building) spoke Choctaw, another French, another English and another some sort of gibberish you would have what you mostly have now —not a very beautiful result.'[11]

Lifeless Latin

Any review of recent Classical tendencies would be incomplete without some mention of Quinlan Terry, who has been modestly pursuing a dull, rather literal Classicism for the last two decades. Perhaps unwillingly, Terry has been pushed into the limelight by that brand of right wing traditionalist opinion that sees all modern architecture as a nasty internationalist intrusion into the calm of English country life, and that imagines 'taste' will somehow restore national cultural glory. Terry's work has little in common with the 'Post-

Quinlan Terry, Thetford Summer House, 1980—83

Mods'. He has expressed disgust at 'Columns made of coloured plastic which give the wrong impression', and of PostModern Classicism he has said:

'It is temporary rubbish. It is even worse than Modernism because it is done with irony. The result of looking at PostModernism is that it makes you hate the real thing. It is awful to be put off a thing that you love by an ironic attack. It is Satan's work.'[12]

Unfortunately more than a critical sense and scholarly grasp of Classicism are necessary to create vital architecture. The Thetford Summer House, for example, is polite and not without inventiveness in its combination of Renais-

William Curtis

sance details, yet it lacks that noble and forceful sense of unity that one experiences before a Palladio façade. The building has the dull air of a piece of Georgian reproduction furniture and puts one in mind of Geoffrey Scott's warning:

'Academic art has its danger. Sometimes it implies a refusal to re-think the problems at issue. Sometimes… it attempts to make the imagination of the past do service for imagination in the present.'[13]

Abstraction: Dilution or Compression?

A scrupulous attention to Latin may end up in dry phases unless it is accompanied by penetration to deeper levels of expression within Classicism. Another approach skips the Latin altogether (except in a stripped and vestigial sense) and attempts to transform the armature of underlying qualities. Some would argue that the results should not therefore be called Classical in the full sense of the word but there are many different ways of referring to a tradition and abstracting its 'sub-structures' simultaneously. What might be called the 'abstract' attitude to tradition has played a major role in the Modern Movement and continues to inspire that extension of it loosely referred to as 'Neo-Rationalist'. It is an outlook containing a number of strands: an Idealist view of primary forms as a key to metaphysical order (Boullée, Ledoux, Le Corbusier, Kahn and Terragni all occupy a place in the pantheon); a preocupation with types and their transformation; attention to construction as a generator of vocabulary (articulation by simple openings, structural joints, etc); the search for consonances between modern and ancient simplicities; and a fascination with the supposed vernacular and natural roots of Classicism. This primitivism links the essentialism of Laugier with Kahn's search for the archetypes behind institutions; it accounts for the obsession with the vernacular and geometrical aspects of Palladio. Geometry, proportion, the compression of meaning through abstraction: these become the keys to the past.

Against Saccharine Historicism

The original Italian Neo-Rationalism crystallised in reaction against mere functionalism on the one hand and against both saccharine historicism and a forced 'Social Realism' on the other. Aldo Rossi has attempted to instate the notion of type as the means for transcending both style and political ideology as if there were a higher realm of ideas that could lead to absolute architectural values. In this connection Terragni has been disinterred purged of his Fascist associations as a suitable father figure who achieved the elision of the International Style and Classicism. Despite the lofty aims, Rossi's production has rarely achieved poetic heights. Reductivism may very easily lead to blandness.

This is certainly the case with many of the imitators: in the United States there are Italophile architecture schools which crank out Rossi clones with facility while in Germany Neo-Rationalist elevations are reportedly sold by the metre. The theorising of O.M. Ungers has attempted to build an idealist bridge over anti-Classical taboos operating since Naziism but built results tend to be diagrammatic. Robert Krier has achieved relative success at infusing housing with Classical urbanity and formality without pretensious and gratuitous displays of pseudo-Classical ornament. With Neo-Rationalism in general the danger lies in lapsing into a simplistic geometrical formula. Analysis by type may lead one to penetrate generic principles or to produce lifeless diagrams. As usual a vital imaginative transformation is required.

Mario Botta, Casa Rotonda, Stabio 1980

The Ticinese group of architects in Southern Switzerland have obvious affinities with their neighbours across the Italian border. The most interesting of them seems to be Mario Botta, and this despite the fact that his forms are in fashion. Botta has never pretended to be anything other than a 'modern architect', a fact which annoys those of his colleagues who spend time trying to hitch up with the latest 'ism'. Indeed Botta has a better claim to the title than most since he was apprenticed briefly to both Kahn and Le Corbusier. Like a number of Indian architects – Dashi, Correa, Raje – Botta has explored the correspondences between these two mentors and has sought to link the dual inheritance to regional concerns but without recourse to a superficial regionalism: there is no straining after the cuckoo clock style. In his case abstraction has served to blend and to compound historical precedents rather than to exclude them. This is also the level on which he has understood Le Corbusier and Kahn: as a way back to the past rather than away from it.

The Casa Rotonda (1980–81) is surely one of the most bizarre of Botta's creations to date. This semi-suburban house is transformed into a solid monument that defies the recent urban sprawl and invokes a return to archaic rural values. Its plan contains an elemental gesture: an axis across a circle. This aligns the cylinder and cuts it in two with the slot containing the stairs. The maintenance of polarities and their gradual unification into the encompassing circular geometry is one of the guiding formal themes of the building. But the plan is also rich in associative qualities which carry through into the volumes. There is the suggestion of a sort of solar calendar as if the slits and openings in the cylinder had been aligned to catch rays at specific times of the day or the year; it is an observatory, a bastion, a tower for spiritual retreat from a world that is becoming increasingly tacky. The penetration of this tower by a stair and shafts of light is not without primal and ritualistic overtones. The building seems to be haunted by a mythical agenda of the artist's own.

The jointing of stair slot and cylinder is handled adeptly on the exterior: the walls step down and away to reveal the curved end of the stairs. Kahn's massive vertical circulation towers or Le Corbusier's use of stacks or silo-like elements for the same purpose come to mind but the form has here been embedded in a new grammatical usage and has heen transmuted into Botta's own terms of reference. The form also evokes a column but one generated from within functionally and in terms of ideas; not just an attached 'sign' or quotation. This 'column' is generalised to possess resonance with Romanesque as well as Roman; it touches on the idea of the column in general.

The forms of the Casa Rotonda have resulted from a thorough assimilation of Kahn, Rossi, Le Corbusier, the rural vernacular, and certain organisational principles from Palladio. The past is present in them in a way that makes the 'Modern versus PostModern' affair seem quite beside the point.

1 Charles Jencks (guest ed), *Architectural Design* 5/6 1980; also Free Style Classicism, London: Academy Editions, 1982.

2 Eugene Viollet le Duc, *Discourses on Architecture*, London: Allen & Unwin, 1959, p455. I have Ware's translation of 1899.

3 Louis Sullivan, 'The Tall Office Building Artistically Considered', *Lippincotts Magazine* March 1896.

4 Geoffrey Scott, *The Architecture of Humanism*, London: 1914.

5 Philip Johnson, see Nory Miller, *Philip Johnson Writings*, 1979.

6 Charles Jencks, *The Language of Post-Modern Architecture*, New York, 1977, p143.

7 Jay Claiborne with Tom Aidala, 'Ethnic Design or Ethnic Slur?' *Places*, Cambridge, Mass: MIT Press, Vol 1, No 2, p18, 1984.

8 Edwin Lutyens, letter to Herbert Baker. Christofer Hussey *The Life of Sir Edwin Lutyens*, London: Hamlyn, 1950 p133.

9 Ricardo Bofill, statement in *Architectural Design* 5/6 1980.

10 Colin Rowe and Fred Koetter, *Collage City*, London: 1978.

11 Frank Lloyd Wright, *The Natural House*, New York: Horizon, 1954.

12 Interview with Quinlan Terry, 'Twentieth Century Renaissance', *Architect's Journal* 14 December 1983, p40.

13 Geoffrey Scott, op cit p199.

The New Spirit

EDITORIAL

E.M. Farrelly
August 1986

PostModernism is dead. Some have known from the start that it was no more than a painted corpse, but for others it has taken a little longer to work through the deceptively populist arguments of the pasticheurs, the quasi-Classicists and the toy-town tarter-uppers towards the realisation that while 'giving the people what they want' may sound like all-too-rare architectural humility, it has, with frightening rapidity, become no more than the pretty plaything of rampant capitalism. The success it has had (and is still, in its obedient, bankable way enjoying) has been achieved by offering an aesthetic path of least resistance and by appealing, after the demands and constraints of Modernism, to some of the least endearing aspects of human nature—indolence, ignorance, oppression and greed.

Now, however, something else is happening. Something new. After the relentless ossification of the PostModern era things are beginning to stir again. Like the first breath of spring after a long and stultifying winter, these first stirrings are signs of hope.

There are, of course, those who prefer winter. Who would choose the closed door, the airless room, the neatly shuttered mind over the demands of even the possibility of freedom. Those for whom the future holds only fear, for whom the past is something known and safe, to be therefore not only

Rudolf Schindler, Janson House, 1949

Darbourne & Darke, Chelsea Football stand, 1970s

preserved but imitated, at any cost. For architecture, however, the cost has been silence, docility and despair; the tacit admission that there is nothing left to discover, nowhere left to go, and nothing left to say—in short, a sell-out.

It began honourably enough. Modernism may have been heroic but it never won the affection of the populace. By the 1970s, widely misinterpreted, and misapplied, it had become brittle and diagrammatic; the revolution when it came was driven by a craving for liberation from its strictures, both moral and aesthetic. PostModernists, in those very early days, seemed like freedom-fighters, dragon-slayers, heroes. From Schumacher to Venturi they fought to legitimise the small scale, the complex, the vernacular, the historical, the decorative and the popular—all things which had been ousted in the single-minded drive for a clean and brave new world.

Before long, however, the inevitable became apparent, and it was clear that PostModernism was not an independent freedom force at all, but a sort of mutant isotope of elemental Modernism; initially radiant but highly derivative, insidious, and programmed to decay. The rebellion, never anything more than a reaction against Modernism, had been doomed from the start to have a short half-life. Its freedom-fighters – unwittingly no doubt – were in fact architecture's harbingers of death.

56

Cedric Price, Regent's Park Aviary, 1962

What Price Popularity?

In retrospect, it should have been obvious. Exuberant at first in its new-won freedoms, but lacking a positive direction of its own, PostModernism[1] has quickly become a meaningless mannerist charade. With the rules of Modernism removed, but not replaced, liberty quickly degenerated into licence, 'vernacular' into pastiche, and decoration into the flabby mass mediocrity that has become so unresisting a pawn of monetarism.

Even so, Post-Modernism soon proved to be easy, popular and saleable. Anyone could do it, and anyone did. Students and developers were equally quick to discover that the essentials of the style – the graceless, overscaled columns and arches, the pitched roofs and broken pediments, the half-round barrel-vaults, and gratuitous decorative squiggles that now distinguish mainstreet architecture all over the Western world – were effortlessly imitable, and provided easy answers for crits and planning-committees alike. Architects themselves, eager to keep up and lacking any more real discipline, soon followed suit. Long-chastised for their monkish elitism, they shed their principles with alacrity, donning instead the gaudy coats of born-again capitalism and strutting in the market-place with the rest, fervent now only in their desire for money and acclaim.

And who, you might say, can blame them? There was a cold wind blowing, and an ominous clanging in the corridors of power; one by one, minds were being closed, bolted against the future in favour of some mythical golden past. Venturi's celebrated polemic for pleasure and pluralism in architecture provided too easy an excuse for our natural intellectual laziness, and for the mindless laissez-faire *stylism which has resulted in the directionlessness of current architectural thought, and endless imitative banality of form.*

People, it was said, did not like Modern buildings any more, and if they didn't like them they wouldn't pay for them; something must be done. But in rejecting – perhaps rightly – the buildings, they also unthinkingly rejected the principles behind them; baby and bathwater both. Space, for example, was one of the casualties. Dethroned deity of the Modern Movement, Space had come to be seen as the enemy of the new favourite 'place', and was rejected outright, making way for the more material obsessions of the new regime.[2]

Modernism was out. All other styles, however, were approved, and freely available in the market-place—for a small (and ever-reducing) fee. Of these there was one which was easiest and most obvious: Neo-Classicism, unlike its original model, is about symmetry, stasis, and sheer physical weight. Hopes that it might further the small-scale planning ideals of those early freedom-fighters soon proved vain. On the contrary Neo-Classicism – or that pastel rendering of it that came to be known as PostModern Classicism – already had a long history of pastiche, and a pedigree free of any but the merest hint of spatial quality. For the new Materialism it was perfect, a gift.

Great minds have tried and failed to establish a necessary link between Neo-Classicism and political oppression. But one thing is certain, it is a style which in its various forms has given itself uncomplainingly through the ages to the adoration of cultures like ours in which status depends, once again and increasingly, upon the acquisition and display of material wealth. PostModern Classicism has brought us architecture-as-commodity; the object cult. It is a style which sits heavily and in fundamental opposition to the forward-looking, life-giving ideals of openness, freedom and, in every sense, light which were embodied, however unsatisfactorily, in Modernism (and, ironically, in Classicism itself).[3]

Defensive Squatter Housing, Nueva Habana

E.M. Farrelly

Romantic v. Classical: An Historical Dialectic

Classicism is traditionally regarded as the dialectical opposite of Romanticism, and it is possible to see the history of art for the New Spirit is undoubtedly one which realigns architecture as one of the arts—as a sort of rectified wave form produced by alternating periods of these two principles; regular pulses of questing, Romantic energy interspersed (and even at times coincidental) with periods of Classical calm.

The analogy is clearly simplistic, but if for the sake of argument we define the terms not according to the forms they produce, but to the spirit that guides them – Classicism as defined opposite[3] and Romanticism as a principle of questioning, contingency and change – it will serve for long enough to suit our present purposes.

It allows us, for example, to see Classicism as a point of momentary equilibrium between times of great change; a state of maximum altitude but zero velocity. And to understand Romanticism as something which can be either positive or negative, either a breaking down of the old order, or a building-up of the new. An impulse which may culminate, briefly and almost incidentally, in stasis, but whose primary concern is with the process of change itself; uncomfortable, but invigorating.

Mad Max II

It is clear that in these terms, Modernism – itself initially heroic, explosive and revolutionary in opposition to the perceived decadence of the post-World War I architectural establishment, but becoming gradually accepted and eventually despised – was composed, perhaps even from the start, of both Romantic and Classical impulses encompassing the absolute Rationalist geometries of Mies, the warmth of Aalto and Frank Lloyd Wright, the waywardness of Scharoun —and even the apparent contradiction of Le Corbusier, in whose work both impulses may be clearly seen.

And it is equally clear that PostModernism (having reached zero velocity but hardly maximum altitude) should be regarded as at best an agent of decay, helping only to break down the Modernist dogma into a state of decay from which a fresh Romantic impulse could grow into new life.

The New Spirit is just such a Romantic impulse.[4] Restless, striving, searching; stirring-up and stripping-bare; never sentimental but, on the contrary, tough, iconoclastic, streetwise; acerbic, often aggressive, and very highly-strung. While trying at times to better the world in which we live, it rejects out of hand all tendency towards prettification or escapism, fierce in its determination to accomplish what Modernism shrank from: the acceptance and embrace of what the world is, in all its complexity and squalor.

But, this determination notwithstanding, there is a direct line of descent from many of the early Modern movements; the New Spirit inherits, and extrapolates from, not only Modern architecture's concern with space, openness and honesty (while rejecting its grand utopian vistas—Le Corbusier, after all, would have eradicated if he could the very notion of the street) but also the thrusting, dynamic imagery of Constructivism, and something of Futurism's savage beauty as well. Above all, however, the New Spirit owes its existence to Dada.

Jan Kaplicky—Future Systems, House for Helicopter Pilot, 1982

The Genesis of Freedom

Dada, widely misunderstood as a purely negative force or anti-art, was in fact hugely influential. In a few short years it was to re-evaluate the role of art and artists in society so profoundly that none of the arts – poetry, music, painting, sculpture, photography – would, or could, ever be the same again. It was, in the words of Werner Haftmann,[5] a movement in which 'all the values of human existence …were brought into play, and every object, every thought, turned on its head, mocked and misplaced, as an experiment, in order to see what there was behind it, beneath it, against it, mixed up in it… a state of mind feverishly exalted by the freedom virus, a unique mixture of insatiable curiosity, playfulness, and pure contradiction'.

It may have been shortlived, but it was fecund, numbering amongst its offspring many of the most provocative art movements of the century: Surrealism, Arte Povera, Pop Art, Action Painting, Conceptual Sculpture, Performance Art, '60s Happenings', the Situationists, and Punk/New Wave itself. Unlike other early movements of this century (Futurism, Cubism, NeoPlasticism) Dada was not a new style or technique but, in the words of Tristan Tzara, a 'state of mind'. It could not, therefore, be copied so much as absorbed—and, consciously or unconsciously, and with varying degrees of success and superficiality, Dada's 'freedom virus' has been absorbed, direct into the bloodstream of twentieth-century art.

But in architecture – which, since Modernism, has distanced itself from the other arts – there has been no really comparable attempt to build anew. (The inflatables, geodesics and woodbutchery of the '60s went some way toward questioning the established order but have remained, despite themselves, fringe events.) Until now.

59

E.M. Farrelly

Now there is something new happening in architecture. Something which, no longer constrained either by the reductivist morality of the International Style or by the need to revile it, is able to review, re-evaluate and re-use *the legacy of Modernism in its various manifestations. There is amongst these new designers a resurgent spirit of enquiry, a renewed interest in space and movement, in the use of real materials – steel, concrete, timber, stone, even plastic, appearing as itself – in a stripping-back towards the essentials of architecture and, most importantly of all, in the dynamism of asymmetry, the very genesis of freedom.*

Dadaist Ancestry

But the New Spirit is by no means a straight Modernist revival, since these preoccupations are combined with a freer use of geometry than the

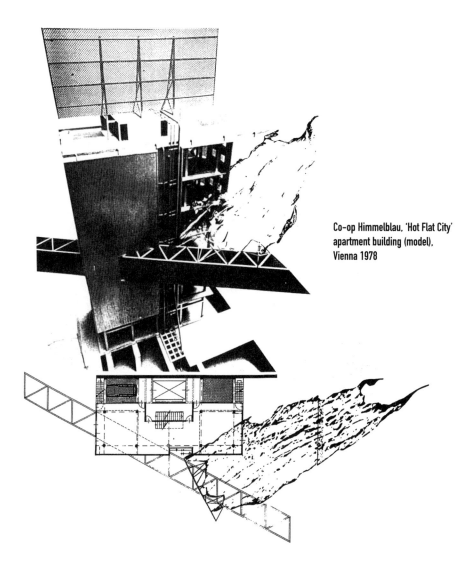

Co-op Himmelblau, 'Hot Flat City' apartment building (model), Vienna 1978

Lyubov Popova, 'The Earth in Turmoil', photomontage, 1923

range of influence than even Modernism could admit. There are, for example, traces not only of Constructivism, Futurism, Cubism and Dadaism, and of the later wood-butchery, Archigram, Technism and Neo-Primitivism, but also (in parallel with the music, fashion and graphics industries) of Rock & Roll, Punk, and New Wave. To all this new vitality only the death-merchants of PostModern Classicism have contributed nothing, except perhaps in provoking at last the contrary determination that architecture should once again LIVE.

Dada's contribution, on the other hand, cannot be overestimated. The New Spirit, like Dada, is, fired in part by the need to break-down and break-through existing patterns of deceit and smug self-interest. It is not only antistasis, anti-concealment, but also profoundly anti-the increasing smoothness, glibness and facile predictability of the established (and by and large unexamined) canons of the prevailing architectural order.

And, like Dada, its chosen weapons in this battle to 'see what lies beneath' are the forces of randomness, accident and chance, giving rise to the apparent anarchy and fragmentation of much of the work shown in this issue. Chance, however, is by its very nature undesigned, you cannot design the accident to happen, so to use such ideas as design principles is clearly problematic (though it didn't seem to worry the Dadaists). Furthermore, the very idea of chance or randomness in design seems to imply a kind of fatalistic acceptance which is patently contradicted by the sheer dynamism of the buildings that result.

But the paradox is only skin deep. For the apparent anarchy is not, in fact, a lack of order so much as a deliberate destruction of the old to make way for a different, subtler and even in some ways more stringent discipline. Chance and randomness are used only as tools, levers to roll away (or dynamite to explode) the tablets of stone, revealing the multitudinous possibilities hitherto concealed by their weight.

In the work of New York's Moser and Goodwin, for example, we see a renewed interest in the apparently accidental collision of forms – reminiscent of Tzara's cut-up poetry – and in the use of real, 'raw' materials. Honold and Pöschl's Bogen 13, in Innsbruck, and their Dragonwing, embrace the grimy godforsaken realities of contemporary urban existence, and celebrate the power of the 'found' environment. The flighty, volatile forms of Vienna's Co-op Himmelblau are like latterday, built versions of Schwitters' Merzbauen, and their very method of working, letting drawings 'emerge' from the unconscious, reminds one of the automatist

61

Ron Herron/Archigram, Monte Carlo Entertainment Centre, 1970

E.M. Farrelly

techniques explored by Arp, Janco and Richter in
Dadaist experiments early this century.

Neville Brody's now highly influential avant-garde
graphics play with ideas of what he calls the 'randomness factor' and the 'found image', inspired by the work
of Rodchenko, El Lissitzky and other experimental
typographers of the 1920s. And Hasegawa's 'sever-
ance', her deliberate participation in the anarchic
chaos of the Japanese city, Zalotay's embrace of accident, or what he calls 'dissonances' and Kevin
Rhowbotham's generative notion of 'spatial collage': all bear the marks of descent, however indirect or unwitting, from Dadaist ancestry.

Political Implications

It is, of course, a political thing. No movement with this kind of pedigree
could possibly be otherwise. Nor is the kind of dynamism and sheer kinetic
energy that so characterises the New Spirit even accessible to those who are
concerned merely to find a new aesthetic sensibility to play with. Its restless
agitation of space and unpredictability of form are built metaphors of the
thought processes involved. For some the forms are highly significant, even
necessary; for others they are almost incidental. But either way it is the
thinking that matters; the hard-edged individualism in a world of passive
consumerist homogeneity, the determined rejection of the conformist ideals
that the Establishment would have us adopt, and the refusal to be manipulated by the huge anonymous forces of authority. There is a fierce defence of
the ordinary – the found object, the despised material, the unloved environment – and a defiant proclamation of the right of the ordinary
human to seize back power from the experts and reassert control over his or
her own life.

This, at root, was what Punk was all about. It underlies Leplastrier's studio near Bellingen, NSW, which, despite its meticulous craftsmanship exhibits a queer sprightliness of form and a love of unmitigatedly
ordinary materials (plastic, 'Caneite' and corrugated iron); Eduard
Samso's quirky but stringent minimalism, Zalotay's stoic self-build, Alfre-
do Vidal's tough, grimy KGB and Himmelblau's defence of the street.

There is, of course, no creed or manifesto—nor could there be in a
movement (if indeed it can be so termed) whose base-line is individual
diversity and freedom. Some of the protagonists of the New Spirit are anti-
materialist, some are not. Some are consciously subversive, some are not.
Some would not even call themselves political. But the political implications are there to be read.

What will come of it all is anyone's guess. It is possible that the New Spirit may meet the same fate as befell Modernism; understood and imitated form, not philosophy. (It is one of the dangers of the kind of dialectical approach to history outlined above that it may seem to lend a spurious inevitability to the unknowable, making the end seem certain and encouraging this sort of premature acceptance of defeat.)

It is possible, but unlikely, for such timid passivity is emphatically not a part of the New Spirit's make-up. Diverse it may be, and by no means unanimously optimistic of the future, but it has at least, at last, outgrown that crippling fear of the present which so unmistakably marks the current architectural scene. The New Spirit can be strange, wilful, even at times subversive, but it is unfailingly vigorous, exploratory and, although it takes no heed of fashion, very much an architecture of now.

1 It should be noted here that PostModernism in architecture is a very different thing from what is meant by 'post-modernism' in literature (and elsewhere). The criticism in this article is aimed solely at PostModernism in architecture.

2 This despite the much more sophisticated understanding of Aldo van Eyck, amongst others, who was fighting for a place *within* the Modern Movement.

3 That is, properly speaking, the architecture of Classical Greece. A distinction must be drawn here between Classicism proper, and Neo-Classicism. By Classicism I mean a guiding principle or mode of thought, a belief in eternal, absolute, trascendent values, perceptible as much in the work of Mies, as that of Ichtinos, or Kallikrates. Neo-Classicism, on the other hand, if it be taken to include everything done in the name (or form) of Classicism, is something quite different.

The sacred buildings of Ancient Greece (the Propylaeum, say, the Parthenon, or even the much later Hellenistic buildings of Pergamon) celebrate, like Mies' National Gallery in Berlin, mankind's sheer joy at being able at last to lighten the burden of gravity, to lift and hold those great weights of stone effortlessly on high. This is Classicism proper.

Neo-Classicism, by contrast – Speer, Boullée, late Lutyens or even the comparatively light-of-heart and spatially-oriented Schinkel – is about weight. Classical in form but not in spirit, it is determinedly earthbound, pinning the transcendent ideals of Classicism firmly and with slow deliberation to the ground for its own worldly purposes: power, prestige, oppression.

Whereas Classicism, striving heavenward, generates space, Neo-Classicism is wholly object-obssesed, bearing heavily, ponderously down on the earth, the spirit, the populace. Where Classicism celebrates the *defiance* of gravity, Neo-Classicism – in which we must now include PostModern Classicism – is a monument to its gratification.

4 Although it should by no means be confused with the so-called 'Neo-Romanticism', which is in the main a sales-pitch for cheap sentimentalism.

5 Postscript to Richter, *Dada; Art and Anti-Art*, Thames & Hudson, 1965, p215.

E.M. Farrelly

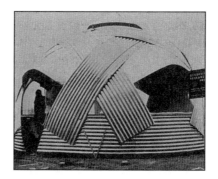

Architecture is on the Wing Again

THEORY

Peter Cook
August 1986

Two winters ago a capacity crowd in a large room on the Dürerstrasse, Frankfurt, heard the words '*Architektur muss brennen*' shrieked by Wolfgang Prix as the film of Himmelblau's 1.5 ton 'Blazing Wing' filled the room and the Rolling Stones thumped away on the soundtrack. The normally phlegmatic Frankfurters and Darmstadters erupted with great clapping and cheering—just some 15 per cent of the audience silently hung their hands (inky, cracked, rationalist hands I wouldn't wonder) and looked grim.

Two days later a capacity crowd in a large room in Bedford Square, London, heard the words 'Architecture must burn' shrieked by Wolfgang Prix as the blazing wing, the music and that whole mastery of enthusiasm represented by Himmelblau's output of the last ten years caused the normally cynical AA kids to clap and cheer—just some 10 per cent of the audience looked rather puzzled (and couldn't wait to creep back to those London polytechnics where the easier games of PostModernism offered safety and orthodoxy).

Buckminster Fuller, corrugated iron 'Indhlu' dome, prototype, SA, 1940

In a single week I had seen young architects really enjoying architecture and getting caught up in the spirit of Himmelblau's battle-cries... 'The tougher the times the tougher the architecture' ... 'Architecture is architecture' ... 'Architecture is *now*' ... 'The city throbs like heart—the city flies like breath'. I could not but recall the excitement and conscious audacity of our earlier Archigram rallies and the recognition that they in turn made towards the inherited audacities and battle-cries of the Smithsons in the '50s, CIAM in the '30s, Bruno Taut or the Constructivists in the '20s. But my instinctive uplift was confirmed in both cities by conversations with students who seriously admired the relentless achievement and growing sureness that accompanied the increasing naughtiness of the architecture. A bridge between the so different worlds of the late '60s and the mid '80s had been made and even consolidated in their work. The passing of time had added to their vocabulary of forms and tricks and had bred its own three-dimensional excitement of wings and diagonals – but a spirit ran through from then to now – an attack upon space – a thrust forward; again and again a thrust into and about space. We were reminded that architecture is essentially to do with stuff —not, thank goodness, semantics, semiotics, supplications or syllogisms.

Some months earlier, another, dual, event had announced, by its own simultaneity as much as anything, a rustle of wings in the architectural nest: Zaha Hadid had won the 'Peak' competition and Tschumi had won 'La Villette'. Both

Richter and Gerngross, Königseder House, Baumgartenberg

with schemes of great verve and thrust, great confidence and a reaching out into space. The subsequent history of architecture (whether or not they got built) could never be the same. An immediate spin-off was a feeling of elation amongst their friends and some students, who knew that these schemes were no flashes in the pan, but a recognition point in years of increasingly dynamic work. Hints of Hadid's talent could have already been seen in her contribution to OMA's Amsterdam City Hall, artistic flair in her sheer elation in her Belgravia apartment proposal. In a different way, Tschumi had long fascinated us, and by the time of

his 'Manhattan Transcripts' he had offered a real challenge to our ideas about architectural dynamic: 'The accident of murder ... they had to get out of the Park—quick... THE PARK', 'Possessed by a woman who was beautiful to look at but lethal to love... THE STREET', 'The elevator ride had turned into a chilling contest with violent death... THE TOWER', 'with its loose yards and its ruthless frames...where everything you want belongs to somebody else, and the only way to get it is illegal,

Bernard Tschumi, Parc de La Villette, Paris 1983

immoral or deadly... THE BLOCK'. Seeing his imagery together with the human analogies, you realised that the whole morphology of nice urban architecture was being, twisted, threatened: violated. The reality of the Parc de La Villette has come merely as a freeze-frame in his equally dynamic architecture.

The subsequent months have seen the results of this ignition: and an acceleration of the thrusting, spatial architecture that is now surely pushing away the torpor of the yuppie-pastel style that has pervaded much of the United States and Northern Europe in recent years with its general sense of coyness and flatness as it rests among the Berlin IBA or the fashionable backdrops for cocktail drinking or child-play grounding (and just about everything else in-between) in every city from Oslo to Melbourne—and it was bound to crack open eventually. Some of us had begun to despair—for the well-developed mechanism of brochures and biennales (masquerading as serious books and manifestations) had flooded most of the arteries. Of course in cussed quarters there had been grumbles: 'We've seen enough of the Americans' said the overfed AA students—and at that place the unthinkable happened in the summer of '84: a Michael Graves audience of 300 melted to 100 after the first hour, through sheer boredom.

An alternative to watching the cracks appear at the traffic junctions of New York, London or Berlin would be to peer at the remote hills, unknown plains and hidden valleys where original work has always continued. At Graz, for instance, where the smell of the Balkans results in an obstinate refusal to be intimidated by the sophistication and arrogance of Vienna and a bevy of strange architects has continued to breed. In the '60s the rivalry between Raimund Abraham, Friedrich St Florian, Günther Domenig and Eilfried Huth gave impetus to their megastructures, inflatables, flying machines and respective diversions into beautiful atmospheric monuments, holograms, or animal-buildings. The second generation of Heidulf Gerngross, Helmut Richter, Michael Szyszkowitz, Karla Kowalski and Volker Giencke seems equally talented...with a third generation of spatialists chasing them. There

Hans Hollein, aircraft carrier, collage, 1964

is a certain raw edge to the Graz work, a refusal to be forced into good manners which runs past the obvious sharing of free-form (and I am trying to avoid the term 'Expressionism').

In this region it has much to do with being surrounded by mountains: the consciousness of hewing rocks, trapping streams, and the honing of forest timbers. Looking at their buildings one can almost imagine Szyszikowitz and Kowalski as a Titan couple wrestling with the landscape and heaving it and twisting it into shelter—hardly restrained by that series of sophistries known elsewhere as 'architectural manners'. I am reminded of a parallel instinct in America which caused the more forgotten parts of the midwest to be a natural context for 'organic', 'craft', 'eccentric' and finally 'alternative' architecture. In a longer analysis it would be fascinating to compare the psychological freedom that this might have offered to Bruce Goff, Buckminster Fuller, Paolo Soleri: alongside Günther Domenig. All their work is ultimately sophisticated, thoughtful and intricate yet none of them are city boys. Certainly, in his lectures, Domenig makes plenty of references to the natural landscape of his own Styrian valley and its surrounding mountains and, in particular, uses this to introduce his three or four year thinking that will soon lead to the building of his own Great House. On closer inspection however, one notices how much sharper and more aggressive are the more recent drawings of this project: how much more demanding it will be of its materials and details: how much more vicious and 'international' is its thrust than in his earlier work. Somehow, he is speaking back to Zaha Hadid and Co-op Himmelblau... the younger 'townies'... 'take a peep down the valley, kids... *that's* where it'll happen'... and he is even willing to flood part of the building in order to grapple further with the elements; part of the structure then re-emerging from within the 'flood' shades of Captain Nemo at the organ in the 'Nautilus'—often, incidentally, quoted by Archigram since it seemed to embody at once the idea of the architect as mad scientist, as musician and romantic, as possessor of both the mysterious cathedral and the ultimate world-encompassing vehicle. In this way, Domenig remains one of the most fascinating figures in our story and throws light upon the vexed question of exposure and suppression in late twentieth-century architecture.

In the manner of things hierarchical and European, it seemed acceptable to the Viennese that Domenig could beaver away expressionistically back in the hills and valleys, and even be permitted to build in a poorer suburb of the city, so long as the world at large didn't know. Visitors were not told about the building for a long time. In the end, however, architectural mafias and politicians (who are notoriously unnoticing of things visual) are doomed to fail. So it is that, eventually, Berlin's Umlauftank by Ludwig Leo and Fraenkelufer Housing by Hinrich and Inken Baller have seeped through the net with Günther Domenig's 'Z' bank as pieces of noticeable, intriguing and discussable architecture. Moreover, his enjoyment of the international scene has caused Domenig to pitch his latest University buildings for Graz up to the levels of refinement that are more character-

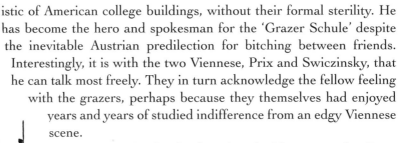

Chernikov, Research & Experimental Station

istic of American college buildings, without their formal sterility. He has become the hero and spokesman for the 'Grazer Schule' despite the inevitable Austrian predilection for bitching between friends. Interestingly, it is with the two Viennese, Prix and Swiczinsky, that he can talk most freely. They in turn acknowledge the fellow feeling with the grazers, perhaps because they themselves had enjoyed years and years of studied indifference from an edgy Viennese scene.

Not for the first time do I have to make direct comparisons between Vienna and London. The differences first: that London is infinitely more international and suffers from the feeling that 'everybody comes through at some time' which can easily lead to complacency —and that London does have more work for architects ('It's just that they're the wrong architects,' etc, etc...). But the similarities are more intriguing: the shared cynicism, the shared amusement at two or three different drinkers in the bar being intellectual enemies but social friends (impossible in new York), the feeling on the part of the *most* outrageous innovators that whatever they do is merely part of the inevitable metamorphosis of the city. It breeds at best that foreknowledge that architecture is a very wide and resilient old territory and that the rise and fall of power, status, monarchies, empires, traditions can be ascribed to the discussion of architecture itself. Certainly in the 1960s and early '70s we felt that only in Vienna and Tokyo did they really share our optimism that architecture *could* and *must* extend its territory and vocabulary – devouring from other territories if necessary – and thrusting forward (metaphorically, technologically and literally) into space. Perhaps Raimund Abraham would be embarrassed that I mention his early designs for robots and space suits. Himmelblau are not embarrassed about theirs: more able to trace the step by step or rather the blow by blow sequence by which the unlikely spaceship is now revealed as the building itself.

When they exhibited in London in 1973 they were regarded as the back runners of the Viennese scene—a long way after the pioneering work of Hans Hollein and Walter Pichler and still behind the somehow more respectable image of Haus-Rucker Co. But they stayed with it, and stayed in Vienna. Rucker – who must have a place in this history – moved both to Düsseldorf and New York. In Düsseldorf they have struggled well against a suspicious and often indifferent German mainstream consciousness as foreign – but (as Austrians) not *very* foreign; as artistic but not *artists*; as weird – but in the end perhaps not weird enough; so that their handsome exhibition at the National Galerie in Berlin two years ago seemed to be saying 'here we are in Mies' basement... *now* will you take us seriously.' The seeming opportunities of Düsseldorf (money, buildings, energy) have also been its trap. In London or Vienna they wouldn't have built much either, but they would have had tougher rivalries, stranger conversations and, perhaps, that curious brotherhood that eventually emerges between creative rivals who become aware that the architectural world at large (maybe 200,000 or 300,000 people) is hardly interested in *any* of them.

John Hejduk, head of New York's Cooper Union, often talks about the essential isolation of really new architecture and about power; in this he is not referring to the mandate enjoyed by Philip Johnson but the issue of trajectory. As he points out, a certain naivety is necessary—perhaps a boyish enthusiasm which certainly links many of the people I am discussing. I can still recall it in the atmosphere of the Archigram Group. Somehow we were conscious that forward-thrust architecture could only come about by pitching it *against* the general stream... 'This'll upset them' was often said as a phrase of encouragement to one's companion. The 'them' was known and understood to be the polite, acquiescent, wanting-to-be-all-right architects of London town. We knew that a studied indifference would be the inevitable reception to our work...but there were unknown allies scattered here and there. The Archigram publication set off the chain: ...'We are a small group in Prague, we call ourselves the "Continualists"' (Dalibor Vesely)... 'Perhaps you might be interested in the catalogue of my exhibition at the Nächst St. Stephen' (Hans Hollein)... 'I am from Florence but teaching alongside your friend Mike Webb' (Adolfo Natalini); later of course they became real faces, friends, sometime allies; but the first contact was very

important seen *against* the studied indifference which could demoralise. At this moment I feel the spirit of alliance once more towards and between the young English who design perilously hung or scrawled shapes that resemble butchers' offal more than they do the Parthenon, and Austrians whose buildings resemble punk hair-dos, and Japanese who live inside beached oildrums with tasteful triangles sticking out, and Americans who place gawky legs up against quilted hangars.

H. & I. Baller, housing, 1984

As might be expected, the most relaxed coterie within this total scenery has existed for some time now in Los Angeles. That city still has a useful tradition for eccentricities, with Hollywood's dream world as some sort of general cultural legitimiser. It has meant that your own theories, however loopy, could find their slot and that somewhere up there in the hills there would be a couple of allies. Archigram first landed there in 1968, backed by a bunch of AA students who later became Chrysalis and later still became the core of Rogers' Pompidou team. In the same department of UCLA there arrived a small group of tutors and students from Graz. The most eccentric of them, Heidulf Gerngross, made the buying of a mattress and the continual sleeping on it in the middle of the school into a simultaneous piece of both conceptual art and opportunism. The humour, though much more perseverance too, remains in his design for the Köigseder house. Somewhere nearby was lurking the embryo Thom Mayne, Eric Moss, Coy Howard and the already known Craig Hodgetts. And busy with his purist output – before the great exciting flip – was Frank Gehry.

For some years there was an inevitable suspicion of the English and Austrian combination of seriousness about language (both formal and verbal), and about drawing. Moss himself has perhaps parodied this period best in a beachside remodel that with its curved corners and pipework excrescences and, essential, lemon-yellow walls, is a source of embarrassment to both him and his Archigram friends. Anyhow, the exuberant and formally inventive series of buildings that are now recognised as the 'Los Angeles Thing' could only evolve directly from the beach, the frame and plywoods, the observation of John Lautner's extraordinary houses, the glamour of Frank Lloyd Wright's son Lloyd when on form, and perhaps the return home to real America after a year at the Harvard Graduate school for these young architects. Michael Rotondi of Morphosis declares – quite aggressively – that it was essential to make an *American* architecture. From London, though, one recognises another aspect of the possessiveness

Bruce Goff, weekend house, Kentucky 1940

of Los Angeles—for here too the companions at the bar make very different buildings from each other and yet feel themselves allied in the face of the disdain from New York. And whilst that city laid down the lines of succession and the new formal rules, the Angelinos felt more and more like running free with bits of wood, sheets of almost anything flat that could be bent at will, and tacky materials like bitumen tiles and staples. Frank Gehry took inspiration directly from his artist friends and did with whole rooms and edifices what they might have done with gallery installations and driftwood—and better. Moreover, he was prepared to go and *live* in them. This more than anything else gave impetus to young architects, who were suspicious of four-square surfaces and impermeable substances, to go out and collage-together buildings in space. The politics of the situation have continued to be a loose collage as well; Gehry, though he is the first to become a world figure, is acknowledged to be supportive of Moss, Morphosis and some of the others to the extent of passing them on work and recommending them to otherwise incredulous clients. The result is a jocular rivalry and a similar down-the-line impetus to odd Sci-Arc graduates whose funny contraptions crop up all over the back blocks of Santa Monica and West Los Angeles.

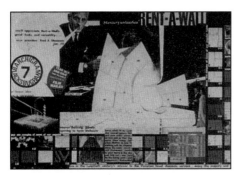

Mike Webb, Rent-a-Wall project, 1967

Not entirely coincidentally, the two best magazines on architecture seemed to come out of California in he early '80s—*Arts and Architecture* and *Archetype*. The former a revival of the pioneering magazine that had sponsored the famous 'Case study' houses in which the '50s men had experimented with the light-tech architecture of Craig Ellwood and Raphael Soriano (to mention only two). In its later series giving a positive boost to the idea that gloss and colour and art and palms and sheer unadulterated form were, of course, linked; but not in any school-marmy way as they might have been in a self-conscious European or East Coast tome. The latter magazine, with an inevitable Austrian, Mark Mack, somewhere at the helm, was noteworthy if for no other reason than that it introduced most of us to Stanley Saitowitz, a South African architect who in his late twenties had already built a most marvellous and original house. Even without the arty two-page photographs in *Archetype*, it commended its sheer relaxedness to anyone with spirit —at a level that made even the LA work seem self-conscious. The proposition was simply that of draping, or gently swinging, long curves of corrugated metal over thin frames and then making occasional house-enclosures below. Taken in fact from the barn-building tradition, but set with great sensibility. Saitowitz has made other houses and designs and drawings that are always fresh and original… as in the case of his sun tracking house (AR February 1986), but this first was shattering.

In what seems to have been no time at all, the scenery has become inhabited by other draped and swung buildings, not in the fields and suburbs of course, but on the drawing-boards of students, particularly at the AA. Demetri Porphyrios has called them 'the architecture of fragmentation, meaninglessness and despair', but then his spirit of architecture is as constipated as his prose. 'Meaning', this dreaded prop of the verbally preoccupied, is always trotted out to validate the spatially turgid at the expense of the formally exuberant. There *isn't* an enormous amount of connotative meaning to be found in the best of the AA work, with the odd exception. What there is, as an alternative, is a lot of running; the running of the edge of the building into other edges; the collage becoming more of a layering process where sheets or wisps or strands or meshes or flimsy filters play amongst each other. The clue was given by Gehry with his chain link and his

Stanley Saitowitz, Halfway House, Transvaal 1978

twisted drapes. To the ferrets it can also be found in the work of some current Australians, like Rex Addison, or Glenn Murcutt, or sometimes Richard Leplastrier, for example, who also rediscovered corrugated metal and decided to drape it and curve it. To other ferrets it can be associated with Hugo Häring in Garkau mood and, of course, to Hans Scharoun in the Philharmonie. The wayward wheel turns full circle, of course, with any mention of the Expressionist stream of European architecture, for in the German-speaking countries one is always aware of the pent-up emotion surrounding Rationalist-Expressionist associations. How did Mies feel about being published in Taut's 'Frülicht' we wonder?

The AA, however, likes to feel itself purely self-generating. At first it has a point: the extraordinary inbreeding that elsewhere would have resulted in the architectural equivalent of cross-eyed dopiness has in fact resulted in a chain of influence, support, rivalry and evolution that puts real meaning into the idea of the academy. Perhaps it is because the English architectural world at large has been jealous or suspicious of the AA since about 1890 that from inside the feeling that 'This'll upset them' is implicit. Just look at a sample of the chain: all of the NATØ Group were students of Nigel Coates, but he in turn was a student of Bernard Tschumi. Neil Porter and Guy Comely were students of Peter Wilson but he was a student of OMA's Koolhaas and Zenghelis. Incidentally, Zaha Hadid was also an OMA student (and, the ferrets will note, a student of Leon Krier at an earlier stage). Kay Ngee Tan and Dimitri Vannas were students of Christine Hawley (and myself), but she had studied with Archigram's Ron Herron who still teaches there. The full chart of cross-fertilisation overlaid on direct-line influence would soon render this piece as boring (or fascinating) as a banquet diagram, but it is the middle generation that forms the key to the real burst of energy and outrageously good drawing—almost across the board. It is the fulsomeness of the thing and the coinciding swirls of inspiration that make the strange but exciting architecture match the strange sociology and, in such cases as Peter Salter and Chris Macdonald, result in a hybrid architecture that combines lyricism with mechanisms and yet is unlike all other.

The Australian buildings might droop similarly, but they never display quite the same lightness of touch. The alumni of New York's Cooper Union may display a similar sensitivity – or even more sensitivity – but nothing like the same range. At times it draws fire through its very self-possessedness; the NATØ work in particular seems always teetering between ugliness and pure masturbation, but just at the point when you might lose sympathy it throws up an exciting reminder of the daft-craft tradition of English work that almost died with the end of the Festival of Britain. Of course, it is now the moment to recall and revivify the spirit of '50s architecture.

So many links can be found and therefore clues to the formal direction of the work under discussion that we know, by extrapolation, that its next stages must be fruitful. In all, it is as if several seams of sustenance have been reopened together in the first four years. First, is the Constructivist inspiration: more and more I come to suspect the dominant authority of the Bauhaus – which was certainly rammed down my throat – of being a filter or gentrification by the middle Europeans of the much more exciting work made by the Russians during and after the Revolution. Airships, agit-trains, theatre sets, paintings, towers, huge creaking abstractions… all this and a host of dynamic buildings too. Perhaps to the teachers of the '40s, '50s, '60s, and early '70s this was all too heady; Bolshie stuff? So we were taught to admire the Bauhaus. No wonder many were bored and looked for easy fun? The mouth-watering kick that the now-fashionable publication of Russian material gives to my own students is also related to the feeling that OMA and Hadid and they themselves can carry on where it left off. There's a post-Constructivism in the air.

In England, the success of the High-Tech suggests that stuff is available that can realise those exotic forms: that the High-Tech offices so far choose to use it sparingly and conservatively is merely a come-on to the imaginative.

That the architecture of the 1950s was highly inventive – even when it stained – is just beginning to dawn, and excite. Oscar Niemeyer (who was not to be mentioned in polite architectural circles three years ago) is once again being heralded as a hero and 'look-no-hands!' becomes, once again, the cry in contemplating the legs and wings of the new architecture.

The present messages being sent out are just the first few hops from branch to branch but those with good hearing can discern a fantastic rustling and the healthy sound of twigs breaking.

73

Architecture is on the wing!

СТИЛЬ и ЭПОХА

Peter Cook

The Quality of Modernism

BUILDING CRITIQUE
Lloyd's Insurance Market, London
by Richard Rogers Partnership

Reyner Banham
October 1986

The new, monochromatic and monumental version of High-Tech that is on view at the recently completed Lloyd's building in the city of London (as well as Foster's Hongkong and Shanghai Bank on the other side of the world) doubtless marks a further stage in the ongoing epic of late modernism, the style that was supposed to die. The falsity of that supposition lay, of course, in construing Modernism as *only* a style, rather than as a style supported by a whole complex of attitudes to design and society inherited ultimately from the latter part of the nineteenth century—the period when so much of the present century was first put in working order.

We all knew this, in one way or another, but what we could not have known at the time of Modernism's first prematurely reported death (Pruitt-Igoe, Ronan Point, *Complexity And Contradiction in Architecture*: choose one), was how deeply ingrained in the minds of architects, and those of clients even more, that modern tradition and its value systems would prove to be. Its fundamental appeal, however delusory, was that it promised a rational and demystified design process, whose triad of Function/Structure/ Materials made sense to the kind of

Le Corbusier, Villa Savoye, Poissy 1929

practical-minded men who manage the building programmes of major corporate and governmental clients.

That was its triumph—but one hardly needs to add it was also its tragedy, because its rationality could not protect its original social idealism and aesthetic vision against the erosions and corrosions of three decades of cost cutting and vote-chasing. The results, as embodied in, say, the truly horrible MACE school-building system, fully deserved the savaging they received from the sharp radical teeth of the critics of the '70s. Unfortunately, those critics have proven to be mostly boys sent to do a man's job, who mistook a complicated civic and professional disaster for a mere stylistic crisis. Manfredo Tafuri, almost alone, with his concept of the inability of architecture as a profession to deliver the 'Utopia of Social Democracy' to which the Modern Movement had been committed, seems to have understood the magnitude of the problem, but one may beg leave to differ from his diagnosis: the problem may have been less to do with social ideology than with the business of actually putting buildings together.

High-Tech, in its British manifestations as epitomised by the elaborate and painstaking detailing of Lloyd's, is clearly preoccupied with putting buildings together properly. In it, Modernism has come back to haunt its critics with a vengeance, but the returned tradition has been properly chastened and transformed as befits the post-critical situation. No virtue is now seen as inheriting automatically in 'being modern'; rather, it now seems to reside in the undertaking of the responsibilities, and the execution of the tasks that are understood as peculiar to a 'modern condition' that refuses to go away.

High on the register of both tasks and responsibilities is that of inventing an architecture appropriate to the times —and that is a task which, despite Rogers' publicly expressed desire for an 'architecture without irony' has produced, at Lloyd's, a monster irony to which we must return in due course. But within the 'project' (as current academic cant would term it) of making architecture modern, lurks the more fundamental task of making modern buildings; the development of methods of design and production appropriate to the times. Too often, in the simplistic and propagandist past, the mere use of a supposedly modern material – typically steel, concrete or glass – was seen as satisfying these criteria, without it being observed that to employ an approved material does not of itself produce an approvable architecture. Or even architecture at all, as the technically brilliant but stylistically depraved use of concrete in Ricardo Bofill's mass-housing schemes makes all too clear.

Mies van der Rohe, Glass Tower project, 1921

Reyner Banham

When one looks back at Modernism's pioneer constructor-architects, such as Auguste Perret – or architect-constructors like Mies van der Rohe – one sees that the actual style and technology of using materials are crucial, that there is some necessary (if perennially inscrutable) connection between the usages that shape the individual pieces of material and the architectural quality of the building that results from them. The Lesson of the Masters (particularly Perret and Mies) is that the architect cannot avoid responsibility for the quality of any single detail of the building, even if it comes standardised and off-the-peg like a brick or patent glazing system. Indeed, one of the modern tradition's continuing problems is that it has been very slow in developing ways of making care in the use of off-the-peg glazing systems as apparent as care in the design of brick-work—although the *reverse* of care in the use of patent glazing is all too easy to see, as in recent work by Philip Johnson and John Burgee.

Clearly it would be easier to see that due care had been exercised if the architect takes it upon purpose-invent every detail, every assembly that is used. But this can only be a crushing task, a killing responsibility that is beyond the capacity of most of those legally qualified to call themselves architects. The masters themselves had to cast about for help or even invent psychological pretences; Perret re-made concrete after detailing wood and the forms of Classicism, and Mies used standard sections, for which he could disclaim responsibility, to build up assemblages so rich and complex that he had to blame them on God.

High-Tech, as an attitude to the making of buildings, pursues a different but related strategy in which support and comfort are found in the methods of making machines. Again, this has long and solid – if often bungled – Modernist traditions behind it, but it is no more a slavish imitation of machine forms than those of Le Corbusier's classic villas were literal cribs from the work of Bugatti, Farman or Voisin. In either case, the specific usages are clearly different from those that engineers might use—indeed the differences are among the considerations that establish the usages as architecture rather than engineering, but at Lloyd's the differences can also be so subtle and minuscule that confusion is understandable.

Confusion becomes inexcusable on close inspection, however; confront any single detail – the fixing of the uprights of the handrails of the external stairs, for instance – and one is looking at a design solution that would be virtually inconceivable in normal engineering practice. An engineer might, indeed, have done a handrail upright for half the price, but the result would not be half as rewarding as the architecture. This is not to say

Richard Rogers, sketch depicting atrium principle

76

that architecture does not still have an enormous amount to learn from even the simplest practices of engineers, and it certainly does not denigrate the crucial importance of the contribution to the total design of Lloyd's by engineers like Peter Rice. Engineering is one way of designing things, architecture is another. The triumph of Lloyd's is, paradoxically, that it is so difficult to tell them apart.

Perret re-made concrete and purpose-invented every detail with loving care but…

Nevertheless, one seems to sense at Lloyd's a new determination to make it clear that, in the last resort, *alles is Architektur*. the more unified the image produced by the almost monochrome finishes, as opposed to the diverse colours of say, Centre Pompidou, which tended to separate the parts, draws attention to the kind of unified general conception that is usually supposed to be the product of architectural designing. If there is, in all this emphatic complexity of engineer-style detailing, a manifest attempt to project an imagery appropriate to the technological times, then the generally monochrome presentation underlines that this is still an architectural projection, and if the equipment in the service towers is indeed meant to be replaced on normal engineering time-cycles of obsolescence, the monumental tonality of the unbelievably good concrete work and of the high-style glass walls assures us of the permanency of the overall concept.

True Quality of Modernity

When the sub-contractors have finished up all the bit and pieces and odd corners and glass-walled lifts that were still not quite right at the time of this writing, Lloyd's will be a fairly shocking reminder of the kind of architectural quality that ought to be part of the heritage of Modernism—and let anyone who says, 'and I should think so at that price!' Try to remember a period when good architecture was ever cheap. But if the architecture has the true quality of modernity, does the client? This is not a frivolous question; it is fundamental to the whole building. When one looks down into the pit of the Room where the business of Lloyd's is actually done, one is suddenly struck by the recognition that its uncanny resemblance to a set piece from some old science fiction movie is less due to the glittering finishes or the exposed structure or the illuminating criss cross escalators, than to the sheer number of grey and brown clad human beings (up to 5000 at a time, it is believed) moving about everywhere. It is like up-market Kafka, or T.S. Eliot's 'many' whom 'death had undone' re-choreographed by Busby Berkely. A great spectacle of financial power, but is it necessary?

Being There

Surely, in the High-Tech world of electronic communications and personal computers most of these people could stay at home – stay in bed, even – and do their business without crowding onto this hopelessly overloaded site. Apparently Richard Rogers did raise this issue tentatively with the client, but without effect. However high the technology they employ, the underwriters see no alternative to their common presence, blocking gangways and getting in one another's way generally, in this single room. Being there is what it's all about; the drama, the boredom, the irritation, the moments of high panic and all that ancient tradition, symbolised by the presence of the Lutine Bell to be rung to announce shipwrecks —under which sits a uniformed attendant calling for missing underwriters by means of a microphone and a current electronic paging system. Every item of high technology at Lloyd's, structural, environmental, mechanical or electrical, services a business that still puts its faith in face-to-face contact and rumours whispered in passing ears.

If one finds this an irony – and it is extremely difficult not to – then it seems to be an irony appropriate to our late-Modern times. Architecture may have abandoned its utopian dreams of changing the world, because the world is perfectly capable of changing itself without architecture's aid, but the compulsion to make sense of the resulting human dilemmas is still the most essential quality of Modernism.

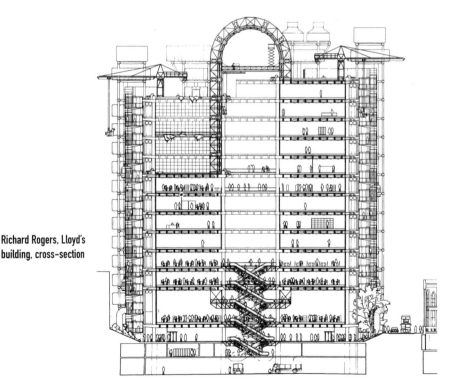

Richard Rogers, Lloyd's building, cross-section

Foster Development

THEORY

Alastair Best

April 1986

It is tempting, to anyone trying to make critical sense out of Foster's career, to regard the Hong Kong Bank as the great central masterpiece, the culmination of over 20 years astonishingly fertile practice and the almost inevitable outcome of a series of ambitions which have never faltered. And in many ways it is. The Bank develops and enormously enriches ideas foreshadowed at Willis Faber (the moving staircase combined with atrium) and at Sainsbury (extensive prototyping of prefabricated components); but one of its most significant features is new in Foster's repertoire: the spatial variety made possible by opening up the building at street level and suspending the office floors in stacks from bridge-like trusses. Willis Faber and Sainsbury, by contrast, are sealed containers; the most seductive examples available of architecture as industrial design. Also new in Foster's work is the emphasis on *movement*. After the somewhat constrained circulation of Sainsbury, the Bank provides an exhilarating journey from public, to semi-public to semi-private and finally to private space.

Norman Foster and Richard Rogers are the only architects of international status who are now practising with their Modern Movement ideals more or less intact. Both still cling tenaciously to an architecture which is anti-suburban in form, committed to social integration, and wholly, even ostentatiously, dedicated to technology at its leading edge. These are values worth fighting for, but

Sainsbury Centre, East Anglia University 1978

Vers une Architecture

they are out of fashion. Those who have abandoned the struggle – through fecklessness or expediency, or both – must now watch from the 10 guinea seats while Foster and Rogers carry on the heroic struggle alone. Heroism is unfashionable too: yet we admire courage and virtuosity, and although we may reassure ourselves from time to time with the cosy reflection that all this Late Modern stuff is drenched in self-parody. We cannot escape experiencing the frisson of excitement, the sense of danger which all Foster's work conveys. A.E. Housman once famously assessed poetry by its effect on the hairs at the back of his neck: if they bristled involuntarily, then it was the genuine article. Judged by this criterion, Foster is a very great architect indeed.

It is perhaps inevitable that one should bracket Rogers and Foster together – although I happen to believe Foster to be Rogers' superior as an architect – for despite the strong dissimilarities in their work, their careers have followed similar paths and their personal and professional lives were once closely intertwined. They came to architecture, however, by very different routes. Rogers, as Bryan Appleyard's newly published biography (Faber & Faber) vividly demonstrates was a late developer, somewhat *depaysé* after what sounds like an idyllic and cultured Italian childhood, a school dropout, and, to begin with at least, a rather indifferent performer at the AA School of Architecture. Foster was not so much a late developer as a late starter. He began life in the accountant's department of Manchester City Hall and only switched to architecture after National Service in the RAF. Both experiences were crucial. Of Waterhouse's magnificent Manchester City Hall interior, what struck Foster most of all were the details: the hand-rails and the light-fittings – even the glass-sided water-cisterns in the lavatories. But apart from this very significant revelation – for what impresses again and again in Foster's work is precisely the beautifully judged sense of detail – very few of Foster's admitted 'influences' could be described as buildings by well-known architects. What fascinates Foster is the language of assembly: the grading of components, the pared down junction, the smooth immaculate fit. His office walls are adorned with blown-up details of key images of heliostats and airstream caravans, for he belongs to the last generation of students to be weaned on the seductive imagery of *Vers une Architecture*. It is hardly surprising that a book which twins the Parthenon with the cockpit of a Caproni sailplane on a double page spread should have left an indelible mark. National service in the RAF as an electronics engineer was the second formative experience of Foster's professional life. It instilled a love of flying and of aircrafts, and the desire – seen by some as quixotic – to reproduce the *svelte* and energy-efficient forms of the flying machine in his own architecture. Nor did the built forms on the airfield escape attention. Foster recalls how he worked in a turf-covered hangar ('high on camouflage and very low natural light'), and it is not entirely fanciful to look forward from this to the turf-covered roof garden at Willis Faber or the sleek, ground-hugging form of the Frankfurt Leichtathletikhalle, or even (a personal favourite of mine) the Computer Technology air tent. In the same way the problem of introducing natural light into deep plan has been a recurring preoccupation. It was completely ignored at IBM Cosham, whose interest does not extend very much further than the glass skin: partially solved at Willis Faber by punching a central light well into the heart of the plan; and brilliantly handled at Sainsbury with its filigree of trusses, grilles and catwalks. The Hongkong Bank's sunscoops which direct light beams into the atrium provide another solution; their precursors are the tracking mirror systems, designed to harness the low winter sun, which Foster mounted on top of the unbuilt 'office in a forest' for Fred Olsen at Vestby on Oslo fjord.

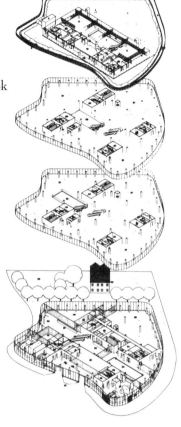

Willis Faber, Ipswich 1975

The third and much the most important influence on Foster was the time spent in America on a Henry Fellowship at Yale. Here he met Richard Rogers and became acquainted with Californian architecture—notably the work of Craig Ellwood and Charles Eames and Ezra Ehrenkrantz's SCSD schools system. At Yale he sharpened up his drawing technique under Paul Rudolph (the exploded section and heavily shaded elevations with which all Foster buildings from Reliance Controls on are presented owe something to Rudolph) and came under the spell of Serge Chermayeff whose theories of community and privacy are resurfacing with interesting results in the Bank. 'I have always believed,' he told the RIBA during his Gold Medal address in 1983, 'that architecture is about people—at the one extreme the private inner sanctum it can create, at the other extreme the outside public spaces… In between the public and private domains the edges can be consciously or self-consciously blurred to create or modify communities by sustaining, erecting or breaking down social barriers.' Those who argue that 'people' are precisely what Foster's architecture is *not* about would claim that this is the empty rhetoric of a man who seems to shun personal relationships and

Reliance Controls (with Richard Rogers), Swindon 1967

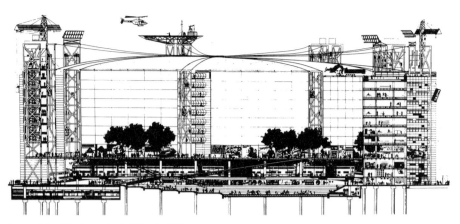

Transportation interchange (project), London 1977

whose buildings, for all their technical brilliance, remain cold and inhuman. I think they are wrong and I feel that Foster's motives are entirely genuine. They are rooted in standard Modern Movement ideology and in Foster's observed experience of American corporate culture. His early work is characterised by a perfectly orthodox social commitment which saw architecture as the instrument for improving the lot of the working man—by, for instance, sweeping away false barriers between management and shop floor. One detail from this early phase sticks in my mind. Foster Associates, retained to convert a small canning factory for Ian Barron's rapidly expanding Computer Technology, installed a fitted carpet on the factory floor. This had a dramatic effect on the working habits of the staff, who began to perform with an almost obsessive neatness, and it also demonstrated that in the new clean industries the old divisions between white- and blue-collar workers need no longer apply. Nothing at all remarkable now, but in 1968, on a scruffy trading estate in Hemel Hempstead, it was a mild sensation.

Foster is not of course a believer in architectural determinism; but he has always maintained that a better working environment can improve morale and labour relations and he has used these arguments with brilliant success. At Willis Faber, for example, he was able to convince the client that an Olympic size swimming pool should be the centrepiece of the main entrance, on the grounds that recreation should form an integral part of the working environment. In the same way Sainsbury is an essay in the art of persuading wary dons of the inherent dangers of a Two Cultures mentality. All this 'strategic questioning' is part of the

Stadium (project), Frankfurt 1981

82

architect's stock in trade but Foster has developed it into an art form in its own right. It has enabled him dramatically to alter or extend his brief, or, as at the BBC, to let the brief slip through his fingers. An architect less concerned with 'challenging preconceptions' (a favourite Foster phrase) would, perhaps, have achieved *something* at Portland Place. Instead, the constraints of the site and the shambolic and impenetrable corporate culture of Broadcasting House have deprived central London of one of its few chances of acquiring a serious modern building.

The proposed Radio Centre at Portland Place and the proposed Mediathèque at Nimes both suggest a new post-Hongkong Bank phase in Foster's development. Here for the first time he is having to grapple with sensitive, historic urban sites. The drawing of Nimes, captioned in Foster's own unmistakable hand which appeared on the May 1985 cover of the AR, told all. 'No diagonals in structure —must *not* look industrial'. This is not so much a loss of nerve, as a sense of realism. Or has Foster, while attempting to resist it with every weapon at his disposal, begun to see the virtues of contextualism in certain circumstances? I think it very improbable that Foster is distancing himself from past concerns – drawings of Stansted terminal and of the Leichtathletikhalle suggest not – but he could claim that his work shows an increasing preoccupation with light, space and movement. And he would be right.

83

Design Study, Nimes 1985

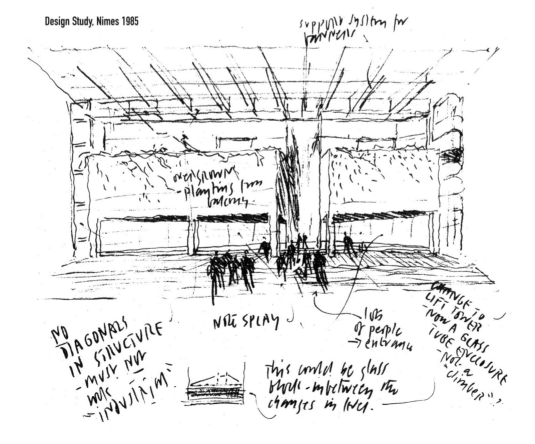

After Eames

BUILDING CRITIQUE
House and Studio, New South Wales
by Richard Leplastrier

Rory Spence
August 1986

Leplastrier's house near Bellingen for a writer and a painter, like all his work, is intimately related to its immediate landscape context, as well as to the lifestyle of its owners. Characteristically, Leplastrier spent three weeks camping on the site with the clients, developing the design for the house on the spot. Simpler and less refined than Leplastrier's other buildings, the Bellingen house had some of the informality of the rural farmhouse, but combined with an unusually formal almost ceremonial relation to its site.

Set in a pastoral valley, the main house closely hugs the tree-lined Never-Never River to the south, and addresses a range of mountains to the north with an almost Classical symmetry and confidence. But it is also reminiscent of the archetypal Australian rural shed with a change of roof pitch. The house is only single storey, but is raised up on tree trunks or 'stumps', a traditional form for timber houses in Northern NSW and Queensland, primarily to escape floods but also to give apparent detachment from the ground, from both inside and out, rather like a tree house. It was his intention the foliage should grow up around the base, so the house would seem to peek out through the upper branches.

Detail of kitchen

The Greek cross plan, orientated to the points of the compass, maximises the external wall area – very favourable in a semi-tropical climate – and gives direction and individuality to the different parts of the house. The essence of the house is the north-south, mountain river axis. All main communal spaces are located on this axis —the river platform to the south, offset to align with the river, the entry porch and bathroom in the south arm of the cross, the kitchen/dinning room in the centre and the living verandah projecting out towards the mountains to the north. As in some of Frank Lloyd Wright's houses, the central kitchen, with its central dining table, is the social core of the house— meals and conversation by implication the focal household activities. The east and west arms of the cross originally contained study/bedroom and studio respectively, but with the later construction of a separate studio the latter has now become an additional, protected sitting room. The bed itself is a retreat, a room within a room, like an English four-poster bed or the enclosed sleeping alcoves of traditional Danish farm-houses, but with its own little window, while views through to the study give a sense of spatial complexity and ambiguity to the small open-plan interior.

One of Leplastrier's primary concerns is designing to suit the Australian climate—houses which can open up in the summer, like shelters or tents rather than solid European-style buildings. In some of his Sydney houses, which have translucent sailcloth walls in lieu of windows, he has tended to *over*-estimate his client's capacity to cope with the winter cold. But semi-tropical Bellingen, where winter is even milder, is more sympathetic to his ideas. Here the whole house operates

South wall of studio in various degrees of openness

like a giant thermal stack gathering warm air from its various arms and releasing it, via hinged panels in the kitchen ceiling, out through the roof ventila-tors in the central skylight above. Hinged wall panels above the door to entry porch and verandah and behind the half pediments on the north facade, as well as windows and doors, can also be opened to allow cross ventilation throughout the building. In winter, all the panels – oper-ated, characteristically, by nautical block and tackle – can be closed to make the retreat from the cold, wind and rain.

The climax of the house is the magnificent main sitting space, which is simply a fly-screened verandah, open on three sides, surveying a 180 degree panorama of moun-tains—a place in which to experience the dramatic semi-tropical weather changes. This is a house for the rain as well as the sun. A full storey below, the foreground falls away and one is thrust out into the valley, apparently at its

Fly-screened living verandah on the north (sunny) side of house

View of studio from south-west

focal point. The bathroom is, similarly, an open, fly-screened box but, like the river platform, it is associated with the trees, birds and sound of running water to the south.

There is a continuing dialogue in Leplastrier's work between respect for tradition, craftsmanship and materials, and an intense desire to experiment and create anew. The former expresses itself in a celebration of the ordinary and a love of natural materials: the traditional Queensland stumps, the simple roof forms, the vertical slats of the gable valences and the use of fine and durable Australian hardwoods —black butt for the structure and brush box for internal walls and floor, beautifully constructed by Hank Mulder, a local builder. The latter expresses itself in a re-interpretation of the ordinary and an interest in modern man-made materials: the open fly-screened bathroom and living area, the ingenious ventilation arrangements, the use of corrugated iron and hardboard for external walls and sliding shutters (in standard aluminium frames, replacing one sheet of glass) and unpainted 'Caneite' pinboard for internal upper walls and ceiling. This dialogue between tradition and innovation contributes towards a sense of freshness and vitality that is characteristic of Leplastrier's work.

The second aspect of Leplastrier's work is particularly apparent in the studio, generally referred to as 'The River Room'. Where the main house, although built of the same materials, is quietly dignified the studio, built two years later, is elegantly vivacious, even capricious, with its asymmetrically tilted, curved roof and its delicate little awning protecting the walls from the sun and rain. The one confronts the distant mountains, breaking free from the line of the river, while the other peers into the trees and, like the open platform, aligns itself with the river. The two-storey south wall, of translucent corrugated plastic (and facing *away* from the sun) gives a beautiful even light suitable for painting, but allows no view out. The central portion of the wall can be opened up, however, to reveal an exquisite backdrop of mossy tree trunks and foliage: two large panels slide back on either side, the opening protected by a curved plastic hood. The lower part of the wall is a proprietary 'up-and-over' garage door, ingeniously turned back to front, so that it forms a projecting external canopy when open. Small top-hung wall panels can also be opened to provide ventilation and views in three directions from the built-in desk on the west wall.

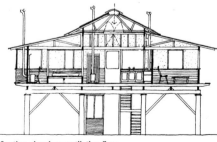

Section showing ventilation flaps

Connecting walkway, from the studio

When opened up to the river and the sounds of water and birds, the workplace had a wonderful contemplative serenity, much appreciated by its painter client, who found it an ideal workplace, and for several months virtually lived there, sleeping on the high-level platform at the east end. Leplastrier's inventiveness is demonstrated above all by the delightfully simple roof —a double skin of curved corrugated iron separated by timber battens and tensioned by steel wires propped out from the ceiling on standard broom handles of Spotted Gum: its elegance further enhanced by the ingenious incorporation of clear plastic piping as a seal along the verge junction, giving a barely perceptible delicate line of light separating ceiling from wall. House and studio are linked by an open, raised walkway, with bent galvanised-steel pipe for roof framing and hand-rails, giving an animated, spidery quality to an otherwise hard industrial material.

The house and studio, each in counterpoint to the other, thus celebrate and intensify the two most natural features of the site —the open valley and chain of mountains to the north and the intimate and mysterious wooded river to the south.

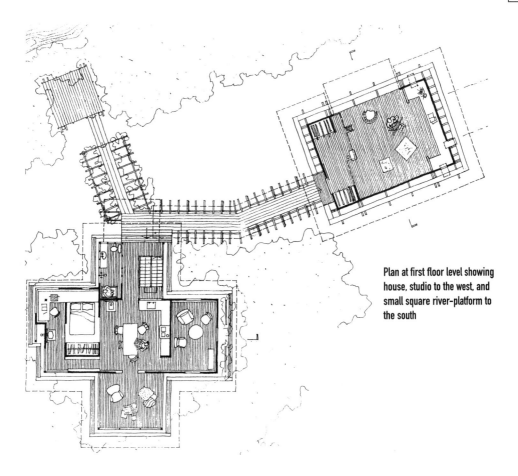

Plan at first floor level showing house, studio to the west, and small square river-platform to the south

right angle is only one possibility among many and to impose it mea

ricting the possibilities   London Docklands—a great exhibition

osable architecture   The new modernism that is taking shape nc

gain sha   the robe   ch off i   lders   nal identi

ns only po   le on   e frin   wh   have   ve   bee   nquered b

mer soci   Th   s a   -C   ru   m in the   You ma

world i   one tha   e cli   eve   es   right angle i

sibility a   g many a   o impo   t me   restric   g the possibilit

Docklan   —a grea   hibition o   le arc   cture   The

at is taking shape now is again shaking the robe of kitsch off its shou

gional i   ty see   ossibl   fringes   have have

quered b   onsu   soci   re is   ost-Con   ctivism in th

ke your   wor   it,   tha   ly th   ient eve   es   The

only on   ssibility a   many a   pose it   ns restricting

Lon   Dockla   —a great e   tion of disp   ble architect

modern   that is   g shape n   s again shaki   the robe of k

oulders   Regional identity seems only possible on the fringes w

ot been conquered by consumer society   There is a Post-Constru

it, one that only the client ever sees   The new modernism tha

1987

1991

The Public Finnish

BUILDING CRITIQUE
Myyrmaki Parish Centre, Helsinki
by Juha Leiviska

Colin St John Wilson
June 1986

The Myyrmaki Parish Centre is the most recent of three centres built by Leiviska in the last sixteen years, all of them depicting as a common theme the elementarist forms exemplified in the most sophisticated way in the Myyrmaki complex itself.

What is remarkable about these churches is the exploration and development of a particular language of forms for the making of a sacred place. Although this language obviously owes a great deal to facet Cubism and its extension in the elementarist canon of Van Doesburg and Rietveld, it constitutes a refreshingly vigorous extension of that canon through compounding it with a spatial distribution of great vitality. This spatial discipline has its roots in those Aalto projects of the mid-'30s in which rhythmical sequences of the echelon form lead to a range of dispersal points of focus. It is the opposite mode to static symmetry: like music its discipline evolves in a framework of movement and counterpoint.

The Myyrmaki church is sited in a suburb of Helsinki in a park that runs in a narrow band on a north-south axis to the east of a railway embankment: and this boundary forms the back of the site against which the church is stretched in order to free most of the area as parkland.

Myyrmaki Parish Centre, side view

This rather defensive strategy pays off remarkable dividends through the formal tactics deployed by Leiviska. The long western wall is set up as a powerful *datum* against which the church, parish and club rooms are freely distributed and it is the fixed plane of this wall that acts as the controlling device for the whole composition.

The most extraordinary spatial result of this *parti* is that the axis towards the altar is not the conventional long axis but the short cross axis. This device results in the altar wall gaining dramatically in intensity of focus from the pews that press towards it in shallow space. Furthermore since the wall is very high, an extraordinary suggestion of spatial pressure is evoked, animating the wall's surface with a pronounced upward directionality. This apparent weightlessness is derived from the veiled modulation of light created by the vertical and horizontal overlapping of planes which makes a space of luminous resonance evoking a trance-like experience of levitation. The aesthetics of light become transformed into the metaphysics of light. The Abbé Suger would have approved... *'per lumina vera ad Verum Lumen'*.

This 'dematerialisation' of form, extended out to the perimeter of the building, dissolves any sense of mass or any conventional assertion of the frontal plane of the facade in favour of melding the front edges of wall planes with the shafts of the silver birch trees of the Park. Landscape and building melt into one another and this has the effect of demonumentalising a powerful sense of presence; and indeed that sense is made broader and more pervasive because of the building's engagement with the wider landscape.

Finland is the one country in which the architecture of the Modern Movement seems to have grown, developed without challenge and come to maturity as if in its natural habitat without the need to reject its past. This thought was brought home to me vividly during a symposium in Venice to which I had been invited as referee to a debate between Italian and Scandinavian architects on the topic 'La Tradizione Moderna'. It was clear that Italy which had fathered Futurism, the first and most violent protest against tradition (experienced as the suffocation of 'living in a Museum'), was now only too ready to relive ancient glories — 'Romanita' reborn in the guise of Rationalism.

For the Finns, however, it was quite natural to believe that Modernism itself had matured to the point at which it had achieved the depth of perspective proper to a tradition of its own. At one level this is a simple fact of life: Tuomo Siitonen for instance pointed out that he had been born and brought up in a world in which only one building in eight was older than 60 years. At the deeper level of architectural intention (one might say of polemic) it is significant that an architect like Christian Gullichsen when he confesses to 'a taste for

Christian Gullichsen, Kauaniainen Parish Centre

clichés' does not have in mind the Arch of Constantine or the Villa Malcontenta so much as references to Corbu, Aalto, Lewerentz, Duiker and so on. In other words, for Finnish architects, the Modern Movement is not only an unchangeable foundation for a living and evolving architecture but has, during the last 85 years, produced a broad enough base and variety of growth upon which to build—a critical tradition of ample depth.

Why is this so? It lies in the chemistry and history of a culture and that is an infinitely complex phenomenon. You might as well ask why Greek culture posed the sort of questions that could only be answered by the invention of entasis—and then pursued the consequences of that answer with the intensity of a moral imperative. Suffice it to say that at a happy moment in history the self-awareness of a growing nation somehow became encoded and embodied in terms of architecture—the moment was happy because it coincided with the genesis, emergence and self-realisation of a worldwide revolution in the experience of architecture itself.

Where that revolution had been greeted in other countries with considerable resistance, in Finland it was welcomed as normal.

From this there has come into being a quality of *rootedness* in the realm of *res publica* and this is a gift beyond price when compared with the position in the UK or the US in which every building has frantically to search for and assert its 'meaning' in a public vacuum. It needs also to be said that this phenomenon was not the achievement of a single man nor of a single generation but something sus-

92

Juha Leiviska, Kirkkonummi church, 1980—84

tained by many talents across a very broad range of values. I say that this quality of diversity has to be emphasised because the popular myth of the domination of the scene by Alvar Aalto has failed to do justice to the debate within—a tension and a complexity remarkable for their intensity. For instance, that myth would not have prepared one for the selection of Tadao Ando for the Aalto award in 1985: to understand that you need to be aware of the background of elementarist abstraction in the very influential work and teaching of the 'Rationalist' Aulis Blomstedt and the equally authoritative Minimalist school of architecture typified in the work of Ruusuvuori, Pitkanen and others. There is a sustained running debate. But then it also has to be said that Finnish Modernism has, always been a complicated affair.

Myyrmaki Parish Centre, south-east view

You merely have to take into account Aalto's Villa Mairea to realise that it is an architecture that has very little to do with that American tourists invention of 'The International Style': and by the same token, it has rather little reason to take too seriously the equally trumped-up invention (born from the same mentality) of 'PostModernism'.

As to the typical Finnish response to that phenomenon one can expect a number of references to Aalto's famous phrase about 'the smell of Hollywood'. But perhaps a better way to illustrate the point would be to take two or three typical case-studies. I immediately place these on a very different plane of reference from Anglo-American practice by taking a building type that is very common in Finland, very rare elsewhere, the Parish Centre. This is the bringing together in one place of a focus for both the social and sacramental life of a community. The requirements of church and recreational centre are brought together in programmes of varying degrees of scale and complexity. The first thing to be said is that in symbolic terms the programme itself does not have to strive for 'meaning' in the way that so many 'PostModern' theatrics do and in doing so reduce themselves to the ludicrous. (Once again the advantages of 'rootedness' assert themselves.) Indeed to take three examples of the type is very instructive not only for their individual excellence but also for the stance that each takes towards the question of 'PostModernism'. I have in mind Leiviska's Myyrmaki, Gullichsen's Kauniainen Parochial Centre, and the Paavilainens' Paimio Parish Centre.

First, Leiviska's Myyrmaki Church and Parish Centre. Here the language is an original extension of the Modernist vocabulary in which the elementarist planes deployed in the Schroder House engage in a renewed version of what Le

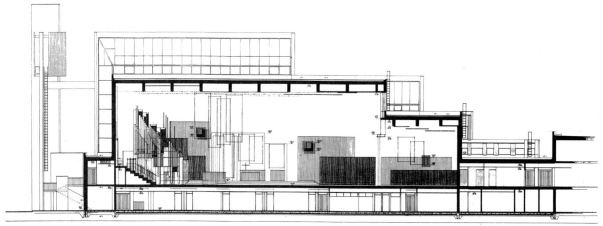

Myyrmaki Parish Church, longitudinal section

Corbusier called 'the cunning and correct play of forms in light', — but in this case in a play that is specifically directed to the creation of a sacred place.

Next Gullichsen's Kauniainen Parish Centre. Here there is a shift in the nature of the language not only in formal terms (it is 'carved') but in a certain propensity for allusion, for representational forms. Here, however, we encounter a range of allusion that is markedly different from the PostModern repertoire: for while there is proclaimed a generalised reference to archaic prototype (the approach by descent as in the catacombs) the specific allusions are, as noted above, to modern precedents — to the pergola of Corbu, the undulating wall of Aalto, the scooped windows of Scarpa... What is reassuring is that not only do these elements 'work' pragmatically (a wall undulates to find a place for a font, a sacristy, a stair) but they also work as references that give something back to their sources while at the same time binding the whole composition together on a difficult piece of topography with the original Parish Hall and Tower built by Petaja twenty years ago.

Finally, in the Paimio Parish Centre by Käpy and Simo Paavilainen, there is some reference to the PostModern mode, but it is of a special kind. I write in this case from experience of the photographs only, but I sense that there is nothing portentous here and the touch is very light (the mannerisms are taken from Venturi, not from Speer). Once again however the allusions are to Modern precedent unless I am very mistaken — the star-spattered ceiling of Asplund's Skandia Cinema, Corbu's billowing Chandigarh cornice, yet carried out in the polychrome metal of his Zurich pavilion and so on. But what is more important because it overrides this game of allusions and 'deliberate mistakes' is the overall spatial planning of the project that is more akin to the spirit of Scharoun and that recalls the fine exuberance of these architects' earlier Parish Centre in Olari.

Compare these three cases to the projects for the extension of London's National Gallery. There architects seemed to have been trying 'to please teacher' with five-finger exercises in what my taxi driver calls 'the Palladium style'. I could swear that in one project at least four of the six Roman Doric columns had real genuine entasis: who knows but that with a little more practice…? What we are confronted with here is the difference between allusions that are authentic to context and those that are merely kitsch. In his crucial essay on 'Tradition and the Individual Talent', T.S. Eliot argued that there is a reciprocity in the exchanges between old and new, such that not only is the new reinforced by energies from the past, but also the old is itself transformed by a shift in realisation that has been won by the new. (To us it is clear that not only was Eliot changed by Dante but that Dante has been changed by Eliot.) My definition of kitsch would accordingly point to those occasions on which some allusion to the past is a one-way transaction only—the new trying to borrow 'meaning' from the past without repayment, that is to say without giving back any new life to the source upon which it has drawn.

It was noticeable in last year's exhibition 'Finland Builds' that, for the most part, the exhibits were public buildings – church, school, parish centre, theatre, housing, etc – and secondly, that the commission was won by competition. In Finland it would seem that competitions are the means by which the whole profession is honed to a high standard: and that standard is ensured by the great professional attention devoted to the competition process in which a carefully chosen board of assessors may spend weeks examining submissions in the course of which they will write a full report on every submission (not just the prize winners). The rigour of this procedure stands in marked contrast to the situation in England where architectural competitions are rare and more often than not end up as the subject of a freak show (of Northampton County Headquarters or the recent National Gallery competitions).

We live in bad times. In the field of architecture it is a time of bad faith; all of a sudden architecture has become a topic profitable to the journalism of spec-

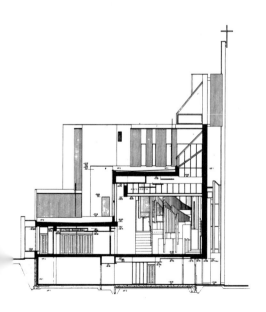 

Sections through main body of church

tacular facts, contrived polemic and nostalgia for the good old days that is the pabulum of middlebrow soul-searching. In America this has taken the form of pure Disneyland (once again we must refer to Aalto's 'smell of Hollywood') but with the sickening overtones of an intellectual pretentiousness that has no more real depth than *Reader's Digest*. In England, purely negatively, it takes the form of a frantic flight back into the nineteenth century cushioned by the sanctimonious belief that although we may have lost an Empire we have gained a Lutyens. In Finland architecture is still vivid without seeking to be sensational, and thoughtful without being doctrinaire. And so it is with inordinate relief that I want to salute the unruffled persistence with which certain potentialities of the Modern Movement largely neglected elsewhere are being broadened and deepened there; and above all, I rejoice at the fact that such a broadening is based upon an unquestioned belief in the sufficiency of resources deployed by a movement which, rightly understood, never lacked depth, never rejected its past—and which has by now its own evolving Tradition.

Main church hall

Operation Overlords

BUILDING CRITIQUE
Cricket Stand, London
by Michael Hopkins

Peter Davey
November 1987

Lord's, remarked Pevsner in one of his heavier moments, is 'a jumble without aesthetic aspirations, quite unthinkable in a country like Sweden or Holland'. For once, the great anglophile missed the point. Of all the many international games invented by the British, cricket has remained the most rooted in England. Its mythical origin on seventeenth-century village greens is still re-enacted all over the country on every summer weekend and, in a sense, Lord's, the centre of world cricket, is a village green writ large. A jumble of miscellaneous buildings of different ages, some solid, some tents, surrounding a central green was the inspiration for Michael Hopkins & Partners' new Mound Stand.

Lords' most venerable building is the Pavilion which faces the wicket from the north-west and dominates the ground. Built by Thomas and Frank Verity in the late 1880s, it is a village pavilion blown up and made formal with the traditional banks of seats flanked by two heavy Classical brick wings (Frank Verity trained at the Beaux Arts). These are topped with metal roofs which, even today after a good deal of unthinking adaptation, float airily above their masonry substructure in a way that recalls the verandas of Empire. In the 1930s, Herbert

The Mound Stand in 1963 showing Frank Verity's 1898 arcade in the foreground

Baker replaced the one-storey covered terrace to the north with the massive and characteristically stolid Grand Stand and in the 1950s, Kenneth Peacock inserted the Warner Stand which connects the Grand Stand with the Pavilion. This is one of Lords' real delights, with enormous elegantly tapering plate-girder cantilevers propped by thin inclined steel columns in a way which would make any present-day AA student drool. Peacock's next insertion, an echoing curved piece on the other side of the Pavilion is as stolid as Baker and is particularly sad because it replaced the picturesque jumble of buildings including the old Lord's Tavern which most recalled the village origins of the game.

A traditional way of watching cricket: concept sketch by Michael Hopkins

This brings us round to the Mound Stand, originally built in 1898–99 by Frank Verity as the earliest of the heavily raked stands. In the easternmost part of the stand (the curved corner) supported the back of his raked concrete Mound to be a pattern for containing the whole ground, but cash ran out and the length of the stand which runs parallel to St Johns Wood Road was supported on an ad hoc, flimsy steel structure which, by the early 1980s was visibly decaying.

In 1984 the Marylebone Cricket Club decided to rebuild the Mound Stand to celebrate the 200th anniversary of Lord's and five firms of architects were invited to compete for the design in February 1985. The Hopkins practice won, partly because they were the only ones who suggested that the Verity terrace with its excellent sight lines should be retained. On top, they proposed a virtually independent three-storey steel structure which would shade the terrace in a similar way to the existing asbestos cement roof. This strategy allowed the whole development to be phased over two seasons. In the winter of the first, the old roof was taken down and Verity's load-bearing brick arcade was extended round the perimeter of the stand, replacing the ramshackle steel structure (the remains of which, carefully disconnected from the ground, are within the new brick piers). In the second winter, the whole of the superstructure was erected.

Extending Verity's arcade entailed a new departure for the Hopkins office into load-bearing English bond masonry but they tackled it with the thoroughness and honesty which they have always brought to detailing in metal, glass and plastic. Second-hand stock bricks were acquired from an old factory and the bricks of the arches were carefully rubbed to form segmental wedges in a way that would have delighted an eighteenth century architect. It is a pity that all this care has been partly defeated by dreadful, clumsy modern pointing. Control over the contemporary craft of welding comes as second nature to the practice; control over masonry, now sadly debased, is plainly much more difficult.

The majestic march of the arches encloses a promenade under the back of the terrace which has on its inside various shops and bars (and the entrances to the terrace seating). This is a much finer space than its equivalent under Baker's Grand Stand which is munic-ipal-lavatorial. In the Hopkins building the sun shines on the busy activities within the enclosure and passers-by in the street are given glimpses of the private mys-teries through high and elegant railings.

In the new arcade

The new superstructure, erected last winter, is a masterpiece of simplicity. It is a truly temperate climate building because, by definition, it is not used in winter (and indeed Lord's is only packed to capacity on about eight days a year). So it needs no heating or cooling and many conventional devices for protection against the elements become irrelevant. The only threats from nature that had to be considered were rain and exces-sive sun. So this part of the building could become the contemporary equivalent of the eighteenth century ideal of the primitive hut—demonstrating a direct rela-tionship between structure and human use which is denied to buildings that have to be occupied all year round.

In functional terms, the new part consists of a layer of private boxes with, on top, a raked layer of debenture seating. Between the two is a mezzanine con-taining lavatories and water tanks (virtually the only service elements). On the box level there are private dining rooms overlooking the road at the back. At the top, a series of restaurants and bars lies behind the debenture seating and the

Stand during play

Peter Davey

whole is covered with a fabric tent-like roof. All of this immense mass floats above the old terrace with a poise which matches Verity's pavilion roofs and far outdistances them in extent and elegance. Its structural ingenuity (Ove Arup & Partners were the engineers) is, for our times, at least as daring as that of Peacock's Warner stand. The whole lot is fundamentally supported on a mere six 406 mm tubular steel columns which, at mezzanine level, carry a great plate girder that forms the spine of the structure. From this spine, ribs in a compound of plate and lattice project to support the cantilever forwards towards the green and backwards towards the road. (The private box level

is hung from the skeleton above.) This asymmetrical section is prevented from toppling forwards by steel ties which anchor the structure down at the back. Occasionally, when the wind blows from the north, these members are in compression so they are prevented from buckling by straps which tie them back to the brick structure underneath—the only time the two act together.

The rest of the structure is equally simple. A rear plate girder catches the out-of-balance loads and transfers them to the ties. The six columns project as masts which, with great spars strung together with galvanised-steel cables, provide a framework for the tent topping. Tubular steel cross bracing at each end provides transverse stability.

The spaces are just as simple and elementary as the structure. The private boxes have sliding glass walls towards the wicket which are free of obtrusive gaskets because they do not need to keep out the cold or wet. At the back of the boxes is an equally simply detailed glass block wall which allows daylight into the corridor which runs round the line of the spine girder above. Fair faced lock walls separate the boxes.

The spaces in the mezzanine have the steel plates of the girders for walls and so become like ships' lavatories—this nautical feeling is of course greatly intensified at the top level with its sails, spans and rigging. The roof fabric is woven polyester with PVC and PVDF coating. In this, it differs from the same practice's Schlumberger building at Cambridge where PTFE fabric was used; recently, worries have been raised about the tendency of fluoro-polymers to produce toxic fumes in fire and large-scale use of PTFE is now banned in the UK. And the Lord's tent differs from the Schlumberger one in that it does not have to make weather tight joints with the building beneath. The tents float in perfect catenary curves, unlike the sometimes tortured seeming Schlumberger roof.

The tent structure is , of course, a conscious re-interpretation of the village green marquee and it works extremely well. Both from under the fabric and seen from the other stands, with the MCC's orange and yellow pennants fluttering in the wind, the whole building seems extraordinarily jolly and festive. It is a successful regionalist building in that it re-interprets traditional life patterns using today's technology. Indeed, the simple elegance of cricket seems to permeate the whole building even down to the pinned movement joints between the transverse bracing and the building proper which recall the fine joined quality of the way in which bails sit on stumps.

There is a rather more unhappy aspect of this re-interpretation of tradition which shows that regionalism is no panacea. When he set up his ground in Dorset Fields 200 years ago, Thomas Lord's great contribution to cricket was to make it socially respectable and the tradition of Gentlemen v Players still lives at Lord's even though the match itself has now been dropped. Lord's continues arcane but very firm distinctions between members of the MCC, debenture holders, box proprietors, and various grades of the general public. It is, in many ways, the built embodiment of the English class system and the new stand very clearly reflects this tradition. But there are changes: instead of being the property of the great landed families, the boxes are now owned by big companies like ICI and Willis Faber (the only personal box is owned by Paul Getty

Relation of new work to existing buildings

Junior, the anglophile American millionaire who nobly put up half the money).

Yet, while British businesses may have provided the other half of the cash, British industry was singularly unable to make the building. The steelwork comes from Germany and Belgium; the roof fabric and even the seats are German. The British contributions are limited to providing concrete blocks and putting everything together. Viewed in this sense, the Mound Stand is a sad parable on British economy and culture. We have brilliant, innovative architects and engineers but lack the industrial infrastructure to back them up.

Peter Davey

Technology Transfer

Theory

Martin Pawley
September 1987

Whenever the principles of architecture become unclear, the rudder of history is moved until they can be understood again. In periods of uncertainty these movements often describe a circle, as they are doing today, until the past once again falls into place. That is what happened when the theorists of the ancient world convinced themselves that Classical architecture was the progressive refinement of prehistoric construction; when the theorists of the nineteenth century claimed the patrimony of the Dark Ages. More recently, in a gyration apparently so drastic as to have no remembered precedent, it happened when the Modernists of the twentieth century claimed – like mutineers – that science, technology and socialism had entirely changed the cosmos so that the whole of architectural history could be compressed into a single category called the past, and cast àdrift in an open boat.[1]

The Great Mutiny and Its Consequences

The architects of the generation of 1914, the monocled mutineers who lived through the invention of the automobile and aeroplane, were the first to embrace science and technology as a substitute for their accumulated cultural legacy, bringing these matters into the mainstream of architectural thought for the first time. They took this step as artists, licensed to find inspiration where they chose,

The remains of Moshe Safdie's Puerto Rico Habitat: Collapse of unchallenged Modernist technological expertise

but they soon found that immersion in science and technology threatened their old identity. Before they died, the mutineers came to realise that their art had been summoned by the machine. As the century progressed, advances in materials engineering, environmental controls and information technology meant that buildings served up as homage to the industry of 1914 were soon as hopelessly obsolete as their Victorian predecessors. Alison and Peter Smithson might naively write in the report that accompanied their 1951 Coventry Cathedral competition design: 'Modern Architecture has at its disposal means of expression which would have sent Brunelleschi wild with joy' – but more insightfully Maxwell Fry had written seven years earlier: 'If the developments that had led to our present technical skill were to continue at the same pace into this century, at a pace that is exceeding our capacity as artists to assimilate them, then our hopes of establishing a workable architecture would be slight.'[2]

Seizing upon the means of expression that would have sent Brunelleschi wild, and yet at the same time assimilating them as artists, proved to be impossible. The logic of their position urged the mutineer architects to make another quantum forward leap, and then another, and another, until a breathless race to keep up with the materials and methods of science and industry became the identity of architecture itself. But chiefly because they chose to remain a collection of individual artists instead if becoming an industry, the architects of the generation of 1914 never did initiate an architecture of continuous technological revolution.[3] Instead the mutineers fell out, and in what can now be seen as something like the restoration of a monarchy, a large part of a building technology chained to the limitations of artistic assimilation.

As a result we live today in an age of Restoration architecture, a period populated by frightened practitioners who, in Jenck's words, know just how far too far they can go; and theorists who believe that their task is to heal the breach caused by the Modern mutiny. Where once the break with tradition was seen as thrilling and final, now creeping tendrils of sentiment are encouraged to grow over it concealing it from view like a crack in a wall. Long-lived practitioners, veterans of the exciting days of the mutiny, now face career prospects like those of French army officers after the defeat of Napoleon. Venerable surviving Modernists are urged, as by priests at their

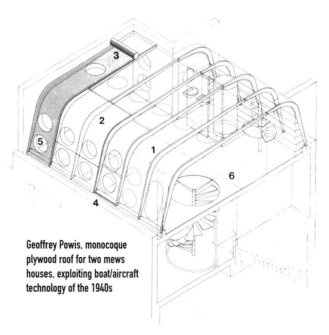

Geoffrey Powis, monocoque plywood roof for two mews houses, exploiting boat/aircraft technology of the 1940s

Martin Pawley

deathbed, to give their blessing to the restoration – the triumph of the voyage in the open boat.[4] Who can blame them when they consent? 'No memory of having starred atones for later disregard' wrote Robert Frost. In return for denying their golden dawn they receive a moment of brief media attention and adulation by young architects. And if they refuse? Edmund Burke truly wrote of those who find themselves at odds with the fashion of the times in which they live: 'They seem deserted by mankind, overpowered by a conspiracy of their whole species.'

Problems of Restoration Life and Times

The great weakness of Restoration architecture is its lack of ideology. It has no unifying theory – 'a supposition explaining something, based on principles independent of the phenomenon to be explained' – as the *Concise Oxford Dictionary* put it. This is despite a veritable explosion of writing about architecture that has taken place since the collapse of consensus support for modern design some fifteen years ago, much of it glorying in the present state of wild opportunism.

A few short years of creeping incorporation and stylistic anarchy have been enough to sink the once clinically lucid language of modern architecture to the level of banality of the fashion page.[5] Fuelled by the unromantic threat of insurance claims; incorporation with shareholders control; the growth of circumscribed 'design consultancy' work; the consumerisation of minor works, and the migration of so much architectural terminology that the word architecture may be found under 'computer' in the dictionaries of the twenty-first century, a terminal demystification of the profession seems entirely possible. Perhaps the darkest portent of all is the fact that it is now widely believed that there is no longer any need for expert judgment where the design of buildings is concerned. 'I know that what I feel in spirit about a building is just as valid a criticism as any professional or technical point of view', the Prince of Wales wrote to Peter Palumbo at the height of the battle for Mansion House Square. And in this as in so many other matters there is no reason to suppose that his opinion differs greatly from those of his future subjects.

Restoration architecture combines a superficial glorification of variety and ornament with a concealed convergence of identity between buildings that can be compared to the process of homogenisation that began on the motor industry twenty years ago. With or without regard to the pace at which 'artists' can assimilate it, global product distribution is overwhelming the construction industry, and with it the architectural profession. Today, just as today the removal of the badge from the nose or tail of a car can reveal its shared parentage with a different make, so can the peeling away of a decorated façade reveal the homogenisation of served floor-space beneath the skin.

Restoration architects have conceded creative hegemony everywhere except in this 'badge engineering' of buildings, the so-called 'signature building' of American architecture. Carbon-copy engineering – in terms of the names of the consultants responsible as well as the structural and environmental control systems used – is now accepted as the norm. From penetrating deep into the genesis of the building, as it did during the Modern mutiny, the power of the architect over construction has shrunk to the literally superficial: a thin skin on the façade like the badge on the nose of a car; a small feature on the outside of the refurbished building; a bureaucratic role in filing of applications and the authorisation of payments. An architect's 'capacity as an artist', still offers him this role, but today only inertia saves him from the modified cry of the small boy: 'The Emperor is as expendable as a light bulb.'

Compared to the great days of the mutiny, when heads of state appealed to architects to replan capital cities, design satellite towns and solve global housing problem, the role of the architect is tragically diminished. In engineering terms he is hardly a designer at all, his work oscillating uneasily between envelopment by a burgeoning design profession and surrender to the reactionary forces of conservation and historicism. For him there is no future apart from button-down slavery as a corporate executive, or the thankless task of acting as an unpaid advisor to community enterprise.

No future unless something that research scientists call a reordering of the data takes place. For in architecture and politics the quickest and most effective way of overcoming and loss of power is a revised perception of the events that brought it about.

A 1936 conception of prefabricated construction from Alexander Korda's film 'the Shape of Things to Come'

Towards an Architecture of Technology Transfer

Technology Transfer is a term used in different ways, but a generally agreed definition might be any process whereby the techniques and materials developed in one field or industry are applied to other fields and industries. A process with a vast unwritten history, Technology Transfer either results from the serendipitous curiosity of individuals, or from a serious marketing effort by corporations intent on developing new outlets for materials or techniques. Modern examples of the latter in building include the use of insulation material as roofing, various spin-offs from aerospace research – like the Teflon coatings and flat wiring now used in a vast range of product applications – and the use of motor industry-developed cold rolled steel structural members of lightweight construction. Perhaps the nearest illustration of the first category comes from one tiny but crucial component in the NASA unmanned Mars landing programme, where the problem of designing a simple lightweight soil-sampling scoop was brilliantly solved by the adaptation of a coiled steel carpenter's rule, whose dished, semi-rigid extending arm provided the model for the light, retractable scoop that was eventually used.[6]

Mies van der Rohe, Mansion House Square project, London 1969

Few architectural historians have concerned themselves with the role of Technology Transfer in architectural design, even though its implications can be of the first importance. In fact the only critical assessment of the phenomenon in recent years occurs in Reyner Banham's *Theory of Design in the First Machine Age*,[7] which was first published in the heyday of the Modern mutiny in 1961. While Banham himself takes the view that architecture and technology may have different evolutionary patterns, so that he stands aside from the suggestion that the collapse of Modernism resulted from its failure to keep pace with technology, he alone among historians writing at the time foresaw that collapse. In *Theory and Design* he drew attention to the already worrying obsolescence of the 'new technologies' annexed by Modern architecture from the nineteenth-century engineering, and identified this area as the one in which its greatest weakness lay. In the final chapter of *Theory and Design*, he quotes from Buckminster Fuller's 1938 book *Nine Chains to the Moon*, to show that the failure of Modern architects to grasp the *endlessness* of technological evolution had sowed the seed of their decline as early as 1927, when Fuller's revolutionary light metal, air-deliverable Dymaxion House adumbrated the frame-hung component structures that were to dominate most other fields of engineering design within 20 years. 'The International Style brought to America by the Bauhaus', wrote Fuller in 1938, 'demonstrated fashion-innoculation without the necessary knowledge of the scientific fundamentals of structural mechanics and chemistry.'[8] Or as Banham interpretatively puts it, Modern architecture 'produced machine-age architecture only in the sense that its monuments were built in a machine age, and expressed an attitude to machinery—in the sense that one might stand on French soil and discuss French politics, and still be speaking English.'

As we now know from developments in related fields, the next step in advanced construction technology after glass, steel and concrete should have been light-frame and monocoque enclosures using the laminated wood, aluminium alloys and plastics developed during the Second World War, ('Enter alloy – exit rust' as Fuller put it in 1944)[9]. But whether a handful of *avant-garde* architects could have dragged the construction industry into a pattern of continuous technological evolution at that time, even with the help of the massive development of light engineering that the War brought about, must remain an open question. Light-frame and monocoque enclosures flowered briefly in the post-war emergency schools and housing programmes, but in the 50 years from Fuller's Dymaxion House to the end of the collapse of the Modern Movement, only a small number of architects published or carried out work based on this method.

Mindful of Fry's wartime dictum, it is tempting to say that failure to keep up with science was the price Modern architecture paid for artistic integrity. Banham is more cautious in suggesting that 'What we have hitherto understood as architecture, and what we are beginning to understand of technology may be incompatible disciplines.' But either way the fact remains that one generation – however much it may have misunderstood what it was doing – seized the initia-

Farman 'Goliath' aircraft: struts and glazing

tive in Technology Transfer, and the next let it slip away. For the generation of Le Corbusier, Gropius, Van der Rohe and Neutra, steel, glass, and concrete were revolutionary new materials that cried out to be used in buildings as different from their brick, stone and timber predecessors as a motor car was different from a horse-drawn wagon. With varying degrees of single-mindedness they spent their lives developing new ways to build using these same materials. But when it transpired that steel, glass and concrete were merely the forerunners of high-strength alloys and composites grown from a science and technology leaping daily further ahead, the ingenuity of their followers was overwhelmed. Tragically it was assumed by the politicians who elevated Modern architecture to global supremacy in the thirty years after 1945 that architects held technological mastery in their hands like an Olympic torch that could be passed on from generation to generation. Seldom can faith on expertise have been more naively placed. Not only did the generation of 1914 misunderstand the process of Technology Transfer, as Banham suggests, but the majority of them did not even think it was a matter of much importance. Taking the permanent architecture of antiquity as their model the Modern masters expected, rightly, that it might take a cen-

Lincoln City Council workshop, constructed with an early version of Terrapin 'Matrex' system, 1983

tury to learn to build properly with concrete and steel. They did not expect to be called upon to explore construction using materials like Nylon, carbon fibre, Kevlar, or Teflon; or to have to contend with an explosion of information technology within buildings, let alone electronic intelligence itself. Only a very few, like Maxwell Fry, even understood how difficult such a task might be.

For a complex of reasons Modern architecture tries to ignore the demands of technological assimilation in an age of science. Like surgeons operating without anaesthetic in a modern hospital, the architects of the great mutiny became dangerously obsolete on their own environment. Towards the end of their lives this became evident, as Fuller had predicted. Despite the spectacular output of synthetic materials and structural technologies that marked the post-war period, their palette remained limited, as did that of their immediate successors. In spite of the defence of their design methodology that is still occasionally advanced, notably by Schon, who still speaks of architects 'knowing how to act correctly in conditions of information overflow',[10] it was precisely because the sons of the pioneers concentrated on formal inventiveness rather than exploring the process of Technology Transfer that had given them their new ways to build, that Modern architecture died of ignorance while new information was exploding around it.

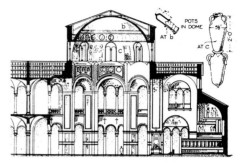

Byzantine Technology Transfer with earthenware techniques: the dome of San Vitale, Ravenna c540–48

What Howard Roark Really Did

The idea that the collapse of Modern architecture was an information failure throws new light on the nature of the great mutiny. Seen as the result of a temporary coincidence of science and building, the equally temporary success of the Moderns assumes less mythological proportions. What Howard Roark, the composite Modern architect hero of the first half of the century, really did was not so much triumph over critics and philistines to bring a new enlightenment, as specify new products and enlarge the market for new materials. Indeed the financial construction came precisely from these materials producers. Two World Wars created massive production capacity in the cement and concrete industry – likewise steel, light metals, plywood, plastics and synthetic fibres; Modern architects created an outlet for them in the civilian economy by rendering their use culturally acceptable in building. That at any rate was the irreversible effect of their work, however far removed it may be from Ayn Rand's conception of their existential struggle.[11] With the hindsight of forty years it is possible to re-order the data of the Modern era so as to see the careers of its great individualists simply as the dramatic, populist elements in an essentially undramatic process—the adaptation of industrial and engineering materials and methods to the design of commercial, cultural and domestic buildings.

What we know about the techniques employed by the most successful of the Modern pioneers is entirely consistent with this view. We know that they literally copied the design and construction of grain silos; stripped the masonry cladding from structural steelwork and put in glass instead; and borrowed from the 'look' of the design of ships and aeroplanes[12] to create 'a new aesthetic'. All these processes involved artistic controversy and public debate but their cultural significance was far less than their economic consequence. In essence they were a resource-shift in building technology, part of the historic process of Technology Transfer whose aesthetic affects have always been better documented than its substance. While sudden and traumatic, the Modern episode can still be shown to take its place in a long line of technology transfers in building whose very antiquity throws doubt on the idea that architecture and technology are incompatible. For if they are, is it not strange that their encounters against the vast backdrop of history have been so frequent and so one-sided in their results?

Wireless aerials derived from sea-going rigging systems, 1923

Head-smashing Winds of Change

Architectural culture is a vast shock absorber against change; like the boom on a gybing yacht it comes over last and it comes over hard, but the driving force, the sail itself, has already taken up its new position by the time the swing occurs.

Perhaps the conversion of timber-frame construction into stone decoration in the ancient world was attended by dramas to match the frustrations endured by modern architects in the 1920s and 1930s, when their work was as fanatically opposed as is the demolition of historic buildings today. Perhaps the use of lightweight earthenware pots in the construction of the dome of S Vitale of Ravenna over 1500 years ago had to be fought through the medieval equivalent of a series of public inquiries. More plausibly the outrage caused by the generation of 1914 came from the pent-up surge of innovation that it directed into building. After the mainsail of industrial production had already swung over onto a new tack, the boom of *avant-garde* architecture finally smashed the head of academic revivalism—making it possible (as it were) to turn the entire technological legacy of the nineteenth century into architecture in an afternoon. The whole process was an architectural transplant of the great nineteenth century engineering boom in which iron shipbuilding took to the land. Camouflaged as an artistic revolution, the Modern Movement in architecture did no more than break free from the technical suppression of nineteenth century revivalism and restore building construction to its correct relationship with the new production industries. In this sense the 'mutiny' was a sudden change in the 'genetic frequency' of Technology Transfer in building.

Seen in this way, as a largely unrecognised logistical process, the history of Technology Transfer in architecture assumes a new importance. But so too do the difficulties that must be overcome in any attempt to bring it, undisguised, to the forefront of design. For not only must the trappings of 'artistic assimilation' be abandoned, but even the idea that the process of building design is 'creative' in the fine art, as opposed to the engineering sense.

In Praise of Uncreative Methods

As the failure of the Archigram Group proves, problems of credibility dog all attempts to separate architecture from permanence. Between 1961 and 1967 this loose alliance of five principal partners produced a dazzling array of projects based on contemporary Technology Transfer, freely drawing on the materials and methods of the Apollo programme. Ultimately none of it came to fruition except in the context of the market for architectural drawings, where the original designs were subsequently sold. Comparable in their predictive authority with the 1914 drawings of Sant Elia and Chiattone, these projects for an indeterminate, intermediate architecture of lightweight mobile enclosure connected with the briefly flowering youth movement of the late 1960s, but failed to enlist the kind of industrial marketing support that once underpinned concrete construction or the idea of prefabrication. With the collapse of the youth movement and

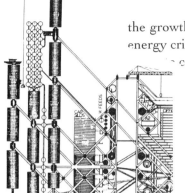

Archigram—Peter Cook,
Plug-in City, 1964

the growth of a reactionary investment market in housing after the energy crisis of 1973 the group abandoned its search for real clients ~ concentrate exclusively in the art market.

The lesson of Archigram's failure to attract investment was that Technology Transfer, even when based on a considerable knowledge of the products of advanced technology, cannot succeed without the support of an industrial base. In the 1960s the nascent aerospace industry itself survived on public funding and lacked anything that might be described as surplus production capacity. What Archigram tried to do was swing the cultural boom over, against the wind of construction investment. In doing so it found itself opposed by the full force of the heavyweight permanent construction industry and its attendant architectural value system. The contrast between Archigram's lightweight, transitional architecture and the heavyweight, 'High-Tech', late Modern architecture of say, Norman Foster or Richard Rogers is instructive. Conceived ten years later than best-known Archigram projects, Richard Rogers' Lloyd's building, for example, was designed as a permanent, flexibly serviced enclosure which promised a 50 year capability to withstand developments in information technology—an absurd claim, as events since its opening in 1986 have already shown.[13] But a truer diagnosis, that only radical flexibility could cope with the space needs of the mushrooming financial services industry, would have produced no £150 million masterpiece. Without a driving mainsail – like resources of the cement yand concrete industry – the case was hopeless. Archigram offered temporary, flexible enclosure and failed: Rogers offered flexible servicing for a heavy concrete-frame structure squarely in a tradition of permanence, and succeeded.

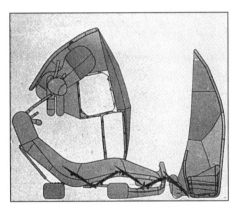

Archigram—Michael Webb, the Cushicle, 1966

Surplus Production Can Supplant Permanence

The obstacle presented by permanence is as great ten years after the design of the Lloyd's Building as it was ten years before it, but the means to overcome it remain the same. Buckminster Fuller was the first to grasp that weight was not irrelevant to building, but ultimatley controlled its cost. He saw that true flexibility or continuous replacement could supplant the concept of permanence, but only with the support of industries with surplus production capacity. Thus it had been with the evolution of machine production under the impact of continual technological innovation, and thus it would be *mutatis mutandis* with architecture.

What was needed to establish an architecture of Technology Transfer was neither more nor less than a real time engineering value base. Unlike the 'historic' contribution of permanent architecture, the architecture of the future must be in continual transition. To make itself financially viable it must draw its value from its performance, which in turn must be as exactly measureable as that of a car or an aeroplane, and be calculated like any other engineering system.

Architects who successfully use Technology Transfer against the background of a Restoration culture do so by compromise with the fine art tradition of permanence. Norman Foster is well known for his ingenious use of components and materials that have their origin on industries far removed from construction: solvent-welded PVC roofing derived originally from swimming pool liners; flexible neoprene gaskets using a material developed originally for cable-jacketing; adhesive-fixed glazing from the automobile industry; superplastic aluminium panels and metallised fabric fire-proofing from aerospace; tensioning devices from trailer side-screens; raised floor systems from jetliners; photochromic glazing from ket bombers. All these and more, including techniques of presentation and colour schemes drawn from aviation magazines, are to be found in his projects and his buildings. But Norman Foster will not agree that his work is a more or less organised search for technology that can be transferred. In his view there is a conflict between this 'redneck' definition of design and the prior claims of the fine art tradition and the role of engineering. As Peter Rice has commented: 'High-Tech architects have concluded that the discipline provided by the engineer is the best framework in which to conduct architecture.' Or, as Michael Hopkins puts it: 'Our architecture comes out of our engineering and our engineering comes out of our engineers.' Perhaps underlying this faith in engineering is a doubt that Technology Transfer can stand on its own as a creative process; a reciprocal of the doubt expressed by some critics that the construction of 108 concept models for a commission (Foster's abandoned BBC Radio Centre at Langham Place) is either intellectual or creative in the traditional fine art sense.[14]

Down With The Heritage Value System

To find total acceptance of the priority of Technology Transfer in architecture today it is necessary to study the work of a former Foster associate Richard Horden, the designer of the purest Technology Transfer building yet constructed in Britain. Horden's 1984 'Yacht House' in Hampshire embodies the principles of Technology Ttransfer that have been sporadically applied by Norman Foster, but concentrated into the generating structural frame of a small domestic building. Horden finds his materials and methods in the high-performance components produced by the yacht spar and standing rigging industry. His unique structure, intended to form the basis of an omni-functional enclosure system, shows not only that architectural design developed from the central principle of multi-sourced industrial component combination is feasible, but that its results can still be culturally acceptable within a fine art design tradition. With it Horden has

gone further than any living architect to show that a true architecture of Technology Transfer need neither be impoverished
nor primitive.

Like Horden, the London and Los Angeles
practice of Future Systems, with its two partners Jan Kaplicky and David Nixon, has
striven for nearly 10 years to develop an
architecture of Technology Transfer.
Future Systems has as yet no completed
building to mark the achievement of
commercial viability, but it does have
the distinction of being the only
British firm of architects involved
in the design of the 1992 NASA
manned space station. Future

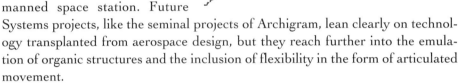

Ian Simpson, hang gliding centre

Systems projects, like the seminal projects of Archigram, lean clearly on technology transplanted from aerospace design, but they reach further into the emula-
tion of organic structures and the inclusion of flexibility in the form of articulated
movement.

Recently, the deliberate presentation of their advanced structural system
projects in the context of conventional Restoration architectural competitions –
such as the 1985 Grand Buildings contest for Trafalgar Square, which Horden
also entered – has begun to enable them to quantify the benefits of monocoque
construction in commercial terms. Exoskeletal construction enabled their Grand
Buildings entry to achieve a far higher net-to-gross ratio of serviced floor-space
than any other competitor, as well as providing a capacity for rapid internal
reconfiguration to deal with information technology changes that would put both
Lloyd's and the Hong Kong & Shanghai Bank to shame.[15]

Today, it is only by such acts of stealth as Foster's carefully metered inclu-
sions of alien technology within a fine art dominated culture, Future Systems'
competition entries, and Horden's unique house design, that the architecture of
Technology Transfer remains visible under the obsolete heritage value system
that has ruled architecture since the Restoration. In reality, because it is a theory of architecture as economic, multi-sourced element combination, it belongs to
a different and more appropriate value system alongside production engineering,
automobile, marine and aerospace design. Eventually, Horden believes, the
entire spectrum of manufactured components, from the smallest rigging screw to
the largest offshore oil-rig assembly, will become a hunting ground for transfer-
able technology. He tends to draw elements for his designs from the smaller end
of the component size continuum, but sees the vast – as yet uncompiled – data
base of all products as the proper area of search for the architect of the future.

None of this can be done without the construction of a bridge from the rot-
ting hulk of contemporary Restoration architecture to this new conception of

112

building as the product of cross-industry component and material combination. At present such a bridge can only be built upon the ability of architects like Foster, Horden, Kaplicky and Nixon to make its results culturally acceptable. It needs the support of expanding industries and, most important of all, an ideological certainty equal to that which enabled the Modern Movement to temporarily overcome obsolete heritage values.

The Need for a Work of History

To begin the process of developing an ideology for this new architecture the best starting point would be a substantial study of its history. Such a document could become the first reference work of the architecture of the information age; a technological and methodical – rather than an art historical – study of Technology Transfer in architecture. A partial model is to be found in Marian Bowley's 1960 *Innovations in Building Materials*,[16] the last authoritative study of Technology Transfer in construction. But this volume has, characteristically, little reference of the actual or possible role of architects. Unlike the historians of construction, architectural historians (with the exception of Banham) have only recognised Technology Transfer as a peripheral matter, remarked in such ancient events as the conversion of the form of decorated tree-trunks into stone columns, or the transfer of plant-derived decoration into carving. No one, even Banham, has ever

Richard Horden, Yacht House system, incorporating marine spars, rigging and panel systems

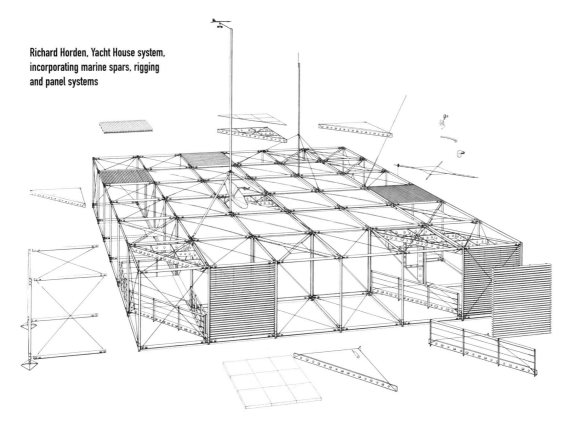

Martin Pawley

treated it as a unitary phenomenon, a continuous process whose evolution can be traced through centuries of craft-construction until, with the coming of the Industrial Revolution, it begins to accelerate out of control.

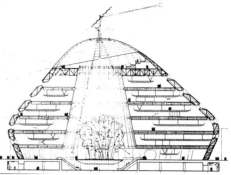

Future Systems, Project 135 section; design for offices in Trafalgar Square, London 1985

It is one of the many serious consequences of the crucial cultural gap that has separated historians and theorists of architecture from the reality of practice, that no such architectural history on the model of Bowley's has ever been written. Even though a pattern of well-documented examples shows this quickening wave-motion with the clarity of an evolutionary diagram. The adaptation of wooden boat building into roof construction in the Middle Ages, for example, took place over hundreds of years: the development of reinforced-concrete building took 50 years;[17] but the adaptation of off-shore oil-rig technology to building types in the present century was achieved in less than a decade. The process is clearly identical and clearly important; only the wave frequency of the transfer has speeded up.

There is a clear relationship between the absence of this crucial field of study and the present predicament of Technology Transfer in the age of Restoration architecture. Without it the delusions of significance that still append to the obsolete categorisation of architecture by style instead of content cannot be swept away, and the progressive marginalisation of architecture will continue.

Photo montage for the above project

Compared to the trivial works of style-history that presently crowd out genuine theory in the body of architectural knowledge, a serious analysis of Technology Transfer in buildings would have the immediate authority of a stock-market analysis coupled with the direct applicability of a consumer report. It would unravel mysteries and explode myths with the clarity and force of the early writings of Loos or Le Corbusier. From the outset it would provide a quantifiable base from which to compare the evolutionary and economic significance of pre-Modern, Modern and PostModern architecture. Placed in a material historical context some PostModern buildings, for example, might show themselves to be more fertile in technology transfers than their High-Tech counterparts—consider Terry Farrell's temporary Clifton Nurseries building in Covent Garden, with its Teflon-coated glass-fibre roof membrane and its Proctor mast roof beams for example. Classical Revival envelopes executed in profiled composite panels might be more impressive still, representing an ingenious way of 'culturalising' the architectural use of such advanced boat building composites as kevlar.

By setting aside the obfuscating camouflage of style, a deep study of the architecture of Technology Transfer would expose the massive material similarity that characterises contemporary architecture, and show more clearly than ever before what are the deep structures and what are the surface structures in the design of buildings.

The Architect and the Bee

By opening such a revolutionary field of study the Byzantine world of Restoration architecture would suddenly become accessible to the quantitative analytical techniques that rule the late twentieth century world of engineering design and manufacture. Architecture, which is now an occult world of ignorance and obsolete mystery, shot through with individual acts of achievement, could become an open-access field of competition. The mighty ocean of product information that presently relies on fragmented, peripheral awareness could be given accessibility with the simplicity and directness of a video game. Architects freed of the tyranny of history for the second time in a century could concentrate on design by assembly, identifying the availability of new materials and techniques, and 'specifying them into culture' with a squeeze on the joystick button. Like bees, architects would be seen to have been carrying out an evolutionary as well as a productive task. Their genetic role: the cross-pollination of materials and methods from a one-world product economy to the new architecture.

Those who doubt that the emergence of this new field of study in architecture could create its own ideology should consider the power of history, which is not only the story of the part but the ultimate proof of the present. When such a record is absent, our actions become as cyclical and unchanging as those of plants and animals, whose history endlessly repeats itself, and our adaptability is forfeit. Nor would such a change in the story of architecture make it untrue – it would make it true again and again

Tery Farrell, Clifton Nurseries in Covent Garden, London

for successive generations – just as the movements of the rudder of a ship, in response to changing winds, changing seas or changing orders, enable it to keep a true course.

1 Barbara Miller Lane (*Architecture and Politics in Germany: 1918 to 1945*, Harvard University Press, 1968) quotes Walter Gropius in 1919; 'The old forms are in ruins, the benumbed world is shaken up, the old human spirit is invalidated and in a flux towards a new form.' Conrads and Sperlich (*Fantastic Architecture*, Architectural Press, 1963) quote Bruno Taut in the first issue of the magazine *Dawn* in 1920: 'Space. Homeland. Style. To hell with them, odious concepts! Destroy them, break them up! Nothing shall remain! Break up your academies, spew out the old fogeys... Let our North wind blow through this musty, threadbare tattered world.' Anatole Kopp (*Constructivist Architecture in the USSR*, Academy Editions, 1985) provides similar quotations from the Russian Constructivists.

2 E. Maxwell Fry, *Fine Building*, Faber & Faber, 1944.

3 'Industrialisation of the process of construction is a question of new materials... Our technologists must and will succeed in inventing materials that can be industrially manufactured and processed and that will be weatherproof, soundproof and insulating. I am convinced that traditional methods of building will disappear.' Mies van der Rohe, *G*, No 3, 1924. Or in a later version; 'It will soon be possible to break altogether with the tradition of putting stone on stone or brick on brick and move in the direction of rational fabrication.' J. D. Bernal, *The Social Function of Science*, 1939 (quoted in Andrew Saint, *Towards a Social Architecture*, Yale, 1987). As late as 1962 Herbert Ohl, the German expert on industrialised building, wrote: 'The artistic and formal interests of the last hundred years have taken the task of the architect away from productivity, in spite of all attempts to rescue him... The architect must realise that the machines, processes and appropriate materials of

industry are effective means for the production of buildings.' *Architectural Design*, April 1962, p162.

4 I have twice witnessed this process at work when Berthold Lubetkin addressed groups of younger architects in 1985 and 1986. Many of the questions put to him take the form: 'But surely if you were in practice now, you would behave as we do and not be as intransigent as you were then?' To his credit. Lubetkin never conceded this point.

5 'The outside of a house should be dictated by the inside, as the form of the animal body is dictated by the skeleton, the disposition of the organs and the functioning of the various systems —blood circulation, nervous and muscular systems and so on... communications, drainage, services and so on.' (Anthony Bertham, *The House, a Machine for Living In*, A.& C. Black, London, 1935.) There are more famous examples of such clarity of thought in the *oeuvre* of Le Corbusier, and earlier ones in Loos, but Bertram is particularly robust, mocking the occupants of 'Tudorbethan' dwellings by demanding to know why they do not wear doublet and hose, *etc*.

6 I am indebted to Richard Horden for this example.

7 Reyner Banham, *Theory and Design in the First Machine Age*, Architectural Press, London, 1961.

8 Quoted in *Theory and Design*, pp325 & 326. A similar thought can be discerned in a quote from Edwin Lutyens dating from seven years earlier still. 'The modern architecture of so-called Functionalism does not seem to me to... show yet a genuine sense of style – a style rooted in feeling for the right use of materials.' (*Country Life*, 20 June 1931.)

9 Quoted in *The Buckminster Fuller Reader*, ed James Meller, Jonathan Cape, London, 1970.

10 Donald Schon, *The Reflective Practitioner: How Professionals Think in Action*, Temple Smith, 1983.

11 Ayn Rand, *The Fountainhead*, New York, 1943. An exhaustive study of the relationship between Rand's hero and stylistic rationality is to be found in Andrew Saint's *The Image of the Architect*, Yale University. 1983.

12 The repeated appearance of the Farman 'Goliath' in *Vers une Architecture* is a case in point. Le Corbusier made no effort to employ the materials and methods of contemporary aircraft construction, but he did emulate the appearance of wing struts seen obliquely – using them as columns – and the visual relationship of planes to solids – as with wings and fuselage. The ability to see complex structures in this formal, unanalytical way may be uniquely architectural. The engineer Peter Rice has described it as 'A fine visual appreciation of the way the engineer's design is perceived. [The architect] refines its form in relation to an image so that ultimately it is explainable at a simpler level.' One of the very few direct technical influences of the aircraft industry on construction on Britain during the Modern period came from the Great War airship programme, when the task of solving the large number of simultaneous equations generated by segmented circular space frames led to the development of the new methods of calculation for lattice girders, Richard Southwell, *Methods of Calculating Tension Coefficients*, London, 1920. The direct copying of American industrial building by the European pioneers is discussed in detail by Banham in
A Concrete Atlantis, MIT Press, 1986.

13 For a discussion of the obsolescence of the Lloyd's building see Martin Pawley, 'Into the Unknown', *AR* October 1986, p88.

14 The Peter Rice quote is from a profile of the engineer published in *The Architects' Journal*, 21 & 28 December 1983. The Michael Hopkins quote from *Building*, 8 November, 1985. The concept of technology transfer as a limited, non- intellectual, non-creative approach to design emerged in conversation with Norman Foster during 1985. The term 'redneck' to describe it was contributed by AR editor Peter Davey.

15 The 1985 Grand Buildings competition brief called for a minimum gross floor area of 18,000m² within the framework of plot ratio, daylight angles and fire regulations governing the site. Future Systems' design provided 23,000 m² gross with a remarkable 89 per cent, 20,500m² net lettable. In addition the repositioning of the suspended floors within the envelope offered unprecedented flexibility —of a type crucially relevant to designs like Lloyd's.

16 Martin Bowley, *Innovations in Building Materials*, Duckworth, London, 1960.

17 The exhibition of a rowing boat made of concrete reinforced with a rectangular mesh of iron rods at the Paris *Exposition Universelle* of 1855 is recorded by S.B. Hamilton (*A Note on the History of Reinforced Concrete Building*, HMSO, 1956) as antedating the first reinforced-concrete building by 10 years, and the first large-scale use of reinforced concrete for building by 40 years.

The Usonian Legacy

Theory

Kenneth Frampton
December 1987

Perhaps one of the most surprising things about Los Angeles is that one can easily spend a month travelling around the megalopolis, and still not exhaust the rich seam of modern architecture that lie embedded there. In this regard it is not only a modern architectural paradox, for which in many respects this is a city where architecture is of little consequence. Unlike Chicago, this is the media capital of the world, where film and television dominate public life and where architecture is, at best, only a poor relation.

None the less, LA is still an astonishing cultural centre where the ethos of what was most vital in American modern architecture is still alive. And when all the dust has finally settled in the great debate that surrounds the rise and fall of a suspect PostModernism, we may possibly look to Los Angeles, to begin again, with an 'other' modernity that has been nurtured in this city for well over 80 years—certainly since Irving Gill's Bailey House and Wilson Acton Hotel, both built in La Jolla around 1908.

Gill inaugurated another important tradition in LA which has unfortunately suffered a serious eclipse, everywhere, except possibly in Latin cultures, and that is a concern on the part of the profession for a socially committed, bioclimatic architecture. This progressive approach was first advanced by Gill in a perimeter block of workers' housing that he realised in Sierra Madre in 1910.

Michael Folonis, Pacific Street Condominiums, Los Angeles

Esther McCoy's sensitive and succinct description of this block, known as Lewis courts, can hardly be improved on: 'One cottage was separated from the next by a long shallow porch intended for lounging or sleeping. On the south and east sides were cottages spaced in such a way that

Rudolf Schindler, El Pueblo Ribera, La Jolla 1925

they did not interfere with garden areas or light and sun for the row houses. Each unit had its own private garden, leading into a community garden, with a large pergola in the centre. Less than a third of the land was used for dwellings. There was a reverence for the individual in the plan that has never been equalled in the field of minimum housing.'

Gill was the first in a whole succession of transplanted Prairie Style architects who first worked in Chicago and then migrated to the West. The emigré Austrian Rudolph Schindler was the next of the Prairie progeny to come to southern California via Chicago and his arrival in Los Angeles in 1920 (to work on Wright's grand mansion for Aline Barnsdall) was to be followed with a migratory pattern by his fellow countryman Richard Neutra, who in the space of two years, worked first for Holabird & Roche in Chicago and then for Wright in Taliesin before coming to Los Angeles in 1925.

This transmigration of Prairie Culture to southern California was reinforced by a genial climate and by a number of other sympathetic factors, such as the indirect influence of the Prairie Style on Kim Weber and J.R. Davidson (both of whom were from Berlin and were active in the area from 1923 onwards) and by the direct presence of Wright himself who built almost continually in the region for the Barnsdall House of 1920 to the Struges House, erected in Brentwood Heights in 1939. It is critical that this last was a Usonian house since nothing could have been closer than Wright's Usonian model to the principles of the other modernity that flourished in the LA region from the late 1920s onwards. Something similar may also be claimed for the Barnsdall House cultural project that in any event served as a training ground for both Schindler and Neutra.

Irving Gill, Lewis Courts, Sierra Madre 1910

It is sobering to have to recognise that Wrights's generic house was the last serious effort to evolve and establish a truly civilised typology for American suburban development. With the exception of the southern Californian school the whole progressive undertaking seems to grind to a halt with Wright's death in 1959, which happened to coincide with a series of articles in *House & Home* popularising Wright's Usonian notions. In

Kenneth Frampton

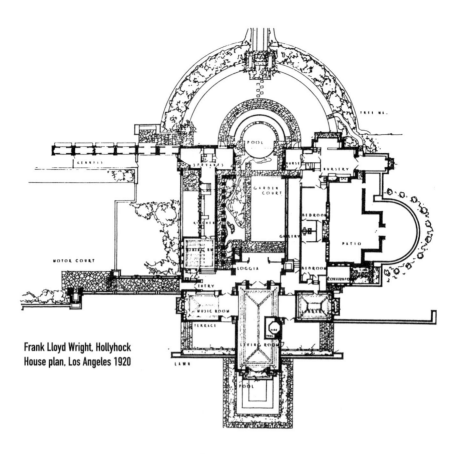

Frank Lloyd Wright, Hollyhock
House plan, Los Angeles 1920

retrospect it was an ironic combination of popular triumph and almost immediate eclipse—the double movement coinciding with Wright's own demise. Of this
widespread but limited Usonian influence John Sergeant has written:

'It didn't matter that the whole message of Wright's popularising activity
was rarely communicated. North Americans all over a continent encountered it
in one garbled form or another, through magazines and radio, often locally produced or syndicated or by the example of local Wrightian design. Advances were
made, and the American home of the late 1950s and early 1960s does represent a
distinct architectural achievement.'

Sergeant reminds us that Wright's definition of the *organic* was ecological,
that it favoured a symbiotic, metabolic relation with nature rather than one of
wilful domination involving air conditioning and the optimisation of energy consumption. As Sergeant put it: 'Wright's attitude welcomes intermediate technology and the use of indigenous material, rather than being reliant on increasingly
distant, impersonal products of centralised technology.'

While neither Schindler nor Neutra publicly subscribed to specific Usonian precepts and while they resisted belabouring the term *organic* in the same way
as Wright, they remained, none the less, continually subject to his influence in the
most creative way imaginable. They were thus able to develop their own Euro-
pean-based modernity along extremely reflexive regional lines. In terms of the

cultural continuity of southern California, it is important to note how Schindler's El Pueblo Ribera development, completed in La Jolla in 1925, really picks up where Gill's Lewis Courts left off and recasts the whole generic project in more Wrightian micro-spatial and tectonic terms. At the same time nothing could be more middle European than the collective paradigm of the *Siedlung*. Here the idea of a socially conscious land-settlement pattern is transplanted and then transformed by being combined with the Californian bungalow tradition. This creative operation was to yield a socio-cultural result of exceptional richness and life-enhancing potential. It is already the essential inspiration that carried Schindler through the rest of his career and it, in turn, sustained a number of LA courtyard settlements of a similar order and intent, above all, perhaps, Neutra's own Strathmore apartments, built in Westwood in 1938. El Pueblo Ribera is as relevant a pattern of land settlement today as it was when it was first completed over 60 years ago. In the interim, save for our current *petit bourgeois* consumerist cupidity, (facilitated by the stylistic degeneracy of PostModernism) little has changed the fundamental socio-economic and technical need to integrate the automobile with low-rise high-density megapolitan housing, for, given the distributive capacity of the freeway it is highly unlikely that we will ever return to the dense pattern of the traditional city.

The luxury and economy of El Pueblo Ribera certainly had to be experienced to be fully appreciated, but something of its appropriateness to the site and its setting may be gleaned from David Gebhard's appraisal:

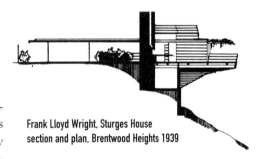

Frank Lloyd Wright, Sturges House
section and plan, Brentwood Heights 1939

'The Pueblo Ribera community is definitely one of the most original urban designs of the period. It is a success in almost every regard—in its blend of coherence and irregularity which it presents as a streetscape, in its provision for maximum privacy for each unit, its use of roof terraces so that each dwelling enjoys a view of the sea, and finally in its adventuresome use of concrete which was formed into walls through the employment of moveable forms.'

This last brings to our attention Schindler's significant critique of the American balloon frame that, much like Gill, he deemed to be a technically degenerate method of construction. He once described it with ironic disdain as 'an inorganic, unelastic plaster swab supported by means of shrinking skeleton'. In this regard

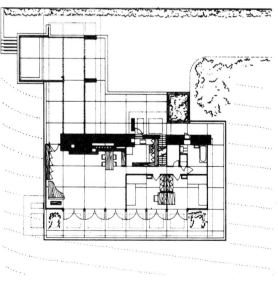

of shrinking skeleton'. In this regard Schindler, like Wright, constantly tried to ground the poetic of his work in a direct relation of the way in which it was built.

Inspiration of Neutra

It is to be greatly regretted that Schindler's long overdue re-evaluation (starting with Gebhard's Los Angeles County Museum retrospective of 1967), should have been achieved at the expense of Neutra's reputation, despite recent ambiguous repertory efforts made on Neutra's behalf by the Californian historian Tom Hines. Far from being little more than a ruthlessly competitive plagiarising ego-

Harwell Hamilton Harris, solar house for Libby-Owens-Ford, model

ist, which is how he has been commonly represented in recent years, Neutra was an architect of extraordinary commitment, sensitivity and power. His role in the cultivation of a modern regional school of architecture in LA throughout the '30s and '40s was seminal and the careers of many distinguished southern Californian architects of the second generation are virtually inconceivable without Neutra's inspiring influence. I am thinking of the brilliant work produced by Gregory Ain, J.R. Davidson, Harwell Hamilton Harris, Raphael Soriano and last but not least, the pre-Miesian career of Craig Ellwood (1952–58) as this is evidenced in Ellwood's Hollywood courtyard apartments of 1953 or in his finely tuned and delicately detailed Case Study House, built in 1958.

Neutra's initial contribution to southern Californian architecture lay in four main areas: in the compelling dynamism of his topographically inflated Neo-Cubistic compositions, in the building techniques, in the formulation of a metabolic, liberating, almost therapeutic, approach to the organisation of space and finally in the pursuit of a proto-eco-

Raphael Soriano, Colby Apartments, Los Angeles 1952

logical sensibility towards the climate and topography of the region. With regard to the last, it should be noted that Neutra is one of the great unrecognised landscape architects of the first half of this century. Trained in plant materials by the Swiss landscape designer Gustav Amman, it was Neutra rather than Schindler, who designed the diminutive, cactus garden below Schindler's elevated Lovell Beach house, built at Newport Beach in 1926.

Caught in the disenchanted labyrinth of the late twentieth century, it is hard for us to imagine the existence of clients like Philip and Leah Lovell who were progressive from almost every conceivable standpoint, be it radical politics or preventative medicine. If they were not quite as insistently anarcho-socialist as

Rudolph and Pauline Schindler, with whom they were intimate friends, they were certainly equally therapeutic in their attitude toward the maintenance of psychological and physical well-being in modern industrialised society. Thus, as Gebhard has written of Lovell: 'Lovell was a characteristic southern California product. It is doubtful whether his career could have been repeated anywhere else. Through his *Los Angeles Times* column, "Care of the body", and through "Dr Lovell's Physical Culture Center", he had an influence which extended far beyond the physical care of the body. He was, and he wished to be considered progressive, whether in physical culture, permissive education, or architecture.'

Theory of Biorealism

The ideology of Lovell and its direct expression in Neutra's Health House, designed for Lovell in 1926, was to exercise a decisive influence over the rest of Neutra's career. From now on his work was at its best where the building programme could be interpreted as making a direct contribution to the psycho-physiological well-being of its occupants. The central theme of both Neutra's work and his writings was the beneficial impact of a well-designed environment upon the functioning of the nervous system. And while his theory of 'biorealism' sometimes rested on dubious causal arguments linking architectural form to overall health, it is difficult to discredit the extraordinary sensitivity and supra-functional attitude that coloured his whole approach; let alone the direct connection between our increasingly abrasive post-industrial environment and the incidence of cancer. Nothing could be further removed from the exclusively formal motivations attributed to the International Style by Hitchcock and Johnson than the overall biological concerns addressed by Neutra in his book *Survival Through Design* (1954) where he wrote: 'It has become imperative that in designing our physical environment we should consciously raise the fundamental question of survival in the broadest sense of the term. Any design that impairs or imposes excessive strain on the natural human equipment should be eliminated or modified in accordance with the requirements of our nervous, and more gradually, our total physiological functioning.'

Thus, the primary concern of Schindler and Neutra (both of whom

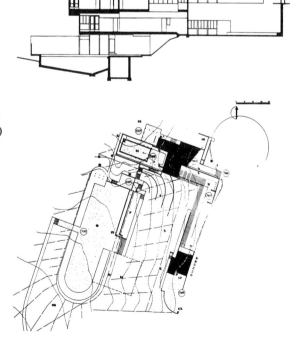

Richard Neutra, Health House section and plan

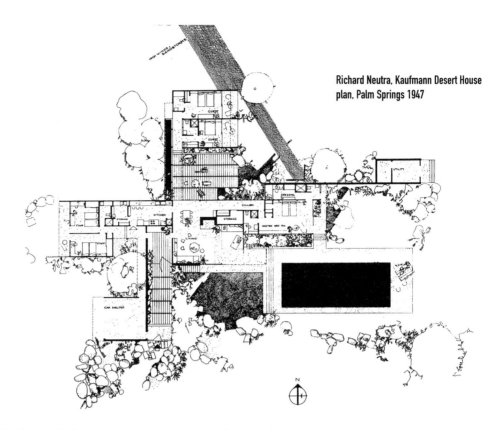

Richard Neutra, Kaufmann Desert House plan, Palm Springs 1947

had served their American apprenticeships with Wright) was not abstract form as such, but rather the articulation of sun and light, combined with a sensitive integration of vegetation and tectonic form into an existing fabric. This ambient hedonism was never more subtly expressed than in Sachs apartments, Los Angeles, built to Schindler's design in 1928; or in Neutra's second masterwork, his Kaufmann Desert House built at Palm Springs, California, in 1947.

That an architect could conceive of his work as transcending both self-conscious aesthetics and the needs and resources of the middle class, 'imperialist' client on whom he or she would invariably depend for patronage is as about as foreign to us today as it was normal for southern Californian architects in the period of the New Deal.

Neutra wrote of his interest in progressive educational methods and of their dissemination to the Third World:

'The briefly illustrated Ringplan School designed in 1926 has rooms in which by monitor-like ceiling openings and the guarded influx of light from above, brightness differentials were kept down with care throughout the enclosed space. This space is… extended to an open-air classroom, with many activities possible on the equally extended ground and floor, so naturally close to children. Undoubtedly the first teaching of geometry and geography took place on the ground, not just on vertical blackboards.

'The ideas presented in these designs have now been broadly accepted in California and in other states. To be commissioned to give thought to the design of an entire school system of a country like Puerto Rico is indeed a fascinating task; and to consider herein a most economical budget gives it world significance, because the world consists mostly of poor countries, where means are not as plentiful as in the State of New York or even in Stockholm or Zurich.'

Rudolf Schindler, Sachs Apartments, Los Angeles 1928

The Usonian legacy was never more prominent in Neutra's work than in his inflected elaboration of single-storey residential accommodation with internal volumes fusing into planted patios at every turn and with bedrooms and corridors being invariably treated as incidental living space, as galleries, libraries, storage walls and the like. He was, in this particular respect, the prime mentor of the school and those who worked for him in the '30s and '40s, architects such as Ain, Pfisterer, Harris, Soriano and even Ellwood (who, as a young man, was to supervise the construction of some of his houses) followed him faithfully in this regard, designing residences that were always ingeniously articulated in terms of their microspace. Certainly one cannot claim that there are decisive masterpieces among the highly civilised houses realised by this group of architects, but this hardly justifies our current snobbish tendency to dismiss the level of domestic civility generally achieved in southern California during the '40s and '50s, and still evident, as continuing culture, even today.

Usonian Superiority

In our search for more socially accessible and economic patterns of land settlement the Usonian model surely still surpasses the virtues of the only other prevalent residential paradigm that is available for future megalopolitan development. Certainly one may claim that it is *ecologically* superior to the AngloSaxon suburban garden city pattern, above all for its tendency to proliferate interstitial microclimatic conditions throughout the built-up area. Other cultural differences between the two are equally apparent for where Ebenezer Howard's Rurisville is a compensatory *petit bourgeois* pattern of private land settlement, that still simulates the nostalgic iconography of an idealised but lost agrarian past, Wright's Usonia continues to project a hedonistic and ecologically viable post-industrial future. And where the former invariably results in an unending expanse of freestanding pitched roofed brick boxes, relieved only by puritanical overworked lawns and flowerbeds and by the generally meaningless *lacunae* of leftover space, the latter results in a semi-collective pattern of carpet housing where built/unbuilt, culture/nature, public/private, all continually interpenetrate each other throughout the built-up area. The socio-familial and bio-regional advantages of this last have already been convincingly advanced, many times since Wright's death (above all by Roland Rainer) but this unfortunately has not led to its widespread adoption as the normative mode of our time. The reactionary and ultimately uneconomic prejudices of mortgage companies, banks and bureaucrats continue to prevail more or less everywhere and it is these forces rather than the critically creative intellect that continue to determine the received image of home as this is reflected on the market and in the general pattern of land settlement. As Antonio Gramsci was to put it: 'The old is dying and the new cannot be born and in this interregnum many disturbing symptoms appear.'

Among the very few exceptions to this depressing rule, vestiges of sensitive, low-rise, high-density development may still be found in southern Califor-

Frank Lloyd Wright, Usonian Lewis House, Illnois 1940

nia today, above all in the recent planned unit-developments built on a relatively small scale by young architects and developers. I am thinking of a whole series of condominium terrace houses recently built in Santa Monica to the designs of such architects as David Cooper, Michael Folonis, James Stafford, Ricky Binder and Steve Andre. Of these works perhaps the most spectacular and generic, from the point of view of positing a model for future development, are the so-called Sun-Tech town houses realised in Santa Monica to the designs of Andre in 1981. While Wright's Usonian house can no longer be claimed as the conceptual origin of this work and while pre-war European housing models are as much an influence on the Sun-Tech houses as Schindler's El Pueblo Ribera block (see the influence of Roger Sherwood's *Modern Housing Prototypes*) there, none the less, remains that particular interpenetration of interstitial interior and exterior micro-space that has become the hallmark of the southern Californian school.

Outram's Iconography

THEORY

John Outram
January 1988

The imagination is a territory with its own exclusive structure. It requires organisation as do the other components of architecture. Iconography is the professional technique for organising pictorial images and their meanings. Iconology is today an unusual territory for conscious and rational design and so it is explained here at some length. But this does not make it more important than other elements of the design.

The iconographic context in this essay mainly concerns two buildings: Albert Richardson's Bracken House, and St Paul's. Both are Classical buildings. The Classical iconology might describe the imaginative structure of St Paul's as:

a The cubic form of the Earth (the nave) on which is placed.

b The sphere of the Cosmos (the dome).

c Their superposition together makes up the profile of the 'sacred mountain'.

∂ A temple (the lantern of the dome) is built on the summit of this conceptual mountain. The cavernous interior of the mountain is entered through.

e A sacred grove of trees (the floriated columns of the portico). These trees, as with other floriated columns around the exterior walls of the church, support a heavy entablature.

This 'heavy roof' was essential to stone construction as it placed the walls and columns into high compression to stabilise them against overturning by wind

Hypostyle island in Pompeian mural

and earth tremors. The separate, but coincident, iconic function of the entablature was to erect a table (Fr: *entablement*, It: *intavolatura*, Lat: *tablinum* – terrace, art gallery, archive), as an elevated territory (or 'new earth') on which to place statues and emblematic objects.

These statues and emblems were personifications, or impersonations of ideas which they represented dramatically, exactly as do actors on a stage. The roof-line of the traditional city was populated by ideas, food for the imagination. All this was a perfectly understood, practical and efficient piece of iconic engineering. (Reyner Banham proposed that Le Corbusier himself used this architectural figure in the Villa Savoye, where he placed objects on its roof derived from the abstracted forms of Cubist still lifes of bottles on 'tables'. In this case it was the five Phileban solids that Le Corbusier held aloft as touchstones.)

What are the idea-things we wish to put on our 'high tables'? Are they the great ventilating fan enclosures of the Centre Pompidou, the blue cranes of Lloyd's, the comic pediment of Philip Johnson's AT&T Chippendale Classical, or real plants and animals, as the environmentalists might advise? Or have we something else of value in mind? An understanding of the traditional rules of architecture makes one conscious that all architecture is inevitably a public statement, and that most of what is not worth lifting one's eyes off the pavement to 'hear'.

The iconic structure of the traditional city allowed few structures to rise above the cornice-level of the entablature. This formal discipline was not mere Neo-Classical tidiness. It accorded with a clear pictorial reasoning: only the domes and spires of monuments broke through the 'new, ideal, earth' to be born again, like the pyramid from the ocean, in that ideal landscape on which stood the statues, the legitimate population of the 'landscape of ideas'.

The rentable skyscraper (perhaps only possible under the writ of the ideological iconoclasm of the New World) broke with this comprehensive and credible tradition. So, to preserve the 'cornice-logic' around St Paul's, the 1930s had to invent its analogue in the form of the 'St Paul's Heights'.

This is a typical example of modern town planning. One takes the disposition of cities that are admired, but that have arisen under the discipline of traditional formal rules, and deracinates them into an abstract (therefore 'rational')

Project logo

geometrical construction. The professionals then play inventively, as they must and should, with these given geometries, but without either asking after, or being in any way referred to, their original formal model. Huge buildings are planned that respond intelligently and directly to these new facts by slicing diagonal chunks off their bodies at the precise point that the St Paul's height line occurs on the map of the City. Architectural nonsense ensues. Modern town planning becomes an irksome set of trivial restrictions in which the natural and intelligible shapes are distorted by abstract rules that serve no credible purpose.

Bracken House is a striking example of a building that conforms exactly, but inventively, to the iconic formalities of the Classical city. It is, for this reason, an extremely valuable contemporary building. It should only be replaced by a building of even greater value to the project of re-ordering the conceptual fabric of urban architecture.

VILLA SAVOYE 1929

Iconography: External Design

The proposed replacement presented here takes up the iconic theme of the great city as an infinite field (a sea) in which the city block is pictured as an individual 'island' (the Classical *insula*). The city is conceptualised, as it has been and still is by millions of imaginations, as a labyrinthic archipelago of such islands, traversed by the rivers and rivulets of streets and alleyways. The tops of these islands would be their most 'original' part: little patches of primal vegetation, or roof gardens with their shelters. When this iconography is combined with that of the elevated cornice-field of roof-level statues, crockets, and other emblems, then the city proper exists conceptuallly as a 'submarine' environment. Within this combined iconic logic the streets become the 'beds and walls of dried-up rivers'.

Bracken House clearly depicts a cornice-level topped by a fabric that is both as green as vegetation and as lightly-built (the columns are made of electric light) as the temples and huts of the Arcadian island tops. This superstructure is supported by a grove of masonry trees —a Classical understanding, or image, of the column. The brick of the columnar flanks is red-brown, the natural colour of earth, the raw sides of the isola(ted) mountain blocks of the city archipelago.

The project logo we created is a masonry tower supporting a winged raft or table and encircled at its base by a serpent. Traditional iconography uses these conventional components. The winged table is the Ark, which was a raft that came to rest on the top of the first island (masonry tower) to rise from the flood (the serpentine waves).

Pavements of streets are imaged as the memory of the water that once (conceptually) flowed down them. The metaphor conventionally used to imper- sonate water (for greater dramatic effect), is the snake, or serpent. Scaly skin is

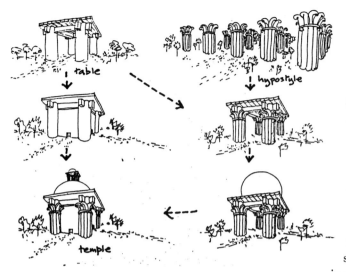

imitated by the glistening cobble-stones, the traditional paving for several millennia. The snake is also the icon of infinitude—the original derivation of its mathematical symbol. Thus the serpent stands for both the idea of water and the idea that the sea is a metaphor for infinity. Hence, the serpent (instead of water) at the foot of the tower indicates that one is dealing in an iconic script for the imagination and not in photographs of lighthouses.

The design adopts the following structures of Classical iconology:

1 The City imaged as an infinite ocean filled with island blocks.
2 The streets imaged as the courses of dried-out rivers.
3 The building imaged as a mountain that was once submarine and supported its rooftop at the original level of the sea.
4 The upper part of the city-block imaged as a green island of vegetation supported on this masonry base that once had the sea lapping around it.
5 The upper part of the building imaged as an entablature, raft or Ark, supporting a landscape of ideas in personified and dramatised form.
6 The lower part of the building pictured as a grove of masonry trees, architecturally a hypostyle hall, the aboriginal forest of standing beings (cf Serlio), that support the entablature.

Iconographical Design: Interior

The interior of the proposed design is structured by the elements of interior planning: geometry, structure, services, and daylighting. The device of a 'river valley' is suggested to connect-up the horizontally and vertically displaced atria. The valley offers both a diagonal sight-line up the mass of this otherwise deep and solid building (40 m by 70 m) and a river whose water falls from the roof garden to the lower ground floor, connecting it conceptually with the open sky and rain above. Hence the 'fresh air' of the outdoors comes right down into the building.

The icon of the river valley has a long history. It underlies the architectural order of many historical building types, from Roman house to Christian church and formal garden. The paintings of Claude Lorraine confirmed its fundamental elements and brought them back from the interior into the exterior, natural world of the Classical landscape. From here they entered English landscape design, through Pope and Kent.

The suggestion that this device has an important conceptual function in an office block may surprise some, yet is perfectly rational. In large offices one can become detached from external circumstances by inner pressures of the organisation and the abstract nature of the work. It is important that office workers have some shared circumstance that reminds them of the greater reality within which they pursue their ends.

The river valley is a basic image of the macrocosm, the whole reality of the living world. It is one that the modern sensibility is likely to find most congenial, because it has an easy natural truthfulness, an absolute value where ecological balance is threatened by pollution: river valleys are the green ecological basis of life—besides having a more 'learned' function in iconography.

Tradition and Modernity

THEORY

Juhani Pallasmaa

May 1988

Motto: '...*everything which is not tradition is plagiarism*...' Igor Stravinski[1]

Techno-Utopia and Identity

In his book *Homo Faber* the Swiss writer and playwright Max Frisch, an architect by training, portrays a UNESCO expert, an engineer – symbol of Modern Man – who continuously travels around the world on his missions. He is a rational and realistic man whose life should be under perfect control. However, he slowly loses contact with locality and place, and finally with his own identity, so much so that he ends up falling in love with his own daughter whom he does not know as the tragic consequence of his loss of roots, the ultimate criterion of reality. Their love ends violently in the daughter's death. *Homo Faber's* grave mistake was his conviction that with technology the world could be transformed so that it need not be experienced through emotions.

The Modern Movement enthusiastically aspired to create a universal culture. The new 'machines for living in' set in 'space, light and greenery' were to emancipate their inhabitants from their bonds with the past, and to cultivate a New Universal Man.

Half a century later, however, the techno-rationally biased and economy-obsessed buildings that have become only too familiar everywhere impair our

Cohesion of local colour

sense of locality and identity. The standard building of today accelerates estrangement and alienation of integrating our world-view and sense of self. Simply, we have lost our faith in utopia.

Meanwhile, we have learned to admire unique and authentic forms of indigenous and vernacular traditions which were earlier hardly considered part of the realm of architecture. We admire the tangible integration of natural and material conditions, patterns of life and forms of building in traditional societies, and this gives us a strengthened sense of causality and existence.

The diversity of building in traditional societies is brought about by the impact of local conditions and the specificity of culture. In our own culture the sheer force of industrial technology, combined with mobility, mass-communication and uniformity of lifestyle is causing cultural entropy that minimalises diversity. What is the feasibility of regional culture and architecture in a world in which two billion people gather simultaneously around TV sets to watch the same football match? Are we not gradually becoming detached from our foothold in geographic and cultural soil and going to live in a fictitious and fabricated culture, the culture of *simulacra* that Umberto Eco has written about? Are we not moving towards a worldwide consumerist folklore, a mosaic of impacts and information detached from their origin. Isn't our culture doomed to lose all its authenticity and turn into a planetary waxworks-show?

Diversification versus Unification

Beyond doubt, the gradual disappearance of a sense of human message and locality from our buildings is the result of cultural factors underlying the act of building—the values and ways of thinking and action that govern our civilisation.

Is it possible to alter the course of our culture? Is the resuscitation of regional architecture in post-industrial and PostModern society feasible? Indeed, can authentic architecture exist in the metaphysical materialism that we live in?

Clearly our identity, and mental well-being, cannot be supported by a universally standardised and abstracted environment. Cultural anthropology has revealed that we do not live in separate physical and mental worlds. The two realms are totally fused and, consequently, the organisation of our physical world is a projection of the mental one and vice-versa.

An architecture capable of supporting our identity has to be situationally, culturally and symbolically articulated. I am disturbed by the notion of regionalism because of its geographic and ethnological connotations. I would rather speak of situational or culture-specific architecture.

The fundamental message of architecture is the very basic existential expression: how does it feel to be a human being in this world? And the task of architecture is to make us experience our existence with deeper significance and purpose. Architecture is to make us know and remember who we are. In the words of Aldo van Evck: 'Architecture must facilitate Man's homecoming.'

133

Constituents of Locality

What are the constituents of a sense of specific locality? They are, of course, reflections of natural, physical and social realities. They are expressions and experiences of specific nature, geography, landscape, local materials, skills and cultural patterns. But they are not detached elements; the qualities of culturally adapted architecture are inseparably integrated in tradition. Without continuity of an authentic tradition even a well-intentioned use of surface elements of regional character is doomed to sentimental scenography, to be a naively shallow architectural souvenir.

Culture is not composed of elements which can be disassembled and recomposed; culture has to be lived. Cultures mature and sediment slowly as they become fused into the context and continuity of tradition. Culture is an entity of facts and beliefs, history and present, material realities and mental conditions. It proceeds unconsciously and cannot be manipulated from outside. Hence, an authentic culturally differentiated architecture can only be born from differentiated patterns of culture, not from fashionable ideals in design. But do such conditions really exist in our time?

The profoundly Mexican architecture of Luis Barragán, for instance, echoes distinct deep-structure features of Mexican culture and life, particularly the presence of death as an accepted dimension of life, and turns these cultural ingredients into his unique metaphysical and surreal art which is traditional and individual, timeless and radical at the same time.

The architecture of Alvaro Siza is an abstraction and condensation of social and building traditions of Oporto. His architecture is abstracted to the degree that one can hardly trace this tradition but its presence is felt in the authoritative quality of his architecture.

The regionalist architecture of Hungarian Imre Makovecz is more explicitly generated from images of Hungarian mythology and folklore and there is a feeling of cultural scenography in his work that suggests archaic rites: one expects people to appear on the scene dressed in Medieval tunics.

It seems that in our time regional identity is possible only on the fringes which have not been conquered by consumer society.

The Hidden Dimensions of Culture

As structural anthropology has taught us, the relations of man, artefacts and culture are complex. The difficulties of rationally conceiving these relations arise mainly because decisive interaction takes place on an unconscious biocultural level. These hidden dimensions have been pointed out by Edward T. Hall, whose books on unconscious and culturally-conditioned uses of space are invaluable to an architect. To deny these differences is now pure ignorance. Knowledge of the cultural conditioning of our behaviour in space and place is rapidly increasing. Studies on the spatial geometry within language, for instance, show that language conditions man's spatial behaviour in a way specific to that particular language.

134

The disappearance of situational character: Casares, Spain...   and apartments in Gladsaxe, Denmark

The psycho-linguistic studies of the Norwegian-born Finn, Frode Strømnes, have revealed astonishing differences in spatial imagery and use of space between Finnish and Swedish speaking people for instance, and these differences are no doubt reflected in Finnish and Swedish architecture. It is difficult to analyse what constitutes Swedishness or Finnishness in architecture but it is perceived at a glance. Language itself can be used to generate architecture. In addition to his morphological studies of Finnish landscapes, Reima Pietila has deliberately attempted to project the rhythms, complexities and topological nature of Finnish language in his architecture.

We Finns tend to organise space topologically on the basis of an amorphous 'forest geometry' as opposed to the 'geometry of town' that guides European thinking. The geometry of the forest is most clearly expressed in Alvar Aalto's work, in the elaborate use of forest metaphor at Villa Mairea and the New York Pavilion. This assumption is not at all surprising if one knows Hall's observations on the radial pattern of thinking among the French and the *gridiron* thinking of the Americans.

Certain deep-structure properties specific to local culture vigorously resist change. For instance, the tone of speech characteristic to a region has been observed to persist through many successive generations after a family has moved from the region. I have been astonished by the persistence of gestural and body language characteristic to a given culture. There is no way of mistaking a French or an Italian by his gesturing or an American by his way of walking, or of not instantly spotting an American in European context by his higher level of voice.

Body and muscle system are strongly connected with cultural identity. Evidently an authentic building tradition must be related to such unconscious factors. Mud-building traditions, in west Africa for instance, seem more related to man's tactile sense than visual. Culturally there is a tendency to develop away from the tactile towards the visual. Yet we return to the tactile mode in certain emotional states, for instance caressing our dear ones.

Consequently, a culturally-adapted architecture is not merely a matter of visual style but of integration of culture, behaviour and environment. To deny cultural differentiation is foolish. A culturally-specific character or style cannot be consciously learned and added on the surface of design, it is a result of being

Edward Hopper, 'Office in a Small Town', 1953   Peter Brueghel, 'Netherlandish Proverbs', 1559

profoundly subject to a specific pattern of culture and of the creative synthesis which fuses conscious intentions and unconscious conditioning, memories and experience, in a dialogue between the individual and the collective.

All artists elaborate their self-image in their art and a differentiated building tradition supports the collective self-image of an entire culture. This applies also to apparently traditionless building in America, the Strip, for instance.

Individual and Tradition

The creative artist's relation to history is equally complex. Authentic artists are usually more concerned with a general feeling for time and history than any factual history or its products. In an essay written in 1919, entitled 'Tradition and the Individual Talent', T.S. Eliot describes perceptively this 'historical sense' and a poet's position in the challenge of tradition: 'Tradition is a matter of much wider significance. It cannot be inherited, and if you want it you must obtain it by great labour. It involves, in the first place, the historical sense … and the historical sense involves a perception, not only of the pastness of the past, but of its presence; the historical sense compels a man to write not merely with his own generation in his bones, but with a feeling that the whole of the literature … has a simultaneous existence and composes a simultaneous order.' This historical sense, which is a sense of the timeless as well as of the temporal and of the timeless and of the temporal together, is what makes a writer traditional and it is at the same time what makes a writer most acutely conscious of his place in time, of his own contemporaneity.

'No poet, no artist of any art, has his complete meaning alone. His significance, his appreciation is the appreciation of his relation to the dead poets and artists. You cannot value him alone; you must set him, for contrast and comparison, among the dead.'[2]

Today's fashionable attempts to recreate a sense of place and rootedness in history through application of historical and regional motifs usually fail because of the one-dimensionally literal use of reference and a manipulation of motifs on the surface level.

Instead of being born from an integrity of cultural forces – the inner necessity, as Kandinsky named it – the historicism of today is a form of intellectual manipulation. Culture is taken as an objectified, external and given reality which

Luis Barragán, Mexico Society, San Cristobal 1967–68

can be consciously applied and expressed in design. The past is taken as a source from which to select instead of being the continuum and context of creative work. Instead of being accepted as an autonomous process, culture has been turned into an object of deliberate fabrication.

The present concern with regionalism has the evident danger of turning into sentimental provincialism, whereas vital products of art in our specialised culture are always born from an open confrontation between the universal and the unique, the individual and the collective. the traditional and the revolutionary.

In an essay entitled 'What is a Classic', T.S. Eliot describes mental provincialism: '... a provincialism, not of space, but of time: one for which history is merely the chronicle of human devices which have served their turn and been scrapped, one for which the world is the property solely of the living, a property in which the dead hold no shares.'[3]

Alvar Aalto's Regional Strategies

The most outspoken advocate of situationally adapted Modernity in the Nordic countries as well as within the Modern Movement as a whole was, of course, Alvar Aalto.

After his short enthusiasm for the main stream of the Modern Movement and its universalist ideals, Aalto emphatically expressed his suspicion of universal and techno-utopian ideology. In Aalto's thinking the task of architecture was to mediate between man and technology and support his social and cultural integration.

There is an unexplainable sense of rootedness and Finnishness in Aalto's designs. His architecture seems to activate certain deep responses in the observer. His biomorphisms give subconscious associations with the organic world and his layered compositions give an impression of environments formed by tradition and history. Aalto uses imagery that activates subconscious association. He uses, for instance, metaphorically condensed images of town and landscape reminiscent of medieval paintings. In one of his early essays – presumably an introduction to a planned book which never progressed beyond this introduction – he praises Andrea Mantegna's painting 'Christ in the Vineyard' as a magnificent representation of 'an architectonic landscape' and a 'synthetic landscape'. The desire to create a 'synthetic landscape' seems to have persisted in his own work throughout his life, and it clearly contributes to the adaptive character of his architecture. He synthesised not only the Finnish landscape in his architecture but also the Finnish temperament.

In his compositions Aalto tended to understate main compositional elements, like the entrance and guided one's attention elsewhere. This understatement is reminiscent of Peter Brueghel's paintings in which the mythical event is hidden in the middle of everyday life. There is a relaxed vernacular feeling, an air of invitation and curiosity rather than an attempt to impose and silence.

Aalto's architecture is connected with a general sense of time and place rather than with any specific style or place. His work gives simultaneously faint hints of archaic history, antiquity, vernacular Mediterranean building and anonymous Finnish peasant tradition.

The work of Henry Moore evokes a similar abundance of imagery related to nature, geology, plant forms, animal skulls and bones, as well as of archaic products of Man.

Aalto's architecture did not aim at the absoluteness typical of the main line of the Modern Movement. As a result, he could use motifs of history and vernacular tradition, combined with a Modern language, and create architecture remarkably rooted in place and time.

Vernacular style is usually an unorthodox mixture of influences and motifs which have lost much of their original meaning and intactness. In a similar manner, Aalto used the Modernist vocabulary in shamelessly unorthodox combinations with romantic, historicist and folk motifs. But Aalto's motifs are not borrowings; they are recreations and they merely hint at a possible origin elsewhere. The use of vernacular motifs gives his buildings a relaxed and unpretentious atmosphere and certainly has facilitated the public's acceptance of his Modernity. This applies also to Aalto's furniture designs which represent the very few examples of Modernist vernacular. Innumerable variations and modifications by other designers are a clear indication of the acceptance of Aalto's design as a modern vernacular.

Interaction between the self-conscious high-style of the academic discipline of architecture and unself-conscious vernacular application, is an essential aspect of the evolution. A style becomes socially significant as it generates a tradition of anonymous application. And one of the shortcomings of the Modern Movement at large has been its inability to produce a positive vernacular.

Culturally adapted architecture reverberates with tradition. It fuses and reflects the timeless vernacular idiom and, consequently, an authentic culture-specific architecture cannot be invented. It has to rediscover and revitalise aspects of tradition, either explicit characteristics of style or more convincingly, the hidden dimensions of culture.

Uniting Opposites

The architectures of Alvar Aalto and Luis Barragán reveal that culture-specific character of architecture is not a matter of simple manipulation of recognisable elements. Cultural isolationism and protectionism do not offer any guarantee of unique architecture.

Regional character may be achieved – and usually is – from totally contradictory ingredients. Frank Lloyd Wright's American architecture synthesised

138

themes from North American and Mexican Indian cultures, and European architectural history as well as traditional Japanese architecture. The impact of traditional Japanese art on today's Western aesthetic ideals is another example of the incredibly composite nature of culture. On the other hand, Le Corbusier's work — strongly influenced by Mediterranean

Alvar Aalto, Maison Carré, 1956–58

vernacular tradition—has given rise to one of the strongest contemporary traditions in Japan and India. And this influence is again reflected back to Europe and other parts of the world in the work of Ando, Correa and many others.

The journey of Louis Kahn's architecture from his native Estonian island of Saarenmaa via Philadelphia to Bangladesh where his geometric architecture has created a strong school, is equally astonishing.

The most outspoken regionalist group in Finland today, the northern Oulu School, has been most strongly influenced by Charles Moore, whereas today's strong Estonian *avant-garde* is a curious fusion of Russian Constructivism and American Post Modernism, an artistic marriage of Leonidov and Graves.

A colleague recently made a comment that regional architecture today looks the same all over the world. All great art tends to be regional for the simple reason that it is open to interpretation and, consequently, can echo any cultural conditions. All great art is the common property and heritage of mankind.

But these crusades of inspirations and impulses in the development of culturally-adapted architecture are not just products of our communication age.

Peasant churches in Finland which are usually considered to be genuine products of an indigenous tradition are clearly echoes of continental high-styles. Similarly, the architectural identity of the Grand Duchy of autonomous Finland was created in Neo-Hellenic spirit which, of course, was totally alien for the underdeveloped forest land of the time. The National Romanticism of the turn of the century, which deliberately aimed at creating a national style and overtly

sought its inspiration from indigenous mythology and tradition was, in fact, closer to contemporary examples in Germany and Scotland, or even on the other side of the Atlantic in the American Midwest. The Nordic Classicism of the 1920s found its inspiration in the Classical vernacular of northern Italy. And half a century later the universal ideals of the International Style were turned into a humane and somewhat romantic version of postwar Modernity in the Nordic countries.

Andrea Mantegna, 'Christ in the Vineyard', 1455

139

One of the most convincing achievements of Western architecture in an alien cultural context is Henning Larsen's Saudi Arabian Foreign Ministry in Riyadh which clearly shows the Nordic sensibility of cultural assimilation. This building is an exceptionally successful example of architectural diplomacy (AR July 1985). Psychologists speak of 'situational personality' referring to the fact that the behaviour of a single individual varies more under different environmental conditions than the behaviour of different individuals under the same circumstances. Maybe we should credit the designer's exceptional cultural adaptability to a particularly adaptable situational personality.

One more note in this concoction of regionalism: as Saarinen created the prototype of the American skyscraper, in Chicago Tribune Tower, in the woods of southern Finland, his painter friend, Gallen-Kallela started his illustrations of Greater Kalevala, the Finnish folk epic, in Chicago. 'Only in the desert of Chicago did my father's imagination burst into bloom', wrote the painter's daughter.

Constituents of Style

Architecture is not an expression of knowledge and certainty, but of existence and faith and a perpetual search for reconciliation.

An architectural style is defined, both on individual and collective levels, by a combination of certain mental orientations. Stylistic evolution seems to take place in a pendulum fashion as priorities shift from one polarity to the other. The orientations are exemplified by the opposite notions like those in the table.

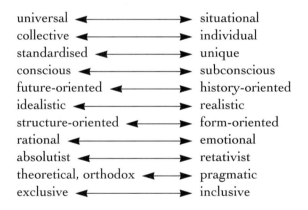

universal	situational
collective	individual
standardised	unique
conscious	subconscious
future-oriented	history-oriented
idealistic	realistic
structure-oriented	form-oriented
rational	emotional
absolutist	retativist
theoretical, orthodox	pragmatic
exclusive	inclusive

The first set of orientations clustered together in the main stream of International Style, whereas the second set of orientations have characterised Nordic architecture through the century. Today there seems to be a rather universal shift towards the latter orientations, away from the mental construction of the International Style. Consequently, a culture specific trend is gaining strength universally and one could foresee a renewed interest in Nordic architecture.

Without wanting to expand the vague terminology of architectural debate, I would argue that Modernity has progressed to a new phase during the past two decades. I would like to speak of a 'First' and a 'Second' Modernity. This implies a change in external stylistic features, but, above all, in mental factors and a new understanding of culture.

In his thought-provoking book *Art of the Novel* Milan Kundera declares that Modernity has transformed to kitsch: 'The aesthetics of mass media are by necessity the aesthetics of kitsch; as the mass media gradually extend and penetrate into every aspect of our life, kitsch becomes our everyday aesthetics and morality. Only some time ago Modernism implied a non-conformist rebellion against received thought and kitsch. Nowadays Modernity blends into the immense vitality of mass media and to be Modern means a fierce attempt to keep up with time and adapt, to be even more adaptive than the most adaptive. Modernity has pulled the robe of kitsch on its shoulders.'[4]

There is no reason to deny Kundera's severe verdict, but I think that only the Modernist dialectical relation to history, culture and society can re-emancipate architecture from kitsch. And I am convinced that the New Modernism that is taking shape now is again shaking the robe of kitsch off its shoulders.

The Two Modernisms

The First Modernism was a utopian, idealistic, purist and demagogic movement, which drew its artistic strength from an innocent faith in a future brought about by new architecture and art. It was a fighting movement with impetus and polemic. It believed in the possibility of cultural expansion and radical change, which could quickly lead to a humane, healthy and sane world.

The Second Modernism is a realistic view of culture unblinded by illusions. It has lost its innocent faith in an immediate victory of humanism and it sees its potential merely as a strategy of cultural resistance in slowing down undesirable anti-human development.

Stylistic change has been equally multifaceted. The First Modernism aspired to immaterial and weightless movement, whereas the Second frequently expresses gravity and stability and a sense of materiality and earth. The return of earth and gravity as expressive means of architecture has more than metaphoric meaning; after its arrogant and utopian journey, architecture has returned to the safety of Mother Earth, back to the source of rebirth and creativity.

In its aspiration for pure plastic expression the First Modernism avoided symbolism, allusion and metaphor, which have become an essential part of the expression of the Second. As the first phase aimed at an impression of timelessness, new Modernism seeks an experience of time through material, memory and metaphor. The First Modernism admired perfection and finiteness, while unfinishedness, process and imperfection, are part of the new expression. The First Modernism aimed at perpetual innovation, the Second consciously uses stylistic borrowings. I want to stress, however, that the contemporary use of quotation

Robert Smithson, 'Spiral Jetty', 1970

takes place in two directions in history and it gives the past a new meaning as opposed to the unidirectional appropriation of eclecticism. There is always an air of necrophilia in eclectic art because of its inability to resurrect the dead.

Motifs of Change

The motive forces behind the change are alterations in consciousness that have taken place during the past two decades and which are more radical than most of us are willing to accept. The Third World, the energy crisis, the university revolution, the development of mass-communication and data-processing are all part of the mosaic of change as well as the whole PostModern debate. But also an awareness of the dangers implied by the technical development and a disappointment with the achievements of Western democracy lie behind the Second Modernity.

The transformation of Modernity did not happen at once. Even in the early phases of Modernism, expressionist, organic and regionalist tendencies existed within the Movement. The momentum of the First Modernism began to run out in the '50s and the emerging change was revealed in the discussions of CIAM. Louis Kahn and Aldo van Eyck appeared as the most outspoken heralds of change. Kahn brought back the archaic and metaphysical dimensions and van Eyck introduced an anthropological and structuralist view.

My view of continuous Modernity is based on a view of the dialectics of evolution which is more explanatory and hopeful than the popular thought of a bankruptcy of Modernity. Fundamentally I see Modernity as a dialectic view of culture that perpetually challenges and resurrects the past.

The New Tradition

The touching and optimistic vitality of early Modernism arises from its origins at the confrontation of tradition and reform. Modernity lost its spiritual depth through the generations, which accepted the style as a ready-made aesthetic without its cultural background and the continuity of tradition implied by Modernism.

The interdependence of architecture and culture has not been sufficiently recognised. The international, consumerist architectural journalism of today violently detaches buildings from their cultural context and presents them in an arena of individual architectural showmanship.

The Second Modernity has to relearn a way of seeing architecture as part of cultural tradition as well as analysing the timeless essence of architecture. It is also significant that the creators of First Modernism were themselves artists or collaborated closely with artists. The spiritual withering of Modernism is associated with the postwar generations that alienated themselves from the fine arts both through prevailing educational practice and shallow professionalism. The New Modernism of today seeks again inspiration from the soil of the arts.

Frank Gehry, house in Santa Monica 1978

Populism

The assumed failure of the mythical hero architect has given rise to a populism and a reverence for consensus or popular taste as the sole authority of design. This view denies the essential dynamism of cultural development, the dialogue and opposition between the creative individual and the convention. In the epilogue to his novel *The Name of the Rose* (one of the literary successes in terms of popularity in recent years), Umberto Eco states that there are two types of writers, the ones that attempt to write what they expect their readers to want to read, and others that construct their ideal reader as they write. And only the latter type of writer is able to write significant literature. Only an architect who mentally constructs an ideal client and ultimately an ideal society as he designs can create memorable architecture. This view does not imply empty utopianism or a belief in a messianic mission of architecture. Simply, touching art is born from the reality of hope and idealisation, a belief in a better future. The art of architecture turns into production of commodities for the consumer society when it loses its poetic and metaphysical content and sees as its duty the mere fulfilment of popular desire. 'To caress a cat to death', is the wise warning of a Polish proverb.

In my view, architecture, like all art, is simultaneously autonomous and culture-bound. It is culture-bound in the sense that tradition, the cultural context, provides the basis for individual creativity, and it is autonomous in the sense that an authentic artistic expression is never an answer to prescribed expectation or definition. The fundamental existential mystery is the core of architecture and the confrontation of this mystery is always unique and autonomous, totally independent of the specifications of the 'social commission'. A church and a cellulose factory do not differ at all as commissions for an architect.

The human task of architecture is not to beautify or to humanise the world of everyday facts, but to open up a view into the second dimension of our consciousness, the reality of images, memories and dreams.

Quasi-Intellectualisation

In today's neurotic architectural climate, the intellectual construction seems to be often more important and more central than a sensory and emotional encounter with the architectural work. The fierce quasi-theorising and intellectualisation accelerates alienation and separation from social reality, instead of supporting the integration of architecture and culture, artefact and mankind.

143

Philip Johnson, College of Architecture, University of Houston 1983–85   Graveyard, San Pedro de Alcántara, Spain

A number of architects today seem to attempt being cleverer and wiser than their work. Milan Kundera speaks of 'the wisdom of the novel' and states that all authentic writers listen to this supra-individual wisdom which explains that all great novels are always more intelligent than their authors. Writers who are more intelligent than their works ought to change their profession, says Kundera. In my view, Kundera's argument also holds in our profession—that is 'the wisdom of architecture'.

Although it probably sounds like an empty word, I believe that there is a 'natural philosophy of architecture' that ties together theory, practice and experience. I believe that such a natural philosophy is the silent message of the Nordic architectural tradition.

Is there a shared Nordic consciousness that could have given rise to a shared Nordic tradition in architecture?

Particular geographic, climatic, as well as political and cultural circumstances have certainly moulded an identifiable Nordic mentality regardless of the national differences. Nordic culture is a combination of agrarian and small-town world-views with a distinct sense of scale, an appreciation of understatement and smallness, compared to the desire for monumentality and grandeur in many other near-by cultures.

The Nordic mentality is characterised by a strong sense of causality and contextuality combined with a rather pragmatic and *non-doctrinaire* attitude to life. This is united with a strong sense of social cohesion and solidarity based on a shared cultural and social horizon.

An attempt to avoid polarisation both in thinking and in the social scene is also common. Consequently, it has been characteristic of Nordic architecture that extreme or purist attitudes have generally been avoided. Architecture has developed as a process of gradual assimilation which has fused impacts and inspirations from various sources. The assimilation of De Stijl planar aesthetics, a Gustavian Rococo delicacy, the rich articulation of light of Bavarian Baroque and an Aaltoesque modern imagery in Juha Leiviska's work is a current example of this sensibility. The fusion of motifs from Finnish Medieval churches, direct quotes from Le Corbusier (the entrance structure is from page 123 of Le Corbusier & Jeanneret, *Oeuvre complète 1910–1921*, according to the author), a

Danish sense of scale and, again, Aalto's sense of materials in Kristian Gullichsen's recent church is another example of this assimilation.

The fusion of the polarities of Romanticism and rationality is a specific characteristic of Nordic art and culture. This, I think, is the essence of 'Northern Light' or 'Dreams of the Summer Night' to paraphrase titles of two recent international exhibitions on turn-of-the-century Nordic painting. This sensible *petit bourgeois* attitude is well illustrated in the idyllic scenes of Carl Larsson.

An innate sensitivity to nature with mystical and pantheistic overtones and the impact of peasant background has further softened intellectual aspirations. A rational and constructive tradition has been surprisingly strong in Finnish visual arts. The ideal of simplicity and asceticism related to peasant life seems to motivate Nordic Constructivism and Purism more than Cartesian ideals.

Finnish peasant chair, late nineteenth century

145

Nordic architecture and everyday aesthetics have developed remarkably organically from ageless peasant tradition through various Classicist phases and through Functionalism to today. The transformation of Nordic Classicism in the 1920s to Functionalism, for instance, is a rare example of a decisive cultural transformation without confrontation. Although there is an overt conflict between Classicist and Modernist ideals, the shift was surprisingly smooth, as we know. The aesthetic asceticism and spirituality of Nordic Classicism paved the way for Modernity. And the ideals of social empathy and responsibility which have characterised Nordic architecture were already planted during the Classical era. The most significant feature of Nordic architecture, however, is the integration of architecture and society. The degree to which the philosophy and aesthetics of Modernity have become part of social reality is unique. Modernity is the self-evident condition of Nordic democracy and it is impossible to imagine a wider eclectic revival in Nordic culture.

In our obsessive consumerist culture which gradually detaches objects and buildings from their use, and turns everything into marketable signs, the traditional Nordic functionalist morality restraint and asceticism acquire a wider cultural value. In a culture that tends to turn into a sort of *Sargasso Sea* of too many goods, too much information, too many ideologies, too much of everything, the ideal and aesthetics of noble poverty have a new moral value. As our materialist culture hysterically produces new marketable images and turns even crime, violence and decadence into profit, the Nordic tradition represents a philosophy of common sense and a poetry of the common place.

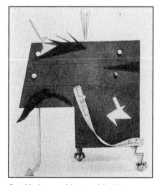

PostModern architectural furniture

Regionalism in the industrial world cannot any longer be founded on a set of isolated and perfectly integrated conditions. Perhaps the most meaningful form of cultural survival that remains is a regionalism of the mind, the strategy of resistance, the subculture that believes in and searches for authenticity. Not authenticity on ethnographic grounds but that of human experience and interaction.

The mission of Nordic architecture lies in the continuous development of the tradition of socially concerned, responsive and assimilative Modernity.

1 Igor Stravinski, *Poetics of Music in the Form of Six Lessons*, Harvard University Press, Cambridge, 1970, p75.

2 T.S. Eliot, *Selected Essays*, new edition, Harcourt, Brace & World, New York, 1964 (1932). Quoted in: Colin St John Wilson, 'The Historical Sense', *AR* October 1984.

3 *Ibid*.

4 Milan Kundera, *Romaanin taide* (*Art of the Novel*), WSOY, Helsinki 1986, p165 (trnslated by J. Pallasmaa).

Split on the Seine

BUILDING CRITIQUE
Arab Cultural Centre, Paris
by Jean Nouvel

Charlotte Ellis
October 1987

The new Institute of the Arab World building is due to open in Paris later this autumn.[1] With an officially approved budget of 50.3 million francs (about £5.3 million) and a total floor area of 26,900 m², this is the smallest and least costly of the Parisian *grands projets* (see AR December 1986).

Set up by France and 19 Arab countries in 1980, the purpose of the Institute is to increase knowledge of the Arab World, its language, cultural and spiritual values: to promote exchange and cooperation between France and the Arab World, particularly in the fields of science and industry; and to enhance relations between the Arab World and Europe.

A site near the Eiffel Tower was chosen originally for the Institute's building but, after the Socialist government was elected in 1981, these plans were abandoned and the architectural aspects of the project radically reconsidered. A new site was selected, at the very end of the Boulevard St Germain, on the Left Bank of the Seine at Jussieu, facing the Ile St Louis. A limited architectural competition followed, won by Jean Nouvel with Pierre Soria, Gilbert Lézénès and Architecture Studio.

Detail of the tower of books

As a parting gesture just before the March 1986 elections, the outgoing Culture Minister, Jack Lang, made over to the Institute the Louvre Museum's Arab and Islamic collections as well as some of those from the Musée des Arts Décoratifs and the Musée des Arts Africains et Océaniens.

A wide range of events – concerts, temporary exhibitions, meetings and the like – is anticipated as well as more permanent attractions. The library, for instance, has a three-fold function: to inform the public on matters of current interest, to provide general information and to cater for specialist research. Meeting rooms, events and exhibition spaces, audiovisual and computer facilities (adapted both to French and Arabic) are therefore included in the library accommodation as well as more conventional reading rooms, books and magazines. Likewise, the museum, which has several departments, is equipped with both temporary and permanent display areas.

Give or take some detailed refinements and a certain amount of juggling with floor areas allocated to the Institute's various functions, Nouvel says the design concept has remained unchanged from the winning competition scheme.[2] Architecturally, the approach is highly symbolic, in that the design addresses three principal dichotomies: 'the traditional and modern aspects of the site; Arab and Western cultures; interiority and openness'. For Nouvel, none of this implies literal-minded mimicry of Arab or Parisian forms, but an opportunity to pursue his own preoccupations with stratification, surface tension and diffraction to create an architectural form and image of the present.

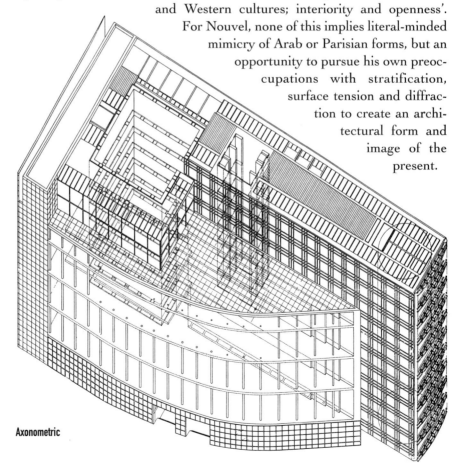

Axonometric

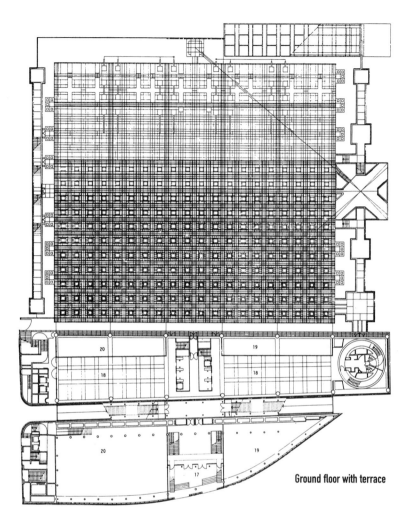

Ground floor with terrace

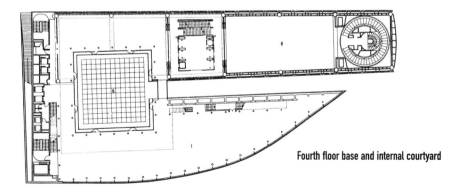

Fourth floor base and internal courtyard

View from river Seine

The form of the building came from an analysis of the site and its central Paris context. The great curve to the northern wing rounds off a notional line, projected in plan between the Boulevard St Germain and the Quai; the southern face of the building lines through with the existing university block next door (from which it is symbolically separated by a narrow gap) and defines a rectilinear open space which, notionally at least, could be linked to the Jardin des Plantes. The dramatic slit between the northern and southern ranges is seen as a suitable response to the apse of Notre Dame cathedral, while the Tower of Books' spiralling upwards within a grid of glazed cladding at the building's western extremity is intended as a landmark, terminating the vistas at the end of the Boulevard St Germain, from the Ile St Louis and from the Sully bridge. But if 'the Institute is the result of the contradictions of the site',[3] Nouvel says the 'architectural approach is entirely based on attractiveness to, and reception of, the public; on the notion of a show case for Arab culture'[4] Most obvious in this last category is the use on the southern elevation of 16,000 moving parts similar to camera diaphragms, designed to open and contract to control sunlight. Their form and the pattern of light and shade they create provide an immediate visual allusion to traditional Arab culture by modern Western means. In contrast, the view over the Seine will be seen through a glazed wall set behind a rectilinear aluminium grille, intended to furnish the transition between the Arab culture as displayed in the museum and the Institute's Parisian setting.

How well such devices will work is impossible to predict before the building has been fully fit-

Central court lined with marble squares clamped in metal frame creating a translucent screen outside the glazing

ted out. Indeed, the future success of the building may well hinge more on politics than architecture. But the new Institute of the Arab World should certainly fulfil Jean Nouvel in 'my greatest wish, which is that later on, when seeing my buildings, people will say "those were the 1980s".'[5] The odds are the majority will be French.

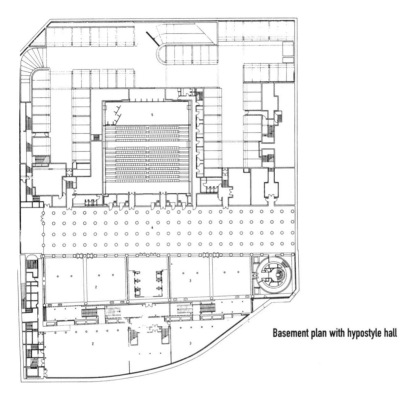

Basement plan with hypostyle hall

1 As built, the Institute's new premises include: museum 44oo m²; library 1900 m²; audio-visual room 160 m²: restaurant and canteen 600 m²; 129 place car park 3350 m²; terraces, patio etc 5780 m²; plant, circulation 7290 m².

2 *Jean Nouvel* by Patrice Goulet, published IFA/Electa Moniteur, Paris 1987, p39.

3 *L'Architecture d'Aujourd'hui*, No 231, February 1984, p24.

4 *Jean Nouvel, op cit*, p66.

5 *Ibid*, p69.

Iris diaphragm which responds electronically to sunlight

Charlotte Ellis

Docklands Double Act

BUILDING CRITIQUE
Housing, Isle of Dogs and Bermondsey, London
by Piers Gough CZGW

Francis Anderton
April 1989

It is now accepted wisdom that London Docklands – through lack of vision, planning controls, infrastructure, civic amenities and so on – is not a real piece of city. It is in fact a showcase, a sort of Great Exhibition of disposable architecture (such is the rate of change that the unfinished Heron Quays, begun in 1983 – a development lauded in the AR as model new dockland design (February 1987) – is due to be flattened under the clumping feet of the Canary Wharf giants. Rather than a confident celebration of a booming industrial economy this exhibition is a risky exploitation of our marketing economy, but it has thrown up a panoply of paper-thin, imagery buildings whose mediocrity triggers the alarm and foreign sniggers that the clumsy, florid *candelabras* and mass-produced porcelain trinkets did in 1851.

But, as sometimes happens at product showcases, amongst the dross – the pastiche, kitsch and plain shoddy – there are a few gems; genuinely innovative, exciting ideas that, but for the *laissez-faire* nature of this experiment, would never have been built, and bode well for the future of British architecture.

China Wharf façade, Bermondsey

Amongst these can be counted the Financial Times printing works by Nicholas Grimshaw (AR November 1988), the water-pumping station by John Outram, hopefully the Reuters building by Richard Rogers, and two residential buildings by Campbell Zogolovitch Wilkinson & Gough.

CZWG are one of the young practices for whom Docklands, in terms of their own talents, really has proved a development zone. Hitherto they have been known as the astonishingly prolific and eclectic designers of, amongst others, artful conversions (AR January 1979, January 1981), small decorative speculative housing schemes (February 1979), private houses, an elegant office and a noble school building; each an individual, noted for the witty, and wise, improvisations on cheap materials and simple construction methods, and liberal application of historical motifs—by turns Art Deco, Neo-Classical and Arts and Crafts (AR March 1977). In Docklands designers Piers Gough and Rex Williamson have found the financial backing to 'get away with anything' and have unleashed a full-blooded Baroque expansiveness on to their two waterside apartment buildings, at Tower Bridge and the Isle of Dogs respectively. They are going on to rebuild a stretch of land, to be called Jacob's Island, by the Thames in Bermondsey. The Isle of Dogs, formerly a boat-building and docking community and one of the most woebegone of the abandoned Docklands areas, is now the Enterprise Zone, the commercial heart of the whole venture. It is here that one finds the

Vertical circulation expressed on exterior

most curious cityscape: consisting of the fledgling developments – small industrial sheds in primary coloured claddings and neo-noddy housing estates – which hover close to the ground the later, more confident, glass-fronted, multi-storey offices and Neo-Vernacular by serious architects; and the recent developments, now reaching to the skies, the ubiquitous pilings and cranes for Canary Wharf and… Cascades.

At 20 storeys high, standing alone on the quayside at Sufferance Wharf and surrounded by water on two sides, Cascades flaunts itself to an audience from miles around. It is the brainchild of Rex Wilkinson and enlightened developers Kentish Homes (with whom CZWG have collaborated on 12 low-rise housing schemes), a calculated risk – testing a bleak location, new fast-track construction methods, discredited typology and strange appearance – which has paid off (flats in Cascades have sold like hot cakes, proving that the punters are more daring than most would believe) .

Cascades is the first among giants. With its head in Canary Wharf and tail in the low-rise buildings to the south, it will fit in humbly with its future neighbours, which will house the amenities and company at present lacking. The

Francis Anderton

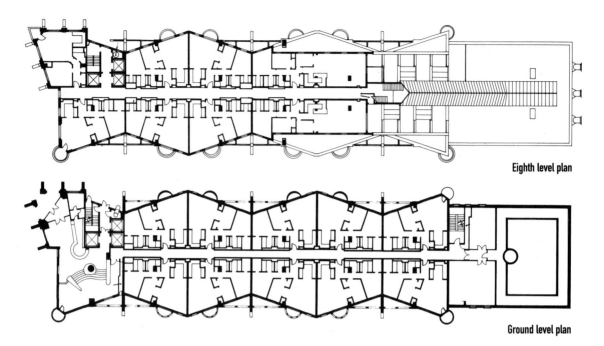

Eighth level plan

Ground level plan

building was completed, on schedule, in an extraordinary eighteen months – the 20 storey concrete lift core was slip-formed in under three weeks – and achieved several technical firsts, such as an anti-condensation detail for the cantilevered concrete balconies, which are now used elsewhere. Boasting a communal swimming pool, gymnasium, outdoor tennis courts, meetings room, fax and telex facilities, Cascades has re-established a taste for the luxury highrise flat. This highly desirable form of accommodation, which is commonplace abroad, was eagerly promoted by English Moderns in the '30s and last tested at the Barbican, but fell generally out of favour due to the failure of post-war council housing blocks, four of which stand as a grim reminder nearby. Hence the emphasis on a block of flats that would look nothing like a systems building.

The one thing that cannot be said about the appearance of Cascades is that it is trying to peddle a familiar image of home. There are no pitched roofs, pediments, dormers or lintels. There is comforting brick cladding, but in bold bands of blue engineering and extruded yellows it makes no attempt to play at being phoney arches or copings; in fact, it combines with portholes, funnels, lighthouse balconies and tower to form a homage to the (fictional) existing Docklands riverscape of ships and warehouses. The building is a maverick, an architectural abstraction, which, unlike most of the other buildings whose impact barely exceeds the three-minute attention span, offers many readings and looks different depending on where you are.

Seen from a distance in its solid, rather solemn, state with its great ramp shooting up at 45 degrees, it reminds me of the mighty sundial, built by the visionary Jai Singh in his observatory in Jaipur in the eighteenth century. Since the building lies due north-south and almost exactly on the Greenwich Meridian line, Cascades could almost serve this purpose as well, but presumably cosmic

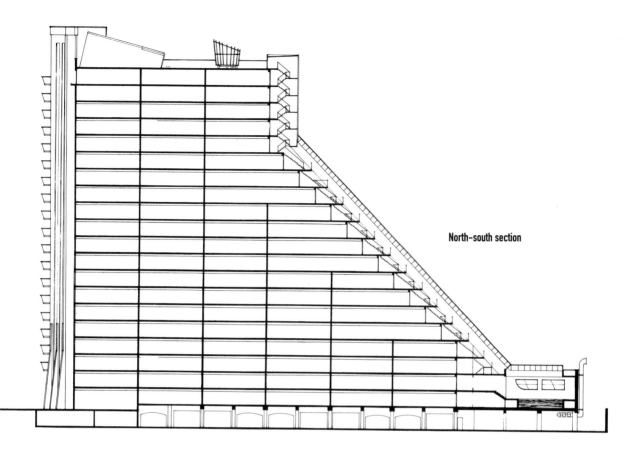

North-south section

consciousness is not in the brief for commercial buildings in Docklands. Close to, the composition fragments; it becomes a multi-faceted manmade rock, broken up by undulating walls, brick banding, orioles, balconies, bays and many shapes and sizes of window into a light, human-scale, crystalline creation. A six-storey, stock-bricked, traditional style quayside building, containing flats and three shop spaces (so far an estate agent and dry cleaners have opened up), marks the way past a shared landscaped garden, to the smart foyer in the towering entrance and circulation zone of this unlikely residence, which contains, dispersed on either side of central corridors, 164 one, two and three-bedroom, single-aspect, flats. The asymmetric plans – generated from large depth living room and smaller bed-rooms – and complex form of the building arise from the desire to give each flat the best possible orientation. Hence the faceted walls, various projections and windows and the south-facing slope which creates a cascade (whence the name) of sun-terraces and alternating greenhouses for the penthouses. This slope also incorporates the fire escape, beneath a canopy of corrugated steel and glass which extends over the swimming-pool to form a skylight. Flying endlessly down through 15 floors with a terrific view, this fire-escape is truly a remarkable expe-rience. But unless the residents see its potential as a communal conservatory or covered circuit-training ground, it will unfortunately go unused.

The pains taken by architect and developer have paid off. The building is interesting and the occupant, in his 'highest specification in Docklands' (accord-

Francis Anderton

ing to a resident) flat, does enjoy spectacular views. The pioneer residents in the west side look on to a panorama of the historic London they chose to leave behind: Hampstead, Tower Bridge, Greenwich. For the braver ones on the east it is future shock: the sun rises over burgeoning Canary Wharf and endless other developments.

CZWG have a reputation, partly perpetuated by vocal partner Piers Gough who gives himself self-deprecating titles like 'pop' or 'B-movie' architect, for being wilful and superficial. On the contrary. Having far too much creative imagination to need the prop of a dogma or style Wilkinson and Gough seem to be amongst the few who manage to combine stylistic abandon with sound, practical considerations and achieve buildings which are delightful, comfortable and, one hopes, enduring.

Such are the qualities of China Wharf, a dashing red building further up river. Filling in one of the last waterfront gaps in the Victorian warehouse development at Tower Bridge, China Wharf, designed by Piers Gough, was CZWG's first really big building. However, when it becomes part of their gargantuan Jacob's Island scheme (a little to the east), whose shapes and gaiety it anticipates, it will look very small and perfectly formed indeed. It was commissioned by developer/patron Andrew Wadsworth (CZWG designed Wadsworth's apartment in the tower of his first development, the conversion of New Concordia

Wharf) who remained closely involved with the scheme. The name was inspired as much by personal associations as by the (fictional) whiff of the spice-trade wharves, and he was keen to propel Gough into greater theatricality than even the architect thought necessary. The building is a bold, bright gesture. Unlike Cascades, which is surrounded by space, China Wharf is wedged ingeniously into a tight site. A perky newcomer in a family of old warehouses, it links on the riverside to form a continuous façade and closes the gap to create a courtyard on the other. Like Cascades, it is multi-faceted; but it has three different faces, each a logical, and mannerist, response to its position. With offices on the ground floor, it contains 17 flats, approached from a central corridor, which are

organised in a complicated scissor-plan ('Never again,' says Gough) so that each has its living-room facing the river and bedrooms at the back. The ideal river façade, to make the most of the north light and fabulous river views, would be predominantly glass. To visually separate the adjoining three flats, to provide privacy, and imply support for the cantilevered balconies, the central panel with wings and flanges was introduced. Hence the delicious pastry-cut pagoda, constructed in poured concrete (with steel flanges) and painted poppy red, which so impressed a French magazine they featured it as a masterpiece of metal design. Sitting on sturdy concrete columns, harbouring a disappearing boat/balcony, it looks inevitable.

The Mill Street elevation, seen best from the river, has the bathroom and bedroom windows. It is also where China Wharf meets Reeds Wharf, with which they curiously share circulation, and its other warehouse neighbours. Hence the warehouse look-alike façade, the reducing window openings (inducing a false perspective effect which partly emphasises the opening size and partly graduates between the different windows of the neighbouring buildings), and the smartly black-painted loophole opening, framing shared entrance, lift and staircase, into which plunges Reeds Wharf like a train going into a tunnel.

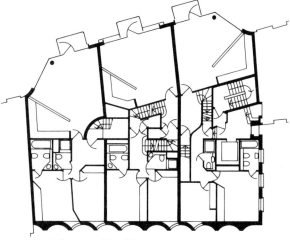

Fourth floor plan, China Wharf

The courtyard side can be overlooked. Hence the small windows, turned away from direct onlookers, and towards the south-easterly morning sun. So that it should not look like a saw-toothed student hostel, the wall is fluted, paying homage in a negative print to former silos, and painted bright red and white — not, sadly, to represent yin and yang, but for light, and to be silo-like, above, and to conceal dirt, below. The use of Chinese symbolism is relaxed. There is, according to the laws of geomancy, a certain number of studs (jokily including the peephole) around the door frames. The lifts, lined with billowing fabric, transport the occupants in an abstracted Chinese lantern. The red on the river side certainly could represent 'ceremony, longevity, excitement and wealth' but it is also about sunshine on a cloudy London day on a gloomy London dockland.

If my emphasis appears to have been on the elevations of this immaculately finished building (executed by enlightened builders Harry Neal) that is because it is not necessary to linger on the plans. As at Cascades, the apartments are as good as they can be, given the spatial constraints of these high-density developments. Suffice it to say that the kitchen/living rooms are open-plan, separated only by a sweeping curved panel, enjoy muted light and fabulous, framed views of Tower Bridge. The bedrooms are compact and have fitted cupboards.

What Wilkinson and Gough have endeavoured not to do is come up with the answer to the problem of finding a new Docklands building typology. What they have done is find sensible, entertaining empirical solutions, drawing on existing types, to a specific situation. But what these private housing developments are itching to do is go public. Their designs have the pomp, vigour and civic presence of an age which preceded the invention of architectural angst. It is to be hoped that if the state ever recovers from its miserable parsimony and cultural indifference it will ask CZWG to design a few buildings we all can enjoy.

Francis Anderton

Store Street Snowline

BUILDING CRITIQUE
Design Studios and Offices, London
by Ron Herron

Martin Pawley
January 1990

Today Ron Herron looks older than he did when, with Peter Cook, Warren Chalk, Dennis Crompton, David Greene and Michael Webb, he contributed to the magazine Archigram.

But looking through the pages of Archigram now is like looking through the resumé of everyone in British architecture: even John Outram once contributed designs for a 'Motorway City'. Archigram in all its manifestations was devoured by enthusiasts from Tokyo to Budapest. Even today the modest Milton Keynes playground that is the only Archigram building open to the public – the other was a swimming pool for Rod Stewart – still receives the occasional student visitor on a pilgrimage.

In 1967 Ron Herron drew a project for a 'tuned' suburb that appeared in Archigram magazine. Herron's idea was that, without changing the existing houses, all sorts of mixed-use HighTech interventions like inflatables, domes, tents and tension structures might be strung from them, like climbing plants in a garden, to intensify land use without requiring new infrastructure. Three years later Peter Cook took up the same theme. In a 1970 drawing called 'Cheek by

Jowl' he moved the scene from the suburbs to the city and showed the same kind of metamorphosis taking place on a larger scale. 'The streets still handle everything' he wrote prophetically, 'but the basic structure of some buildings can have new flesh added, people can wire up a tent, or add loose floppy skins bugged with sound, but still cheek by jowl with the old buildings... You will not know which is building and which is growth.'

Seldom can a more accurate salvo have been fired into the future. A bare 20 years later, in cities and suburbs where demand for covered floorspace is bursting through the existing street patterns like the muscles of the Incredible Hulk, there is nowhere for it to go but into the gaps between the buildings that are already there. The old façades are protected and redevelopment is off the agenda: but behind the building line backlands and infill development – 'tuning up' – has been going on for years.

High Tech Tune-Up

Appropriately an older and wiser Ron Herron has come along with the last piece of the jigsaw, the right HighTech aesthetic and materials to give an identity to this 'tuning up' process. In a historic way Herron has brought the 'loose floppy skin' that Cook wrote about so long ago back to its proper home, for the 'tuned up suburb' is now a reality only a stone's throw away from the Architectural Association, where most of the Archigram Group taught at one time or another, and Herron himself has taught for 22 years.

At Staffordshire House in Store Street, just off Tottenham Court Road, Herron Associates, the partnership formed in 1982 by Ron Herron with his two sons Andrew and Simon, ably assisted by John Randall, has so successfully 'tuned up' an uninspiring 60,000 sq ft Edwardian building with an unused lightwell that it has become a paradigm of HighTech refurbishment success. Indeed Herron Associates have since merged with the client for this building, the design consultancy Imagination Ltd. This firm manages musical events, designs interiors, masterminds light shows – including the Lloyd's building illuminations – launches cars for Ford and has advertising agency type accounts with British Telecom, British Steel and the BBC: it is a spread of activities that promises further opportunities for imaginative Herron structures.

The Imagination refurbishment cost £4.5 million and added about 6000 sq ft of non-airconditioned floorspace to a building consisting of two nearly-parallel six- and five-storey blocks separated by a 7 m lightwell. Externally almost invisible, but utterly transformatory in its impact on its host building, the most important part of Herron Associates' treatment is its skin, a translucent white pvc envelope that now encloses the lightwell. This was only initially 'loose and floppy' before it was tensioned

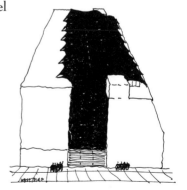

'A skin which tunes up the backlands'

and sprung, but otherwise it fits the 1967 bill. Ironically it can only be seen from outside by looking north from the southwest corner of Bedford Square, where it pours like a snowdrift over the rooftops behind Tottenham Court Road. Supported on a frame of lattice steel beams, tension rods and compression umbrellas, the big pvc membrane vaults lightly over one roof and the lightwell of the old Imagination building with only minimal anchorage.

Sixth Time Successful

Herron Associates had prepared five schemes for five different buildings before

'Archigrammic idealism realised in the heart of the City'

Imagination took the 1902 brick-fronted, concretefloored sixstorey former school with a second five-storey block behind it in Store Street. Knowing that the entire building would have to be refurbished because the facade was sacrosanct, the Herrons started off by thinking of converting the lightwell into an atrium by means of a glass roof. It was while pondering the complexity of this glazing – because the two blocks are not exactly parallel – that Herron thought of using a flexible translucent pvc canopy instead, tensioned with flying struts. He checked with his engineer, Ian Liddell at Buro Happold, and found that it would last at least 15 years, be five times cheaper than glazing, and weigh only one sixth as much.

Now, with the canopy in position over its whitepainted and stainless steel rigging, it seems unfortunate that the magnificent 20 ft by 120 ft by 60 ft atrium the Herrons have created, literally out of the thin air in the lightwell between the buildings, should be closed to the public, although there are plans to open the staff restaurant at ground level to a wider clientele in the future. It is however the essence of backlands architecture that, as Ron Herron says: 'You make your own world in it, one that only the client ever sees.'

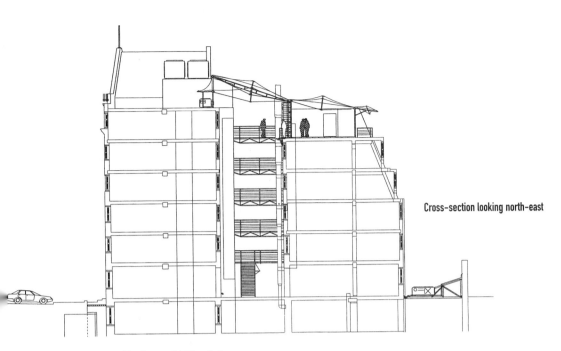

White Painted World

Within Imagination's 'world' the atrium end walls, east and west, are lined with white-enamelled perforated steel tiles so that the membrane can only be seen directly overhead, right through the most impressive feature of the design, the array of superbly detailed steel and aluminium stairs and gang planks crisscrossing the space between the two white-painted facades at different levels and

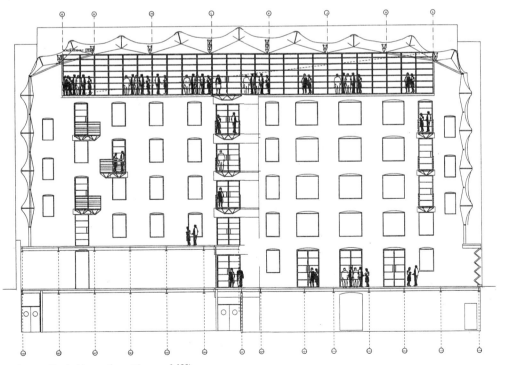

Long section looking south-east (approx. 1:400)

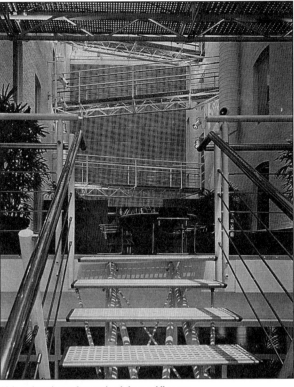

angles. Slight differences in level between the two blocks, as well as the non-synchronisation of the existing window openings and deft new lighting, have enabled the architects to produce a pleasing dissonance here that creates an impressively Piranesian spectacle where previously there was only gloom. Higher up, at the rooftop level of the lower block, the membrane passes over a new exhibition and presentation space giving on to a southfacing covered balcony with the open lightwell to the north.

The heart of Imagination is an essentially simple concept brought to success by an indulgent client and an absence of regulatory interference. While

Main stair to the conference level, from public space

it is certainly no matter for congratulation that much of the favourable press garnered by the project has focused on the fact that it is 'secret' and 'invisible' – and thus not an obvious candidate for aesthetic censorship – in fact the refurbishment shows how essentially practical the technological superhumanism of the Archigram era really was. Hopefully the critical and commercial success of Imagination means that at long last Archigram can be profitably revisited.

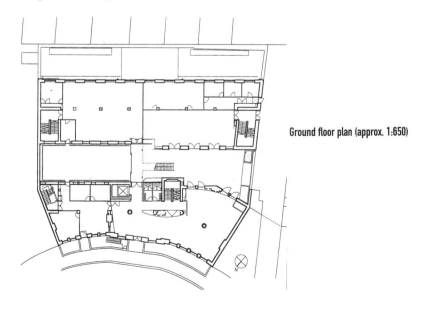

Ground floor plan (approx. 1:650)

Regional Meaning

EDITORIAL

Peter Davey
November 1990

The one overriding need in architectural practice at the moment is to give buildings meaning, a sense of fitness belonging to place and us. This may seem to be an absurd statement at a time when workloads of architects are declining all over the world as the capitalist economy goes into one of its periodic recessions.

But far more important than periodic downturns in economies, more important than the workload of individual practices, is the fact that architects influence less and less the built environment. We are the only people who, by our calling, are concerned to make the world a better place to live in and not just make profits from providing more enclosed space. Yet however much we have tried, our efforts have often seemed fruitless.

The heroic aspirations of the post-war generation, which sought with architectural imagination to solve the terrible crises of lack of housing, and public buildings like schools, now seem left by the tide on a grey and rocky shore of anomie and vandalism, covered by the endless tentacles of bureaucracy. The riposte by the advocates of PostModern Classicism, which sought to make architecture a branch of marketing – turning it into a trade of exterior design – has been so transparently false and ridiculous that it has only been embraced by the most facile designers, critics and developers.

The author

Real architecture, even at its most eclectic periods, has always had integrity, so that the people looking on it, and the people inside, could all enjoy the spaces and forms. There was a generally agreed conception of what people wanted to do and how to make the places to lead their lives in.

We desperately want to get back to this integral world, yet it is always elusive. We keep looking for the philosopher's stone that will transmute the mundane to a built poetry that can unite us all, of whatever background, in homecoming.

One of the most promising approaches to finding the magical stone has been regionalism. This magazine has always been supportive of particular and idiosyncratic local approaches to architecture from its foundations in the Arts and Crafts movement to the present day. We believe that architecture should grow out of a very deep understanding of local need and local circumstance.

Yet how are we to get such contiguities between past and present in big multi-racial and multi-cultural nations like France and Britain? Of course, the Muslim, Hindu, Jewish, Buddhist and Parsee people who belong to our societies must be themselves; make the buildings that they feel most at home in. Of course, all together have to subscribe to the ideal of a multi-valent society. Yet every family who lives in Britain or France has in some sense chosen to do so, and it is sensible that we try to make our countries different, so that by building on the past we may make meaning for the future.

It is very much easier to call for regionalist architecture in places like Scandinavia or Spain, where there has been relatively little immigration, than in the old colonial countries with their multi-cultural population. Indeed, seen askance by some committed hardline Modernists of the International Style school, regionalisn can be presented as a form of nationalism verging on racism. Even when seen with less blinkered eyes, regionalism often seems to be an excuse for indulgence in Neo-Vernacular kitsch in which bits of the past are collaged together to create populist buildings that have no more inner meaning than the worst superficialities of PoMo.

True regionalism in art is far deeper than eclectic copying of the past. It strives to establish an imaginative response to particular place and to traditional ways of doing and seeing things which are conditioned by factors as fundamental as climate, vegetation and topography. By understanding these, the best architects of a new multi-cultural nation like Australia can evolve a regionalist approach—vital in the creation of a new society that is as convincing in its authenticity as the (very different) regional schools of the much older cultures of Scandinavia.

The best products of the regionalist approach do not necessarily look in the least like the buildings that have been made before in the same parts. But they often occasion the same sensations and feelings as the old ones. (Ove Hidemark's crematorium at Linköping with its celebration of the traditional Swedish sensitivity to nature is a case in point.)

And sometimes regionally-inspired buildings create new authentic perceptions of place, of time and culture that are only possible because regionalists are, by definition, people who have taken on board the possibilities offered by Modernism, possibilities of, for instance, transparency and interpenetration of outside and inner space that were denied to our ancestors. (Cowplain school in Hampshire is an instance of this.)

As Juhani Pallasmaa remarked in our last issue devoted to this theme, 'The human task of architecture is not to beautify or to humanise the world of everyday facts, but to open up a view into the second dimension of our consciousness, the reality of images, memories and dreams'.

Regionalism is one way (but not the only one) of trying to achieve this heroic aim. But it must be properly understood—not as a generator of styles but as an approach to distilling the essence of place and culture through the alembic of Modernism so that we can be related to our past yet build for tomorrow.

165

Peter Davey

Earth Architecture

THEORY

Jean Dethier
September 1990

Architecture achieves solid reality only through its realisation in appropriate construction materials, industrialised or natural. Of the latter, our environment offers us many resources wood or stone, but also earth. Until its eclipse in the twentieth century, earth was in many countries one of the most well-used traditional building materials. Earth architecture can now be considered in two related ways.

First, in terms of heritage (and its protection); we have recently awoken, throughout the world, to the value of innumerable masterpieces created from this material. In France, England, Germany and Spain, there are many hundreds of thousands of buildings constructed using traditional earth techniques.

Second, we have to think about earth architecture in terms of the present and future. For 12 years, teams of scientists and practitioners have convincingly demonstrated the reliability of this material for many constructional purposes thanks to the noted advancements made in modern technology. France has acquired the reputation of being the most advanced country in research and education in earth building. This has been achieved principally due to the efforts in France of the group CRATerre, a multi-disciplinary European team established in 1979 within the architecture school and linked to the Scientific University at Grenoble.

CRATerre housing units in the island of Mayotte, Africa

The interest in following and expanding this new and significant development is clearly. but not exclusively, for ecological reasons. The real advantages of a mastery of earth construction are multiple and complementary.

Economics

Appropriate use of the material considerably reduces construction costs and therefore stimulates the economy. Moreover, in the context of an economy generally threatened – as in 1973 and now in 1990 – by excessive expenditure of energy, earth construction allows appreciable economies. It constitutes an asset that one can neither ignore, nor underestimate. Its clean technologies can assure the countries that master them of new internal and external markets.

Iranian image of 'pisé' construction

Energy

Since this natural material can be used locally with reduced transport costs and without secondary industrial transformation, it permits significant reduction of energy use, especially compared to the high-energy consuming industries of cement, steel and bricks. In addition, other economies in energy are appreciable, because the thermal inertia of the earth walls can assist in reducing heating and air-conditioning of buildings.

Ecology

The absence of a very high temperature phase in manufacture of earth buildings reduces the pollution which contributes to destruction of the ozone layer of the planet threatened by heavy industry (which produces the most widely used building materials). It is revealing that the first national prize given in France by the Minister of the Environment, which aims to encourage the production and use of ecologically-sound building materials, was given in March 1990 to CRATerre for its research and building work.

Politics

Raw earth is by definition a locally-used material, conforming to the resources of each region and country. It lends itself to a decentralisation of activity in terms of land management. This logic takes on a political dimension when conceived at the scale of the third world. It allows developing countries, faced with massive urbanisation and a vertiginous housing shortage (400 million dwellings need to be built over the next 15 years), the chance to face these problems themselves in

167

Jean Dethier

a real and achievable way. Up until now the dependence of developing countries on imported techniques and materials has made an economic and political problem which aggravates their enormous foreign debt. Earth construction can help solve this problem, once people have been taught the building techniques which are easily assimilable.

Social

Earth technologies allow reduction in the cost of housing. Increasingly there is a demand in certain countries (France, Germany and the US) for a habitat that takes ecological and environmental needs into account, for warmer and less impersonal architectural forms afforded by this natural and sculptural material.

Cultural

Earth has always lent itself to a creative architectural language responsive to regional differences The exceptional success of the exhibition 'Earth Architecture', at the Pompidou in 1981 (AR October 1981), is an indication of the deep resonances of this cultural step in international opinion.

It is necessary to reinforce and expand the actions already undertaken since 1981 by CRATerre with the Grenoble Architecture School. It has already earned the confidence of many governments and international organisations and, in France, with support from the State and regional authorities, it is building the new town of L'Isle d'Abeau near Lyons (see AR May 1990). Since 1983 CRATerre has put its technical know-how into construction of the first European area of social housing built in earth. It consists of

Seven-storey tower in Morocco

63 dwellings, grouped in buildings of three to five doors. Proof of the success of this 'Domaine de la Terre', is that the leaders and councillors of the new town now want to build a larger and more exemplary housing development in earth.

It is there too, in the heart of this future pilot zone, that the authorities and CRATerre have pooled their efforts to build at last a European institute of scientific research, offering multidisciplinary education and applications for modern construction in earth. This unique institution intends to attract the public with a médiathèque and museums of earth architecture around the world.

It also intends to accept researchers, architects and engineers from all countries. The new buildings should themselves be a living and symbolic demonstration of European expertise. Planned over 5000 m², these buildings should be the object of a European architectural competition to endow them with the cultural quality they merit. CRATerre has, during the '80s, been involved in earth projects in more than 30 countries. It has acted as technical and economic consultant for industrialists, governments or international institutions, under the sphere of influence of the United Nations and the World Bank. It has also conceived strategies for large projects, particularly where the local conditions for assimilation were especially complex or novel.

In addition to the new town at L'Isle d'Abeau CRATerre has planned and designed, in the 1980s, the infrastructure for the largest-ever raw earth construction programme, on the island of Mayotte, off southeast Africa. This much admired pilot operation will result in 5000 cheap dwellings for one of the poorest peoples in the world. CRATerre has also initiated the creation of rural technical schools, essential to help prevent the exodus of rural populations to the big cities.

Ancient and Contemporary Traditions

All traditional architectures have followed (until the industrial era) a common constructional logic: they were built of natural materials – little or unchanged – which were regionally available: stone and wood of course, but especially earth. Cooked earth baked at high temperatures as bricks; or raw earth, which could be used as it is in many proven techniques. Since men began to build cities – 100 centuries ago – raw earth has

French urban earth architecture

been without doubt the most well-used material in the world, across civilisations, urban or rural, used to construct the majority of dwellings – rich and poor – but also many other building types, civil or military, modest or grandiose.

In this vast archaeological and historical heritage spread over five continents, Europe also conserves a remarkable heritage: from Spain to Sweden and from England to Romania. In the heart of Europe, France is the country where this tradition is both the densest (almost 15 per cent of the national dwelling stock was built in raw earth at the time of the consensus, taken at the turn of the century). The region of Grenoble-Lyons-Chacon still contains numerous examples of this art of building in '*pisé de terre*' bourgeois villas, aristocratic houses or five-storey urban buildings. In this region most of the villages and market towns

Recent vernacular earth architecture in Africa

still contain up to 80 percent of traditional homes in raw earth. This technique was used up to the turn of the century to build schools and churches, workshops and factories and even town halls.

Activity was at its peak in the nineteenth century. But from the 1920s it started to disappear in the face of competition from the materials of heavy industry. Raw earth (unlike stone, marble or wood) has never been the object of commerce or of an economic pressure group. It has only been developed locally. It is therefore a material that has been supported neither by industry or public pressure.

The renaissance of a modern earth architecture in the US, Australia and Europe is related to an increasing demand from the public and its leaders. Earth architects are not reviving a defunct tradition but fostering a living one which, given the changes we are experiencing at the end of the twentieth century, could be a tradition for the future.

The renewal of Earth Architecture

The ideal of modernising traditional systems of raw earth construction —to adapt them to new rational demands, to conceive architectures which reconcile scientific resources and this natural material appeared in France two centuries ago. Around the time of the Revolution, François Cointereaux, born in Lyons in 1740, was the first architect of modern times to devote his life and work to raw earth construction. He had considerable international influence. Thousands of buildings, for public or domestic use, were built in France, England, Scandinavia, Germany and Australia, according to his principles. Under the direct influence of this visionary French builder, the architects of raw earth began to adapt to the early demands of the industrial era. At the beginning of the twentieth century, use of natural, local materials rapidly disappeared in favour of steel, concrete or bricks. But when these materials were unavailable for civic purposes (for example during the World Wars) raw earth construction re-appeared as a logical and economic alternative: it was used by Speer in Germany, by Frank Lloyd Wright in the US, and by Le Corbusier in the 40s.

In developing countries, modern earth construction also enables a reduction in construction costs and adaptability to regional contexts. In Algeria, France built in 1947, the regional hospital of Adrar in earth. This is an architectural jewel which demonstrates the feasibility of the material when it is used in a modern creative and appropriate way. At the same time in Egypt, the architect Hassan Fathy (1900–89) started a crusade for the re-use in the third world of raw earth construction to which he devoted his talents. He worked with others on the invention of a new language and ethic for architecture.

From the energy crises in 1973, the US experienced the first re-use at grand scale of raw earth construction to build thousands of luxury villas. For 20 years, it has been a status symbol in California or New Mexico to build a house in adobe. This phenomenon has generated the birth of a lively regional economic activity.

In Eastern Europe particularly in Germany, more than 300,000 raw earth dwellings were built in the 20 years after the War. In Western Europe, since the '60s many architects have learnt from and been strongly motivated by their cooperative technical work in the third world. Following a return to Europe, these practitioners have disseminated their knowledge in their own countries.

The '80s have been a decisive decade for the re-appraisal and development of raw earth construction Its obvious potential for the solution of ecological and economic problems must now be recognised by professionals and government institutions, and used in a longterm, global strategy for the '90s.

171

Shibam City was declared World Heritage by UNESCO in 1987

Jean Dethier

Architects influence less and less the built environment   With space cap
uttles   In mediaeval times it was said that 'city air makes man fr
has progressively become not the edge of the world but its very cen
ernism   premat   reported   — Pruitt   Ronan Point
xity and Contradiction in   hitecture: c   se o   e façade o
l Gallery   tensi   s con   tua   the   t of servi   In media
was said   'city air   man fre   The Pa   has progress
nenot the   ge of the   orld but its v   centre   Modernisms fir
y reporte   eath — P   t-Igoe, Ro   Point, C   nd Contr
ecture: choose one   The façade of the National Gallery Extensi
al to th   t of se   A   influ   d less the
ent   th sp   caps   s an   hutt   mediaeval times i
at 'city ai   akes   n fre   e Pa   c ha   ively becor
dge of th   orld but it   y centre   Modernisms   t prematu
h — Prui   goe, Rona   oint, Comm   ty and Contra   on in arch
e one   The faç   of the Natio   Gallery E   s contextu
f servility   Architects influence less and less the built environm
les and shuttles   In mediaeval times it was said that 'city air mal
ic has progressively become not the edge of the world but its very c

1992
1995

Aperspective Space

Peter Blundell Jones
March 1988

The history of modern architecture is in urgent need of reconstruction. The mythology of Pevsner and Giedion which dominated it for more than half a century has gone sour on us, and remains a real impediment to deeper understanding. In recent years Modernism has been damned on precisely the same grounds that it was once praised: for its pursuit of Functionalism, for exploiting modern technology and for breaking completely with the past. There is a clear basis for this attitude, as almost every city has buildings constructed in the post-war period which exhibit these characteristics in a negative way. They reflect an obsession with the most banal design criteria at the expense of those which are unquantifiable, subservience to the processes of construction, and an autistic indifference both to architectural history and to the local context. This is Modernism at its worst, and it deserved to die, though unfortunately it lives on in different clothes. It should be clearly understood, though, that this is not the architecture which inspired the mythology of Pevsner and Giedion, rather that which resulted from it. The architecture of the 1920s was neither so simple-minded nor so shallow-rooted.

The deeper one looks into it, the more mysterious the question of Functionalism in this period becomes. While it is understandable that the struggling *avant-garde* – a tiny minority, it must be remembered – should have found it con-

Alvar Aalto, Viipuri Library main reading room, 1935

venient to adopt glib pseudo-scientific justifications for their work, it is harder to see why they were believed unquestioningly for so long. Their arguments do not stand much scrutiny, for on deeper analysis design strategies for which a purely pragmatic basis was claimed turn out to be essentially rhetorical.[1] The construction issue also turns out to be far from straightforward, as most of the great pioneering works were handmade in anticipation of what the machine might produce—and much High-Tech is still handmade today.[2] Thus in a strict sense the Modernist pioneers fulfilled neither the requirements of 'form follows function' nor of 'form follows construction', even if they did contribute new interpretations of these perennial themes in architectural history. They were not as new, as different, or as original as early historians hoped.

Most obstructive of all to a deeper understanding of Modernism is the presumed *tabula rasa* whereby Modernist pioneers supposedly renounced their past – all the superstition of 'historicism' – and took a brand new road. Historical examples were carefully chosen to back up this idea, so the early works of the pioneer generation were suppressed, while the choice of key works from the previous generation was extremely selective.[3]

The more one scrutinises the Modern Movement today, the more the exceptions seem to overwhelm the rule, the less valid seems the unified vision so unmistakable in books and magazines of the '30s. Scratch the surface and the illusion of consistency disappears: there is considerable diversity even among the works at the 1927 Weissenhofsiedlung, the event which is supposed to mark the establishment of the new style. Under close examination, its buildings demonstrate the varying concerns and backgrounds of the participants, and though the image of Corbusian Cubism may have had a pervasive influence, the only ones based on the *methodology* of the five points are those of Le Corbusier himself.

In the rush to establish the *tabula rasa* it was all too easy to pass over the fact that the crucial generation of Modernists was born mainly in the 1880s, and was around 40 in 1927. They had not only absorbed a traditional training, with lessons in composition, the orders, proportion and so on, but had also built traditional buildings. They may have wished to liberate themselves from all this, but a great deal of it was built-in irrevocably as part of the implicit structure of their perception and their method of working. An exposure to proportion theory may help develop a good eye, and a training in questions of progression through a building – known in Beaux Arts circles as *marche* – may encourage an architect to seek this quality in creating an architecture altogether different in kind. This tacit persistence of tradition helps explain the evident loss of quality between the work of pioneers and that of later generations trained only according to the impoverished programme of the post-war years.

To understand this tacit persistence we need to reject the *tabula rasa*, and the idea of Modernism as a stable plateau, to see it rather in terms of continuous and continuing evolution; to look at all the work in its sequence of development, and not just at the familiar landmarks chosen to support the old thesis.

Peter Blundell Jones

As an outline sketch for one area of this reconstruction, the following pages examine the development of a spatial sensibility shared between architects of the pioneer generation in Germany and Scandinavia belonging to what has loosely been called the organic tradition.[4] They all produced Classically based projects in their youth, yet went on to develop techniques of free-planning which appear to dispense with traditional ordering entirely .

Gunnar Asplund

The Neo-Classical nature of the Stockholm City Library (1918–28), evident from outline to detail, scarcely requires underlining. Much of the drama of the building, though, is due to the power of the axial route. Starting in the street, it follows a ramp through a slot in the base to the main door, then continues on the same line up the principal stair to arrive right at the heart of the central drum. From this main axis the subsidiary cross axes depart; the central one marking the routes to the side reading rooms, a lesser one binding facilities in the front wing to the entrance hall. Thus the whole organisation is given by axes which define the primary geometry and are main routes. The same kind of approach is evident also in Asplund's Lister

Stockholm City Library main approach

courthouse, though in the slightly earlier Snellman house one finds an asymmetrical layout, skewed plan angles, and false perspective effects, a reminder of the other tradition on which Asplund consistently drew: the National Romantic movement. What both approaches have in common is a concern with the experience of progression and sequence as one moves through a building, which was to remain a major theme in his work.

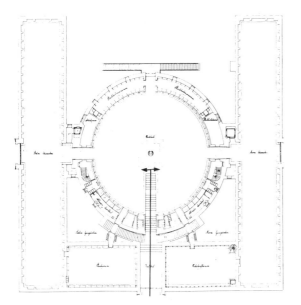

Gunnar Asplund, Stockholm City Library principal floor plan, 1918–28

The transformation which took place between these early works and the mature Modern Asplund are most easily demonstrated in a project which links the two: the Gothenburg law courts' extension and reorganisation, won in a competition of 1913 and completed in 1937.[5] The initial project was set up on a dominant long axis which was both axis of symmetry and principal route, leading from the central entrance across a court, up a double staircase and across a gallery set on the main cross-axis, then

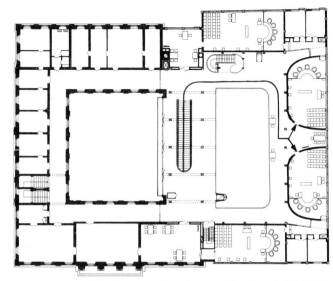

Asplund. Gothenburg Law Courts extension and reconstruction plan, as built in 1937

across a bridge over the second court to the principal courtroom at the end of the site. There were several intermediate projects between this and the final design, which show Asplund coming to terms with the existing building and accepting the essential asymmetry of the problem. In the final version the asymmetry becomes a virtue, and though an underlying axial order gives the complex a clear spatial structure, the routes do not cross the main courts but run along their margins. The boundaries of the main internal hall space are made ambiguous by play with the boundary walls, sometimes straight, sometimes curved, sometimes transparent, suggesting continuity with the external court beyond. The Modernist vocabulary of steel frame, glass, and free partitions conveys an airy lightness completely at odds with the ponderous version of 1925 whose organisation is almost identical. In the late '30s it was obviously necessary to celebrate the qualities that made the final design new and different: today we should also remember the continuity which provided the underlying order against which the new variations were played with such virtuosity.

Alvar Aalto

Aalto's debt to Asplund is well documented,[6] and the parallels between Asplund's library and designs by Aalto like the workers' club at Jyväskylä of 1924 established. Aalto, too, started on a Neo-Classical basis with central axes which were both axes of symmetry and principal route. The library at Viipuri is of special interest because it spans his transition to Modernism, the competition entry was submitted in 1927 and the building completed in 1935.[7] Asplund's model was impossible to ignore, and the competition project even used the same kind of severe forms and Classical details externally.

More crucial though is the persistence of the main organising idea at Stockholm — the axial route which brings you dramatically up into the centre of the building. While the trappings of Neo-Classicism were whittled away this became ever stronger, and the main reading room was made larger and more dominant. In the final building the main entrance leads via three flights of stairs to the reading room, arriving as with Asplund right at the centre in front of the control desk. The main difference is that there are a couple of turns on the way: a 180 degree turn within the reading room, and a 90 degree turn between the axis

177

of entry and the axis of the reading room. The former was a late development reflecting the changed relationship between reading room and reference library. The 90 degree turn was there from the start due to the decision to enter the building on its long side. It is significant that though this turn started off as a traditional axial change marked by a colonnade, it was finally signalled by a Modernist curved wall which underplays the turn in order to dramatise discovery of the room beyond.

In his post-war work Aalto began to plan more freely and to exploit skewed angles. The articulation of volumes each according to its own rules and expressing its own purpose produced dynamic in-between spaces used as entrance halls and foyers, taking their character from the more positive elements around them and from their linking function rather than as defined enclosures in their own right. One example must suffice: the entrance hall to the main lecture theatre at Jyväskylä University completed in 1957.

Two blocks of building collide, the tapered theatre whose stepped shape is due to being partitionable, and the rectangular classroom block.

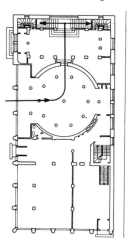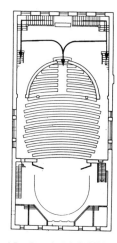

Alvar Aalto, Workers' Club ground and first floor, Jyväskylä 1924

The juxtaposition is exploited externally both at the front, where the stoa-like continuation of the classroom wing runs off at a skew, generously embracing the approach space, and at the rear where the convergence embraces an external amphitheatre. The discipline of the ground floor plan comes from the floor above, which determines the column grid, stair positions and perimeter line. Continuous glazing around the edge emphasises continuity with surroundings, and contrasts with the blind solidity of the volume above. Having set up this general framework – which stresses two axial routes – Aalto introduced a whole series of secondary measures to define and specialise areas of the foyer. Thus the restaurant, placed in a kind of side aisle defined by columns, is given further autonomy by being dropped three steps, carpeted and curtained, and scaled down by a low ceiling over the counter. The other side-aisle is given to cloakroom counters, one of which also serves the

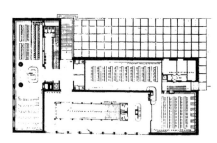

Viipuri Library, ground floor plan, first and final version

classroom block. The end of the counter on the right-hand side is inflected towards the doors of the lavatories, placed at the back of the space where one expects them, yet turned discreetly sideways.

As with the hall at Asplund's Gothenburg law courts there is a distinct hierarchy between the general framework and the local incidents which occur within it, and the spatial dynamic has everything to do with the transition being made between external and internal worlds. The transparency and interpenetration of spaces are not confusing or disorientating because the general order is so clear.

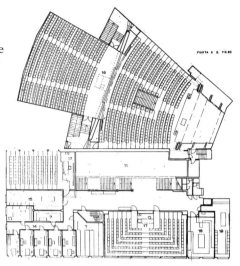

Alvar Aalto, Jyväskylä University, main lecture theatre and classroom plan, 1955

Hugo Häring

Although also the inheritor of the Neo-Gothic tradition of asymmetry and articulated form, Häring produced Neo-Classical projects in his early years, the most significant being competition entries for the Royal Opera House in Berlin and the German Embassy in Washington. The former is a shameless imitation of Garnier's Paris Opera, the predominant model at the time, even borrowing the entry arrangements and grand stair in a square well. Garnier had been obsessed with questions of arrival and departure and with a sequence of rooms appropriate for a parade of fashionable Parisians, generating almost more theatre in the foyers than in the auditorium: he also wrote a book *Le Théâtre* setting out his intentions.[8] These were lessons which Häring evidently absorbed.

The embassy project of 1913 is more original. Unlike other competitors Häring chose to fill the whole site with building, carving holes in it for courts and gardens and though the most important spaces and rooms are both geometrically regular and placed in axial sequence, lesser elements absorb site irregularities, strengthening the hierarchy between formal and informal.[9] The plan is based on a pair of crossing axes, the major one running the entire depth from street entrance through entrance hall to carriage court, and across the internal garden ending with a summer house. The minor axis picks up the centre of the carriage court, the entry to the ambassador's residence and staircase. The reception rooms along the first floor front are reached by a ceremonial

Hugo Häring, Berliner Secession, competition project first version, 1926

stair leading off from the right of the entrance hall through a series of traditional axially-linked antechambers.

The Römer house of 1916–20 could scarcely seem more different from the embassy, with its asymmetrical articulated form and castle-like exterior. Some of

179

the irregularity is due to the fact that it was a conversion; its main rectangular volume built onto an old blockhouse that had been part of the city fortifications, but the ability to take on such a context and exploit it points to lessons learnt from Häring's teacher Theodore Fischer.[10] On the ground floor thick walls delineate the old blockhouse, and the angular walled court in front as also inherited. Häring accepted the main axis and created a vaulted entrance hall on four columns: he then played the stair against this geometry in a remarkably free wall, running off right-ward to take in an adjacent cloakroom, returning to the axis to break through the wall in line with the principal door and gate, then running rightward again into the hall above to arrive conveniently at the centre of the house. The interplay of the dynamic stair with the static geometry of the space anticipates later developments.

In the early '20s, Häring was still producing traditional axial plans while experimenting simultaneously with more fluid forms. A sketch plan of 1921 for a railway station[11] explores the possibility of planning around movement flow, with tapered platforms in sympathy with reducing traffic and minor rooms formed as islands in the stream. This approach, shared also by other German contemporaries, suggested a radical alternative to axial progression, and as pursued through a handful of projects.

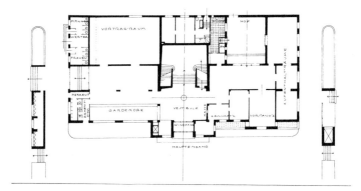

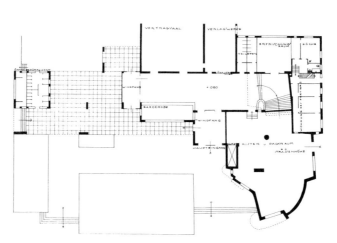

Hugo Häring, Berliner Secession, competition project first and second version of ground floor plan, 1926

Five years later, however, Häring was still uncertain which line to take, producing two designs for the Secession Art Gallery competition which reveal the past and the future in a remarkable way . The first is essentially symmetrical. Its axial entrance leads to a divided stair arriving at two sets of north-lit first floor galleries. In response to the movement of the stair, the stair-hall is slightly tapered, and the lowest treads of the upper flights spill onto the landing. In section the movement on the upper stairs follows the profile of the north-light roof.

In the more radical second version, symmetry is abandoned, the stair is pushed to one end and expanded, becoming a very special head to a tail of plain first floor galleries. The drama of progression from entry to galleries becomes the main theme, with cafe grouping out of the first landing and sculpture hall out of the second. The slight taper of the stair hall in the first scheme is carried over in the skewed side wall and realignment of the stair centres. So while the orthogonal ground floor follows essentially axial discipline, the stair takes over with its own fluidity, declaring its turn into the galleries only with a reduction in width before crossing the void of the hall to reach minor rooms. This design was quite unprecedented in its spatial fluidity and geometric sophistication, anticipating the post-war foyer spaces of Aalto and Scharoun. Unfortunately Häring was never able to realise a building of this kind.

Hans Scharoun

Some of Scharoun's earliest projects, such as a house plan dating from 1912 when he was only 19, show his interest both in spatial continuity between rooms and in highly specific small-scale planning engaging furniture, concerns which were to remain predominant. But equally unmistakable are the axes which tie the house together, defining major and minor spaces. Axial organisation can be found again and again in Scharoun's early work, running right through the so-called Expressionist period, even informing plans which would have burgeoned forth into Tautian crystalline towers. The spatial sequence in a project such as the town hall at Emmerich belongs to the same tradition as Häring's embassy described earlier. Even as late as 1928 Scharoun produced utterly axial projects, naming the axes on drawings. However, this did not prevent him experimenting also in other directions, and in the early '20s he, too, produced plans dictated by movement flow, apparently in ignorance of those by Häring.[12]

The axial sensibility persisted, and axes can be identified throughout the later work, but they do not play the same role. As with Asplund, Aalto and Häring, asymmetry became more frequent and the route tended to depart from the axis and play against it. What makes this kind of architecture radically different from the tradition out of which it grew, however, is the departure from orthogonal discipline, and in Scharoun's case this development can be traced back to a discovery made in 1932.

There is no lack of skewed plans responding to irregular sites among Scharoun's early work so his ingenious hostel block at the Breslau Werkbund

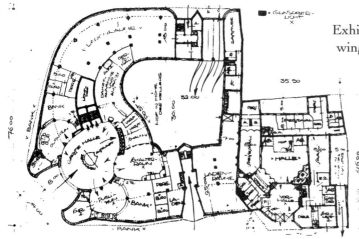

Hans Scharoun, Könisberg Stock Exchange project, ground floor plan, 1922

Exhibition of 1929 with its cranked wings is less extraordinary than it seems. The rarely published site plan reveals the reason for the stated axis locating the glazed central hall and for the various angles. When one looks at the interior spaces, however, the cranking plays no significant role, so the skewed junctions might equally well be straightened out. The same could not be said of the Schminke house, but only thanks to a lastminute change at working drawing stage. The cranked solarium and west wall had already been introduced in response to the site, but the staircase was still placed orthogonally. The re-adjustment cranked it round, giving someone on the stair a preferred direction at the top, while also guiding those on the ground rightward towards the principal rooms. Since the house increases in transparency toward the east end where it projects dramatically over the garden towards a chosen view, the axial transition effected by the stair is of major importance. Having made this discovery, Scharoun went on to explore it in a series of houses during the Nazi period,[13] re-emerging with a new vocabulary.

Among the first post-war projects for public buildings was a small art gallery for Gerd Rosen in Berlin of 1948. Everything focuses on the central staircase, which is also the point of transition between the axis of entry and the dominant cross-axis of the first floor. Two outer staircases in symmetrical positions, though asymmetrically treated mark the lateral ends. The general strategy is thus clear, and the central approach to the building entirely traditional until the point where the route is diverted from the axis. A purely visual axis continues through the glass wall at the front of the building to the main stair, then out to the sculpture court beyond: this would give an impression of considerable depth. The route meanwhile departs to doors on the left before it returns to the central double stair with its choice of four possible paths. The stair leaves visitors orientated to the main axis of the upper floor, which traverses the plan enhanced by end windows. The skewed outer walls emphasise the way the space radiates from the stair, and return patterns of movement to it. As with Häring's second

Hans Scharoun, Schminke House, solarium at east end, 1932

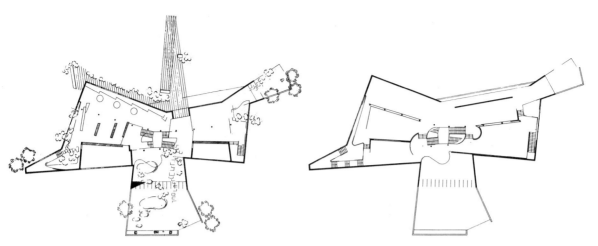

Hans Scharoun, Gerd Rosen Art Gallery project, ground and first floor plans, Berlin 1948

Secession design, the discipline is a mixture of traditional axial progression and Modernist fluidity, but as with all the examples considered here the visual experience of route was a high design priority.

In the Kassel theatre project of four years later the same kind of planning reaches a new level of sophistication. The theatre was to be built into a hill, requiring entry from a road bridge at the top end. The foyer then became the mediating element between bridge and auditorium, taking in box office and cloakrooms on the way. Though the space is asymmetrical in detail, two batteries of staircases for the two sides of the hall do reveal the general symmetry of organisation and imply the central axis still strongly felt within the auditorium. Staircases are placed to indicate direction of flow, with only shallow turns except when they can be controlled unambiguously by landings. By this stage Scharoun had become confident in his use of a free range of angles, operating a kind of hierarchy of directness—the staircase which requires the shallowest turn is the most important, and indicates the continuation of the main route.

While the auditorium for Kassel had been fairly conventional, that of a slightly later project for a theatre at Mannheim was radically different, involving reinterpretation of the very nature of theatre, with some theoretical help from Hugo Häring. They argued that in a traditional theatre the geometrically arranged seating and proscenium arch have an assertive presence which allows the spectator to gauge his or her spatial location in relation to the action quite accurately. This tends to reduce the suspension of disbelief intended for some kinds of play. Scharoun therefore designed what he called the 'aperspective' auditorium, asymmetrically planned with a wide and vaguely defined stage area, no proscenium, and seating converging but unfocused and facing a variety of directions. This Baroque idea has yet to be tried in practice, but some idea of its effect can be gauged from the perceptual elusiveness of the Philharmonie, which seems to change in size and shape as one wanders around it. Indeed, though it does not go so far as the theatre in terms of allowing illusions to be created, the complexity and ambiguity of the space are crucial to the festive atmosphere.

Peter Blundell Jones

Conclusion

These four architects learned a command of axial ordering in their youth, engendering an acute awareness of routes and hierarchies carried over into later work. This sensibility saved them from the trap of diagrammatic planning and gridded order for its own sake which is the hallmark of so much post-war architecture. It also prepared them to exploit the new freedoms available with wide spans, large areas of glass and flat roofs, but was necessary above all when they started to plan with skewed angles, playing off one orthogonal discipline against another.

The use of axes in planning a building is not entirely optional, for they are always implied and cannot simply be omitted: every rectangular room has a major and a minor axis to exploit or ignore, and a door on axis is more important than one off. Their nature is hierarchical, so it is scarcely surprising that axes tend to be deployed by despots to demonstrate centralised power: but our perception is also hierarchical, and to make sense a building needs major and minor elements. That these also have political implications is not to be feared or avoided—every building is also a political statement. For example, the contrast between Garnier's Opera with its acute differentiation of social rank and the communality of Scharoun's Philharmonie reflects the substantial change in political values between mid-nineteenth and mid-twentieth century European society. Similarly the change between Asplund's somewhat authoritarian Lister Courthouse of 1920 and his Gothenburg courts of 1937 reflects Sweden's conversion to social democracy.

The term 'aperspective space' is borrowed from Scharoun, who used it specifically in relation to his Mannheim auditorium,[14] but it can justly be applied more generally. The spaces created by the four architects tend to come across poorly in photographs, because they are not designed to be read statically or from privileged positions. When plans run askew, the whole elaborate convention of perspective, to which our perception is geared and which we take completely for granted, is disrupted.[15] The idea that Modernist space is supposed to be appreciated dynamically, not statically, is commonplace,[16] but while the major medium of dissemination is still photography 'aperspective space' has had no chance.

1 The clearest example is the work of Hannes Meyer, the most literal of Functionalists. Writing about his League of Nations design, he claimed that it had no symbolic content, and represented open government. The extensive acoustic data supposedly justifying the hall are also somewhat spurious as the effect of reflections is not taken into account. All in all. the rhetorical intentions transcend the practical but are not admitted: this is typical for the time.

2 Lucien Kroll makes this point rather well in *The Architecture of Complexity* where he writes of Gropius having a thousand identical windows made by craftsmen who could have made them all differently, and of smooth machine-like white render now falling off '20s buildings to reveal the handmade brickwork behind.

3 For example, architectural histories tend to show Behrens' arc lamps and turbine hall while the almost contemporary and utterly

traditional St Petersburg embassy tends to get overlooked, as is his extraordinary and confusing career as a whole, taking inspiration from sources as diverse as the Arts and Crafts house (1904), San Miniato al Monte (1906), Neo-Classicism (1909–14), Expressionism (1920), Erich Mendelsohn (1927), and finally contributing in the '30s to Speer's Berlin axis.

4 This term was used by Wright, Aalto, Häring, Mendelsohn and several others to describe an approach based on response to specific circumstances, and also by Zevi in his early alternative history *Towards an Organic Architecture*, though it also has some unfortunate associations with zoomorphic form and various strains of irrationalism. For a more extensive coverage see *AR* 'Organic response' June 1985.

5 For a detailed account of the development of the design and an analysis of the finished building see my articles in the 'Masters of Building' series on Asplund in the *AJ*, 'Gothenburg Law Courts' part 1, 14 October 1987, and part 2, 11 November 1987.

6 See the three-volume Aalto biography by Göran Schildt.

7 Competition drawings are printed at the end of Schildt, vol.1, and plans of a second version can be found in Pearson, *Alvar Aalto and the International Style*; the final design is well known.

8 For a clear summary of Garnier's intentions see the essay 'Beaux Arts Composition' by van Zanten; in *The Architecture of the Beaux Arts*, ed Arthur Drexler.

9 Several entries including that of Häring were published in an obscure Hamburg journal, *Die Bau-rundschau*, see vol. 51/52, 1913. The predominantly Classical flavour reflects not just the tendency of the time, but also the fact that Behrens who had just completed his St Petersburg embassy, was among the judges.

10 The similarity of the Römer house to Fischer's Riemerschmid house reinforces this connection.

11 This was a reworking of an old competition for Leipzig railway station of 1907, and seems to have been undertaken as a purely theoretical exercise.

12 They seem not to have met until about 1926, a letter of that year from Häring concerning membership of the Ring being entirely formal.

13 For a detailed account see *AR* December 1983 .

14 Scharoun's use of the term aperspective derives directly from the writings of cultural philosopher Jean Gebser, for whom it was a central concept. Gebser's *Ursprung und Gegenwart* was published in 1949.

15 The extent to which perspective is a convention rather than a natural way of seeing things is not generally appreciated. Nelson Goodman who regards it as entirely a matter of convention. makes much of the anomaly of 'correction' applied to photographs whereby convergence is allowed in the horizontal plane but suppressed in the vertical. For detailed arguments see Goodman, *Languages of Art*.

16 As in Giedion, *Space, Time and Architecture*.

Behnisch: Hysolar

BUILDING CRITIQUE
Solar Research Institute, Stuttgart
by Behnisch & Partners

Peter Blundell Jones
March 1983

After the discipline and thoughtfulness of the Eichstätt library, Behnisch's recently completed solar research institute at Stuttgart University comes as a bit of a shock. It is mostly of stainless steel, with rectangular containers disposed at various angles, services protruding here and there, and scaffolding-like constructions carrying batteries of solar cells. The building itself looks a little like a laboratory test-rig, one of those haphazard constructions of components tied together with pipes and wires and supported by a motley collection of stands and clamps.

There is some underlying logic: the building had to be completed quickly and to a relatively tight budget, so there were advantages in using a series of factory-made containers for laboratory rooms. The two wings are used by different groups: that on the east by university faculties, the west by an independent institute. Oblique placing allows the glazed hall linking the wings to open up towards the main entrance and the sun, while the projecting west-wing room at the north end is isolated because it houses the equipment for producing potentially explosive hydrogen and oxygen from water by electrolysis—the main procedure under investigation. To limit the effects of an explosion, this special room has a light

First floor galleries seen from the north end of the glazed hall roof and light walls on its outer sides so that they can blow out, while heavy concrete isolates it from the rest of the building.

Other elements of the complex are less justifiable in pragmatic terms. Glazing mullions slope for no obvious reason, and bridge-like ramps soar across the hall. The last window on the west side is obliquely placed, and while this helps the composition, the window as window is just silly. The most extravagant formal gesture of all is a red painted steel tube bursting out of the ground to the north of the building, slashing across the hall, and projecting beyond the glazed south end. While this can certainly be read – and was doubtless intended – as a gesture of obeisance to the sun it is almost entirely rhetorical, since its only practical function is to support a short tail of roof.

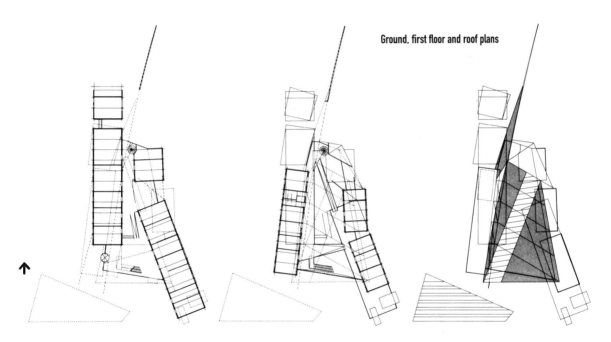

Ground, first floor and roof plans

It is not inappropriate to make an experimental building for experimental purposes, and many of the technical elements attached to scaffolding-like frames will probably be changed in unpredictable ways. The asymmetrical and additive composition will lend itself to transformations of all kinds, and the overall lifespan is uncertain. Placed on the suburban campus at Stuttgart-Vaihingen, with the equally anarchic Sulzer/Hübner self-built student hostel as its only near neighbour, it does not violate contextual duties.

While many such institutes elsewhere are lamentably dull, repressing everything special about their function within a standard grid-planned box, this one is at least provocative and memorable, conveying something of the excitement of the frontier-pushing work taking place within. Even so, the formal manipulations are throw-away gestures rather than deeply founded responses to programmatic imperatives, whether taken at a pragmatic or a rhetorical level. It is a stimulating and amusing building, but rather lightweight, certainly bearing little comparison to such a considered work as the library. When I suggested to Behnisch that it is wilful, to my surprise he readily and candidly agreed. How can the firm produce works so very different in character?

The project architect turns out to have come to Behnisch from Coop Himmelblau, which explains the Formalist tendencies. Such a transfer of loyalties is perhaps unsurprising when one reflects that the Behnisch office must be one of the very few technically equipped to put such ideas into practice at competitive

View from the west showing solar cells on scaffold structure

prices. But why should Behnisch be willing to adopt the wayward ideas of a younger generation and bring them to fruition when he and his partners already have a mature manner of their own? It reflects their open-mindedness and conviction that to keep the office alive, younger members must be allowed some freedom. But even more important, it reflects a deeply held belief in exploration and experiment, in what Lethaby called the 'architecture of adventure'.

In a recent article Günter Behnisch set out to answer a series of questions put by the editor of a German journal about the use of oblique angles, including one about the placing of the containers in the institute. His ironic subtitle, *Schräg ist die Tendenz* – oblique/bent is 'in' – caused some amusement in Stuttgart architectural circles, for this catchphrase turns out not to belong to the current architectural scene – to the so-called New Spirit – but was rather the comment of a furniture rep visiting the Behnisch office around 1955. This anecdote set the time-scale for Behnisch's explanation of the evolution of work its liberation from the excessive technicality of the post-war period, and the gradual discovery of new directions. Others may discover the joys of doing it *schräg* overnight, but Behnisch can claim a deeper more long-standing commitment.

In the 1950s the Behnisch office was involved in systematic design and component systems, constructing some school buildings which are still considered among the best of their kind. They experienced at first hand the inflexibility and monotonous repetitiveness of this approach. Behnisch recalls that 'later on these narrow geometrical ordering systems – systems which resulted from technical demands of production and assembly, but which also arose in the heads of designers for other reasons – became oppressive. Today we consider that such systems can be instruments of domination, taking over first design processes, then moving on to architecture and finally to life itself, whose very vitality and variety soon comes to be regarded as a threat to those in the grip of such systems. Their fears are symptomatic of weakness rather than strength.

'But the danger which later became reality in new university buildings and giant hospitals was already apparent, or at least it could be felt that if architecture were to follow this purely technical direction, it would become one-sided, unable to express wishes and requirements of a differentiated kind, unable to respond to and reflect the possible variety of our world…'.

Detail of junction of glazed central hall with steel-clad containers

From the beginning the office pursued a variety of approaches, and some members were working in a freer manner, which culminated in the triumph of the Olympic buildings designed in collaboration with Frei Otto in 1972. Since then they have produced work which ranges between orthodox (and orthogonal) Modern through the freer approach at the Eichstätt library, and beyond. The angular complexity of the Hysolar Institute represents only the latest move in the search for an architecture which transcends the purely technical. As Behnisch says: 'The right angle is only one possibility among many, and to impose it means restricting the possibilities. There are certainly tasks which find their appropriate embodiment in this customary form, but there are others which work out better with geometrical differentiation and articulation of small elements… With a reduced vocabulary one's powers of expression are also reduced….

'We believe today that architecture should not conceal itself behind technicalities if the wishes and requirements of users are to be given due emphasis; that it should tend generally towards greater openness, not basing itself just on current realities, but also leaning a little towards the future —a future that is not technocratic in nature but geared towards the human world…'.

North elevation

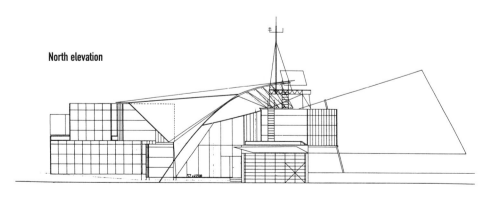

National Gallery

BUILDING CRITIQUE
National Gallery Extension, London
by Robert Venturi and Denise Scott Brown

Rowan Moore
January 1991

The Sainsbury wing of London's National Gallery has been long awaited. Devices like the front elevation, where an extension of the idiom of Wilkins' main building gradually fades away into a blank stone façade, have been promoted by the architects and their supporters as appropriate and respectful ways of causing a contemporary building to mesh with the existing city. How far do their claims stand up?

I blame Owen Luder. He, as readers under 30 may need reminding, was the then RIBA president who praised Richard Rogers' design for the Hampton site for saying 'Sod you': had he forborne, the National Gallery extension might not have become an issue of rudeness versus deference. Carbuncles might never have been mentioned, and we might have been spared the dermatological exercise now filling the northwest corner of Trafalgar Square.

Not that we shouldn't be grateful to the Sainsburys for exercising the ill-advised office element of the original brief. Nor is the finished extension exactly a bad building. It will probably function quite well, and the technical problems of conducting large crowds past fragile objects have been handled with intelli-

Post Office or PostModern, view to National Gallery

gence. The grand staircase does its job of conducting you pleasurably and directly to the galleries, and its semi-external air, as intended, relieves the claustrophobia of museums. From some of the galleries, one looks through deep revealed windows across the stair to the outside which, also as intended, anchors the floating space in which paintings are habitually exhibited in an external reality.

Those collisions of detail which are not excruciating can be satisfying. The fierce incisions in the extended section of Wilkins' front façade introduce a vigour which the original lacks. Against these successes are senseless mouldings as if from Texas Homecare, and, over the stair, some sort of a tribute to Victori-

The borrowings from Wilkins return on to the curtain wall that flanks the stair

an railway stations in the form of patently appliqué steel arches. Too many handrails, fittings and shapes in the plan are composed of odd droops and aimless curves.

But the building's real insufficiency is that so much of it is composed of deference and extenuating circumstance. It has neither a centre nor a pattern, without being decentred or patternless in an interesting way. Venturi compares his rhythmic games on the elevation with music, but there is nothing particularly musical about the dull clunk with which one event, in both plan and elevation, succeeds another. Presumably it was felt that a centre was given by the Wilkins building, but this is to overestimate the potency of its little dome.

Rowan Moore

The plan loops and expands in response to successive contingencies, and the unpredictable moments of theatricality, the sudden appearances of columns and false perspectives, only heighten the incoherence, as in a poorly edited film. The façade is contextual to the point of servility, answering the dreariness of the back streets with dreariness, and the feebleness of the square with feebleness. It is faithful but insubstantial, like mirror glass.

The most obvious reasons for the pervasive indecision lie with the site and with its history. Placed on the least consequential corner of Trafalgar Square, the whole extension project has been subjected to a disproportionate emotional load. Apart from the unwelcome attentions of Luder and the Prince, the project was also an object of Michael Heseltine's zeal for both competitions and the involvement of private enterprise, during his last term as Environment Secretary.

Throughout the project's long history, neither participants nor onlookers have been able to decide whether it should be a National Monument or a modest extension, along the lines of the Orange Street extension built with rather less fuss to the rear. The passion generated suggested the former, but the calls for deference the latter. The matter is still undecided: the replication of Wilkins supports the modest extension theory, but the various assertions of the architects' personality are the attributes of an Important Building.

Given that Venturi has built his career on the celebration of ambiguity, he and Denise Scott Brown were the obvious choice to make the tortuous politics of the site into architecture. But in some of their work, and in the huge number of buildings they have influenced, there is only a fragile distinction between complexity and contradiction, and complication and compromise, between the diffi-

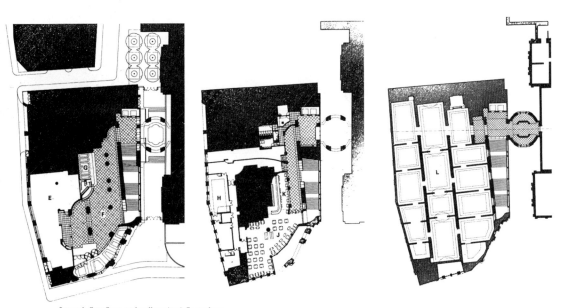

Ground, first floor and gallery (top) floor plans

cult whole and the easy mess. The Sainsbury Wing sustains the distinction only in odd moments.

The plant is fragile because it has shallow roots. Although Venturi has long advocated an architecture in some sense symbolic, which refers to the world beyond architecture, he is transfixed, like a rabbit in a headlight, by respect for architectural history. He seems seriously uncomfortable unless someone, somewhere, has done the same thing before, so the façade comes from Wilkins, the galleries from Soane and the polychrome colonnettes from Thompson. There is no particular reason for this except that these architects occupy about the same time and place in the standard histories.

The idea, presumably, is to plant the building in a cultural context. But the view of

Typical interior of galleries

culture is arid and identifies it with the stylistic ties of early nineteenth century architects. Venturi wants his architecture to be popular and accessible but, by referring only to other architects, he is as hermetic as any Modernist.

Nor is this hermeticism necessary, given the potency of the Sainsbury Wing's content and setting. It contains some of the most treasured items of our culture, and mediates between these and the symbolic centre of London, Trafalgar Square. As Venturi himself points out, the use and character of the National Gallery has utterly changed since it was first built. Designed to accommodate a gentle flow of the interested few, it is now (Venturi's image) more like a sports stadium, and will attract crowds estimated at four million a year. Venturi also points out that the total population of Renaissance Italy was probably less than this, and that the paintings his building houses were originally intended for intimate and private settings, not for the gaze of the multitude. The Sainsbury Wing, more urgently than any London building since the National Theatre, has to contend with the paradoxes of presenting art to a mass culture but, unlike the National Theatre, it ducks the challenge.

Since Venturi's intellect is so sensitive to these issues it is disappointing that his drawing arm responds to them only intermittently. More often his instinct is to neutralise them. The illusion of the Soanian galleries and the Wilkinsesque façade is that nothing has changed, and much of the response to the huge throughput of visitors is at the level of people plumbing. The combined effect is of a Classical building with its openings painfully dilated. His admirable, if tentative efforts to connect the paintings with the outside world are severely impeded by the heavy stone veil which the façade interposes between the interior and Trafalgar Square. The cafe is a further victim of the façade: what could be a natural and direct relation with the square finds itself obstructed by unwelcome quantities of Portland stone.

The hanging of paintings in neutral, evenly lit rooms further increases their distance from any context. Here Venturi and Scott Brown are in good company, since the presentation of deracinated artefacts has baffled designers ever since the museum type was invented, and the top-lit, bare-walled, 'objective' approach has remained the most popular. With due allowance for stylistic difference, Foster is doing exactly the same thing at the Royal Academy. Venturi's galleries are generally thought to be the most successful part of the design, and they are certainly good examples of the *genre*: generously proportioned and well lit, next to which something like the Clore Gallery looks toy-like and cramped.

But, given that the National Gallery already has 50 such rooms, one questions the need for 25 more. It should have been possible to retrieve at least some of the paintings from their well-lit well-proportioned white-walled nirvana, to build out spaces from the paintings which renewed our perception of them, and reconnected them with the present. If they are deprived forever of their original setting on an altar or in a palace, it does not follow that they must always be viewed as if they were specimens in a peculiarly dignified laboratory.

Venturi's galleries have the authority of convention, whereas his liberties with the assumptions of both Modernists and Traditionalists have succeeded in upsetting devotees of both. This seems to please Venturi, who says, 'as an artist the position of being hard to take is not a bad one'. Actually the devotees have missed the point, since the games with stylistic canons are only shocking if, like Venturi, you mistake style for content. A curious side effect of the Sainsbury Wing is that, unless you are a devotee, the Classical quotations are in fact quite easy to take.

The great weakness of the Sainsbury Wing underlies both the elevational games and the hanging of the paintings. It is an understanding which, in spite of claims to the contrary, is hostile to context, since it abstracts and atomises both the present and the past into a set of stylistic objects. The building's real context is the confrontation of delicate devotional images with huge throngs, of Antonello's St Jerome with Trafalgar Square. Venturi and Scott Brown seem to know this, but are too much hampered by art history to act on their knowledge.

The Evolution of the Gallery

THEORY

Dan Cruickshank
January 1992

The collection and organised display of works of art is one of the many cultural innovations of the Renaissance. In sixteenth century Italy, the objects favoured were salvaged remains of Classical antiquity as well as contemporary paintings, bronzes and marbles.

The great and early architectural expression of this enthusiasm for the orchestrated display of the arts is Bramante's very early sixteenth century additions to the Vatican.[1] Towards the middle of the sixteenth century the word 'museum' began to be used, inspired by the example of the Hellenistic cultural buildings of Alexandria where library and buildings for the display of the arts were combined and called the *museion*. Perhaps the earliest Renaissance example is the building in Como which contains the collection of Paolo Giovio which in 1543 had the word Musaeum inscribed on its façade.[2]

These early museums took their forms from established building types: the Vatican statues were displayed in niches in monastic-like cloisters, the Como building possessed a great hall and smaller rooms off a colonnaded cloister. Other museums were organised around palazzo-like cortiles and, of course, there were galleries. Indeed this form of room was so popular that ultimately it became synonymous with buildings for the display of the arts. The Uffizi in Florence, designed in 1560 by Vasari as a block of government offices and adapted in 1581

Zoffany, 'The Tribune in the Uffizi', late eighteenth century

to incorporate rooms for the display of works of art, includes the full gambit of spaces found in later museums, for which the Uffizi became one of the great prototypes. There is a central court flanked on three sides by open colonnades (these, admittedly, were never part of the museum as such) with, on the upper museum floor, a pair of wide loggia-like galleries with large windows on one side and, on the other, sets of smaller rooms. These rooms interconnected to offer a vista through the building, and to allow for the display of works of art in self-contained suites of rooms. The Uffizi also possess one of the most famous and influential of museum rooms, the Tribune. Octagonal, domed and partially top-lit, the Tribune simulated the interior of an antique temple, and it had walls painted a deep, serene red, a colour which from the late eighteenth century in Britain became standard for picture gallery interiors.

The Renaissance museum came to England in about 1615 when the Earl of Arundel built his gallery for the display of his famous collection of antique statues. Probably designed by Iñigo Jones, who had been a member of Arundel's party in Italy in 1613, the gallery was very much in the Renaissance manner; barrel-vaulted with statues on plinths set against a blank wall facing an open arcade which allowed soft lighting to fall across the statues. Methods of lighting works of art, especially sculpture, had become an important issue. Arundel had become a patron of Rubens and may well have known Ruben's own museum for antiques, which was described as 'like the Pantheon' and 'lighted only from the top'.[3]

Certainly by the seventeenth century, top lighting was established as one of the criteria of museum design, for it offered extra wall space, security and an excellent quality of light. Arundel's gallery was attached to his London mansion, and for the next 200 years the museum developed as a building type within the body of the great country house or town mansion.

The integration and development of the museum within the house was to have a profound influence on both the design of domestic architecture (particularly the country house), and ultimately on the design of the public museum when it emerged as an independent building type in the early years of the nineteenth century.

The Earl of Arundel in his gallery

From the late seventeenth century it was usual in Italy and France to incorporate a sculpture or picture gallery when designing a great house —a fashion which reached England in the early eighteenth century and which gave new life and meaning to the traditional long gallery.[4] These had been favoured rooms in England during the sixteenth century but were not intended primarily for the display of art collections.

Holkam Hall, Norfolk, designed in about 1731 by William Kent and Lord Burlington for Thomas Coke, First Earl of Leicester, reveals how the idea of the museum, of the ancient temple of the arts, influenced country house design. Virtually the entire west side of the *piano nobile* is given up to a 'statue gallery' and its related rooms; with statues in every niche facing rows of windows, which terminates at each end in apses leading into octagonal rooms. One of these tribunes also contains antique sculpture displayed in niches while the other is a library. In addition there is, beyond the saloon, the Landscape Room which the Earl dedicated to the display of his famous collection of seventeenth century French landscape paintings. This was hung red fabric, no doubt in tribute to the Uffizi Tribune, and though square in plan, remembers the octagonal form of the Tribune by having its ceiling decoration organised around a central octagon.

With these rooms, and with a mighty marble entrance hall modelled on the prototypes of Vitruvius and Palladio and seen as a reconstruction of a Roman basilica interior, Holkham appears more like a museum than a country house. But it was, of course, not open to the public, although it seems visitors did virtually have right of entry, by demand. Certainly a party visiting Holkham in 1772 were told they could not see the house 'for an hour at least, as there was a party going round' and were ushered to an ante room where they found 'another large party awaiting the guide'.[5] By the end of the century, visiting country houses to see their collections of antique, Renaissance and contemporary art had become a conventional middle-class cultural activity.

Robert Adam, sculpture gallery in Newby Hall, Yorkshire 1767–80

Newby Hall, North Yorkshire, contains a remarkable museum-like interior, designed by Robert Adam in 1767, which comprises a set of three rooms forming a sculpture gallery. They are organised around a circular, domed and top-lit room which represents one of the earliest essays in England on the Pantheon, an ancient building which became a favoured model with early nineteenth century museum designers who, like Rubens, saw it as the prototype of the temple of the arts.

Perhaps even more remarkable is the interior that Charles Townley created in his house in Queen Anne's Gate, St James's, Westminster. The purpose-built terrace house, designed by Samuel Wyatt in 1775, had a ground and first floor conceived almost exclusively as a museum for the display of Townley 's then famous, and now almost forgotten collection of generally over restored Greek and Roman sculpture. They now languish in the basement of the British Museum, very much the poor relation of Elgin's marbles displayed in splendour on the floor above. In Townley's day, the best of his marbles were housed in his ground floor rear room which was treated as a sculpture gallery with walls divided into bays by full-height engaged columns, while on the first floor was a small and cunningly contrived top-lit museum room immortalised by Zoffany's painting of Townley surrounded by his friends and prized pieces.

Dan Cruickshank

John Nash, Attingham Hall picture gallery, Shropshire 1807

By the late eighteenth century galleries were not only being included in new houses of substance, but were regularly added to existing houses, or occasionally, incorporated within public buildings, for example William Chambers' toplit Great Room which he constructed for the Royal Academy at Somerset House in the late 1770s and George Dance's lantern-lit galleries of 1805 within the Royal College of Surgeons. It was largely through these additions that the vocabulary of museum design was evolved. The late seventeenth century Petworth House, Sussex, acquired its sculpture gallery in c1780, a plain north-lit room for the display of the Earl of Egremont's remarkable collection of painting and statuary. In 1792 George Dance added a sculpture gallery to Robert Adam's 1760s Lansdowne House, Berkeley Square, London. The house was reconstructed in the 1930s but Dance's gallery survives with its shallow barrel-vaulted ceiling arcaded walls which would have formed a handsome setting for the display of statues. The gallery was not completed until 1819, a job undertaken by Robert Smirke, the future architect of the British Museum who seems to have been introduced to the problems of museum design during the completion of this project. Dance had cut his teeth on gallery design in 1788 when he created the remarkable Shakespeare Gallery in Pall Mall, a pioneering top-lit space intended for the display of contemporary British engravings. (It was renamed the British Institution in 1805.) In 1800 C.H. Tatham added an influential sculpture gallery and museum to Castle Howard, North Yorkshire. In 1802 Ince Blundell Hall, Merseyside, acquired a remarkably large-scale replica of the Pantheon to house an extensive collection of sculpture, and in 1807 John Nash added a picture gallery, incorporating cast-iron elements in the roof glazing to Attingham Hall, Shropshire. In addition there were two other remarkable London museum houses, Thomas Hope's Duchess

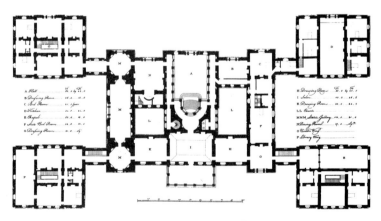

W. Kent and Lord Burlington, *Piano Nobile* with sculpture gallery, Holkham Hall, Norfolk 1731

street house built in 1768 to the designs of Robert Adam and altered in 1799–1803 by Hope who added top-lit statue and picture galleries; and John Soane's museum and office created within and behind 12,13 and 14 Lincoln's Inn Fields from c1808.[6]

A year or two later, in 1811, Soane designed the Dulwich Picture Gallery: the first free-standing, purpose-built public picture gallery in Britain. It was also surprisingly free of overt country house associations. Soane displayed his genius by evolving a definitive public museum interior at the very moment that the building type emerged. The building is single storey so all the main galleries are top-lit by lanterns (Soane had earlier tried his hand at top-lit galleries when designing additions to Fonthill, Wiltshire in 1787). Dulwich con-

Ince Blundell, Pantheon sculpture gallery, Merseyside 1802

sists of a series of square and double square rooms set on axis and interconnected by wide arched openings. By these means rooms can be perceived as individual domestic interiors appropriate for the scale of the paintings they contain. Yet they can also be read as a single monumental space as befits a public building that will have to play host to large gatherings. The walls were painted a Tribune red, as were the walls of the gallery which J.M.W. Turner opened in the West End of London a few years later.[7]

199

The decade after Dulwich saw the construction of the mighty Grecian temples to the arts Leo von Klenze's Glyptothek, Munich designed in 1814 and constructed between 1816–30, Smirke's British Museum, London designed in 1813 and K.F. Schinkel's Altes Museum Berlin which, designed in 1825, contains the last word in the Pantheon-inspired museum interior intended predictably for the display of sculpture. More typical of early public museums than these great national monuments is the Ashmolean in Oxford—a building which shows most clearly how the public museum emerged only painfully and with difficulty out of the museum-like country house.

In the late 1830s the University of Oxford decided to combine its various scattered collections and benefactions within one building. Many of the objects were until then housed in the late seventeenth century Ashmolean Museum which, though an early example of an independent museum, was in effect only a set of small rooms for the display of diverse curios, and which did not utilise any special lighting or display techniques.

The new Ashmolean building was to be shared with an academic institution founded for 'teaching and improving the European languages'. The benefactor for this was the highly successful architect Robert Taylor. This institute – the Taylorian – occupied nearly half of the new building, but this was not in itself so unusual, for Soane's Dulwich Picture Gallery incorporated a mausoleum to its benefactor and at one stage was to include a range of almshouses.

Dan Cruickshank

A competition was launched with a scheme by C.R. Cockerell chosen in 1840, with construction being completed in 1845. Externally the building is a remarkable monument to the final stage of the Greek revival, for Cockerell's design mixes a series of erudite and exquisite Greek details with Roman and even Renaissance forms to create a highly original and successful composition.

Inside, the debt to the countryhouse gallery is only too clear. Facing the main entrance was a rotunda with niched walls (now destroyed) in the manner of Adam's sculpture gallery at Newby Hall. To the left is a long sculpture gallery, with high level lighting above niches which are set into both walls. This gallery was constructed as the result of a special bequest and, strangely enough, was to house what survived of the Arundel marbles.

The first floor was organised like a country house interior with large rooms interconnected by generous corniced doors. Here the major paintings were hung. The second floor is more curious. It has no windows to the main façades but contains a number of smaller rooms top-lit through shallow vaults and by side lights. These rooms housed smaller paintings and objects. The University's decision to divide its collection by type of object was not new in the 1840s; it had been the practice since the very early eighteenth century when the old cabinet of curiosities approach (as exemplified by the old Ashmolean museum) was replaced by the rational approach and specialisation of the Enlightenment. But new in the 1810s was the more scientific approach to methods of display, especially lighting, of the various types of art. Consequently Cockerell's design was subjected to unusually intense scrutiny. In December 1840 two leading connoisseurs – Charles Eastlake and William Dyce – produced a report on the lighting of galleries which made special reference to Cockerell's designs. They concluded that the two first floor rooms above the sculpture gallery would be satisfactory for the display of small pictures if screens were provided (a device which Schinkel had used to divide his long second floor picture galleries at the Museum), while many of the upper rooms were found totally unsuitable for the display of any pictures whatsoever. The dilemmas faced by Cockerell at the Ashmolean still confront designers

John Soane, Dulwich Picture Gallery, 1811

of museums today. Should an attempt be made to simulate the context which the works of art were originally intended? Should traditional methods of presentation be pursued? For example, the niche-filled sculpture gallery is a time-honoured method for the display of antique statues, though it certainly does not necessarily represent the context for which the objects were made. Or should the museum be as neutral as possible with the objects lit to best advantage and with the respectful hush only slightly disturbed by the hum of air-conditioning and sound of visitors making their way from the museum shop to the cafeteria?

K. F. Schinkel, Pantheon sculpture gallery in the Altes Museum, Berlin 1825

1 J.S. Ackerman, in *The Cortile del Belvedere*, 1954, claims that these additions created 'the first museum building since antiquity'.

2 According to Niklaus Pevsner in his *History of Building Types*, 1976. This book provides much useful background information on the origins of the museum.

3 *Rubens* by M. Rooses, London, 1904, pp150–151.

4 G. Tilman Mellinghoff's essay on John Soane's Dulwich Picture Gallery, included in the Academy Editions' architectural monograph on *John Soane*, London, 1983, contains a succinct resumé on the development of the museum in the eighteenth and early nineteenth centuries. He points out that Colen Campbell, in volume three of *Vitruvius Britannicus* of 1725, describes how the traditional long gallery was Classicised: 'the two ends are reduced to cubes… by introducing some columns'. Ideally, this would leave a double cube in-between.

5 *Norfolk Assembly* by R.W. Ketton-Cremer, 1957, p194.

6 Other early galleries include the Picture Gallery and octagon room created in c1762 by Lancelot Brown within Corsham Court, Wiltshire; the Picture Gallery added to Cleveland House, St James's in 1803–06 to the designs of C.H. Tatham; the saucer-domed Picture Gallery designed by Thomas Cundy in 1806 for J. Leicester's house at 24 Hill Street, London; the gallery designed by George Saunders in 1806 and added by the Trustees of the British Museum to Montague house, Bloomsbury to house the Townley marbles and other antiquities; the Gallery and library that Richard Payne Knight added to his own house, 3 Soho Square, in 1809; the Picture Gallery John Nash designed for himself in 1822–24 for 14–16 Regent Street, and the picture Gallery he designed for Buckingham Palace in 1825.

7 According to Joseph Farington (*Diary* ed. J. Greig, VII, p276) the Royal Academy president Benjamin West advised Soane to use red for the Dulwich Gallery walls. However, repair works currently underway at the Soane Museum have produced archaeological evidence which suggests that Soane created a red room in 12 Lincoln's Inn Fields which he built in 1792. The red dining room, which survives in number 13, was created soon after 1812.

Early reactions to Soane's mellow red walls and discreet top lighting at Dulwich were not all favourable. Farington thought they created a 'heavy and unfavourable setting for the paintings', while William Hazlitt, in his essay on the 'Principal Picture Galleries in England', thought the interior 'dim'.

Dan Cruickshank

Aalto Opera Essen

BUILDING CRITIQUE
Opera House, Essen
by Alvar Aalto

Peter Buchanan
March 1991

For almost 30 years Alvar Aalto's competition-winning design for the Essen
Opera House has been a favourite amongst architectural *cognoscenti*; and through
the '70s, following publication of Volume II of Aalto's works, the drawings were
a popular pin-up in many studios. The wriggly cloakroom counters have adorned
countless student schemes—and even many by mature and big name architects.
Most remarkable and admired though is how all the design's sinuous and spacious continuities – and not just the now cliched counters but most especially the
foyer that folds back over these cloakrooms to funnel into the auditorium – are
contained in such a simple and compact overall volume. What was originally only
a single monopitch roof (now at two levels) effortlessly accommodates with very
little looseness of fit all the complex internal volumes and even the full-height fly
tower—all of this in a roughly square if wiggly plan, like some gigantic Aalto ash-
tray. The result is a building of extraordinary experiential and spatial richness,
yet also of stunning conceptual and volumetric economy.

Towards the end of last year this *tour de force*, the model and sketch of the
auditorium as well as the drawings which are so familiar, was at last completed

Aerial view from north-west, direction of main pedestrian approach

—yet to puzzlingly little international fanfare. Aalto had revised the 1959 design in 1961–64 (the Volume II version) and again in 1974, two years before his death. Construction, which started at the end of 1983 was then entirely posthumous, though very substantially in accord with his last plans. These were adjusted and the whole project realised with reverential loyalty by Professor Harold Deilmann (assisted by his son Thomas and others) in consultation with the architect's widow, Elissa Aalto. Inevitably, this delayed completion raises lots of questions.

Where, for instance, should the building be placed within Aalto's complete *oeuvre*? Though finished last it was the first such really grand commission, the original design predating that of Finlandia Hall and reworked both during and after its construction. However loyally executed, both the deference that freezes design (that also lacks on-site fine-tuning by the master himself) and the inevitable changes invite speculation as to what Aalto might have done and so raise questions of authenticity. Yet conversely the prolonged gestation might be deemed to result in this being among the most considered and exemplary of Aalto's designs—indeed its exceptional restraint could be seen as marking it as his most mature work. Though Aalto designed many theatres (most

Aalto's 1959 sketches

of them unbuilt and many, such as the outdoor amphitheatres he occasionally realised, unasked for in the original brief) Essen was the first proper opera house he designed and the only theatre realised with an orchestra pit and full set of backstage areas. How successful as an opera house then is this culmination of such an important and recurrent concern of the architect? And finally, built on foreign soil where some find Aalto's work stiff and less convincing than in Finland, and completed in a very different PostModern age to that in which it was conceived, how good and relevant is the opera house as a work of architecture when judged by today's criteria and prejudices?

Idiosyncrasies of Aalto

Compounding problems of assessment is the idiosyncratic nature of Aalto's architecture. It often combines supreme gracefulness with touches of deliberate awkwardness (dissonance counterpointing the harmony) and an easy obviousness with inscrutable arbitrariness. For instance, the usual inexorable inevitability of

View of vestibule across the café into the park

route and organisation often contrasts with the baffling even jarring application of decoration —especially that used to fragment and layer surfaces. Essen has very little decoration, but if some parts seem a bit fudged as space or surface, does this reflect inadequacy in the executing architects or some dissonance to be appreciated for precisely the effect Aalto intended?

Splendid though it is, the Aalto Theatre, as it is officially named, is a late arrival in North Rhine Westphalia whose 16 million inhabitants are the world's best served with theatres. In the region are at least 30 large opera/theatres (several close enough for an evening out from Essen) and countless smaller theatres. Yet all these and the huge investments in building and running them serve less than 10 per cent of the population and as regular visitors probably only two to five per cent.

Essen, Germany's fifth largest city, is relatively new; it developed with the mining and steel industries of the Ruhr in the late nineteenth century. Flattened in the Second World War, it is now a model of '50s urban ideals. The raised tracks of the railway bisect the town. The station at its centre is a genuine hub with bus station and pleasant ground level arcade of shops and restaurants con-

Dogleg stair with pulpit landing

necting the pedestrianised shopping streets of the original village to the north with larger, straighter, more open streets to the south. It is in this southern section not far from the station that the opera house sits in the corner of a park, the Stadtgarten. As the land falls to its north-east corner the building sweeps up to the tall fly tower and administrative areas that abut closely but quietly the rather drab street that forms the park's eastern boundary. The lowest corner of the monopitch roof juts south-west into the park towards the Saalbau, a '50s building of conference and multi-purpose halls, while the low entry canopy stretches forward to shelter visitors arriving from the park's north-west corner.

First sight of the opera house is a moment of some dismay. Instead of the gleaming Carrara marble Aalto had intended, which has buckled and curled on Finlandia and would badly corrode in the Ruhr's polluted atmosphere, the cladding is a pale grey granite—practical, but lacking any liveliness, and on grey days... gloomily grey. When overcast the extraordinary simplicity of the outer envelope seems too mute, though also striking. Beneath the vast sweeps of the monopitch copper roof the two interlocked main volumes are embraced by a single wavy outer wall. At the top this is simply sliced by the roofs while at the bottom it plunges into the earth without any mediation—there are none of the darker plinths or shadowy overhangs found on Finlandia, for instance. If Finlandia floats like a sparkling iceberg, earthbound Essen thrusts up from the earth like a squat wedge of outcropping rock—except that the cladding is obviously only a thin skin.

As soon as the sun comes out the walls come alive. Even very slight changes in the angle of incident light cause the granite to change colour, accentuating the softest curve, differentiating almost parallel walls and shadowing the smallest projections. This last calls attention to the two contrasting cladding patterns within the constant rhythm of alternating narrow and wide vertical panels of the same two widths. On the lower block of ancillary, administrative and backstage accommodation the cladding forms a smooth skin and the windows are identical rectangles the width of a wider cladding panel. Though they occur with some randomness as necessary they are always in horizontal rows—except those to stairs which occur at half levels. But round the foyer and auditorium the narrow panels project slightly to create an almost imper-

View back down foyer from pulpit landing

ceptible ripple. Between these narrow panels the windows, of the same width as the other but much taller, are placed in random clusters and terminate at top and bottom with some arbitrariness. They even blithely rise past internal floors whose presence is suppressed by masking their spandrels in the same bronze of which the frames are made. And their slight recession combined with masking by the projecting panels makes the windows seem to vary in width with the shifts in angle of the wall.

These contrasting effects are clever and subtle, but many today will find them too understated. In the Volume II elevations the backstage façades are clad in two widths of stone and the foyer/auditorium in three widths—all five widths being different. The model of this version shows both narrower bands in the taller walls projecting appreciably as ribs to produce a more pronounced and varied rippling than on the final building. The effect was probably too decorative and besides would have drawn attention away from what is now perhaps the loveliest of the building's external features—the sinuous contour of the top of the walls against the sky when viewed from fairly nearby. And though marble might have looked splendid in the present rhythm with more pronounced projections, the flatter more bland solution as built seems consistent with granite that we nowadays associate with thin claddings.

Finlandia Hall

Metaphors and Messages

Architects and critics may demur and differ about the colour and restraint of the cladding, but they at least (if very few lay people) will probably be able to read the metaphors and messages implied in the contrasting claddings. The regular windows reflect the floor heights, human scale and mundane activities of the backstage areas and are also a reflection of the windows they face across the street. If this is a very suppressed recognition of and reference to the surrounding city, the tall windows of the foyer obviously relate to the random patterns of nature of the park they face. This interpretation is abundantly confirmed inside.

Leading from the north-west corner of the park, a gentle curve past some potently primitive stone retaining walls by sculptor Ulrich Rückriem, is a row of Aalto street lamps (the graceful wave of their reflectors suggesting to a Post-Modern eye that of welcome, mimicking banner or hand). Reaching forward to meet visitors, and also thrusting out from the body of the theatre, the box office which is open at different hours, is a low copper canopy. On one side it sits on a curved row of idiosyncratic Aalto columns that defines the edge of a *porte-cochère* for dropping off passengers before drivers swing round to plunge down a ramp into the subterranean car park.

Like a prow, the box office divides the stream of arriving pedestrians which then flows through both sets of outer entrance doors. Across the wind lobby (the whole ground floor entry sequence is designed for bitter Nordic winters and their rituals of discarding masses of outer clothing before properly entering the building) more doors open into the vestibule. Prominent in this are fat splayed columns behind which are the wriggly cloakroom counters. With walls and ceilings all white, as are the marble floors and counter tops and the Aalto half round tiles on parts of the fat columns, some find this area clinical or, with the low ceiling, lavatorial. This is strange, for the lighting and the shades and shapes of white it reflects, and the blond wood slats on the counter fronts and the screening all give a feeling of warmth. And the low ceilings and huddles of columns lend a pleasant intimacy as well as some privacy to disrobing and discreetly checking appearances in the mirrors on the sides of the columns: they are also crucial for the contrast they provide with the tall spacious foyer above and for the way they immediately announce the *raison d'être* of the building by revealing the presence and shape of the auditorium.

Enticing the visitor forward with a view out to the park and with the tangible promise of soaring space and light is a broad shallow flight of steps. From the landing, even broader steps drop gently down again to the warmly inviting café set slightly below the level of the park that is visible through the expanse of windows above the head level of the diners—for whom the room thus remains contained and intimate. Turning on the landing, or rising from a café table, visi-

206

tors feel both propelled forward by the unfolding view, yet also compelled into slow motion to extend and savour one of the most breathtakingly beautiful architectural experiences to be found anywhere.

At first the ceiling dominates an upward view; its subtle slopes and bent dashed lines of soft lights set the whole space into a gentle motion that puts a slight spin on that induced by the changing perspective as one rises. Next the

Auditorium seen from the stage

galleries command attention: they are lit by shafts of sunlight from the tall windows opposite, the jittery rhythms of which contrast with the galleries' smoothly serene and hovering forms. Rising further, these focus the eye on the dogleg stair with its pulpit-like projecting landing. This is reached by another broad shallow flight of stairs that invites one forward to its foot and beyond, to where the foyer funnels around the auditorium and into its far side. The auditorium is also entered by doors under and along the galleries—reached from the dogleg stair, the landing of which gives splendid views back down the foyer. And just as the auditorium doors match those of Finlandia, with black woven horsehair covering and leather wound brass handles, so too do the leather wound brass handrails, some free-standing, on 'I' section brass posts.

Aalto was always the master of stairs and the climbing route. Following his Essen stairs, flowing with them, has the easy and pleasurable inevitability of following well-worn paths and terraces on a hill slope. Never for a moment are you at a loss as to where to go. You are always beckoned forward, up to, into and through the building which places everything to hand when and where you need it, as well as preparing you for each new experience. There are also alternative routes, clearly played down as short-cuts that miss some of the drama, but that always lead where you want.

Such seemingly natural routes are choreography as artful as any found on stage. And as precisely as space and vistas unfold to the visitor so the visitor is presented to the rest of the audience.

View from the north

Peter Buchanan

207

Long section through foyer, auditorium, stage and flyover and backstage areas

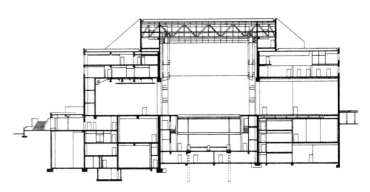

Cross-section through stage and side stages looking towards auditorium

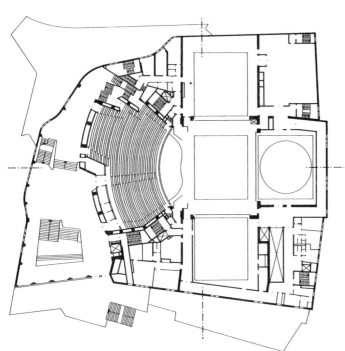

Foyer level (first floor) plan (approx 1:1000)

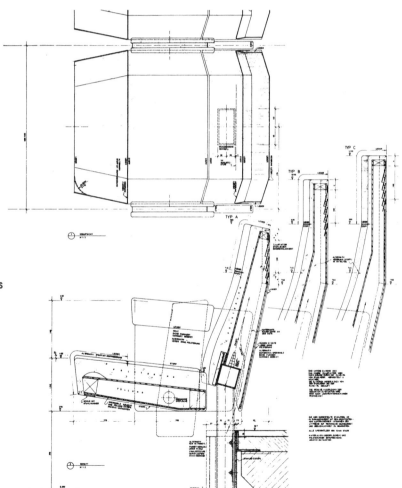

Elevation of 1964 with contrasting cladding rythms

Details of auditorium seating; fresh air is ducted up support-posts and distributed through slats in top of chair backs

Nonsense has been written about Aalto's so-called heterotopic sensibility, his conjoining of very disparate forms and spaces. Yet in essence Aalto's is not an art of disjuncture: instead it is one of flowing continuities, that achieves unities of extraordinary spaciousness and coherence in tight constraining envelopes. Even when a composition is distended it is to achieve dialogue and reciprocity between the parts.

Photographs show the foyer as a bit sparse. It is. Yet paradoxically it is precisely because the foyer is so large that this sparseness is so marvellous. There is little distracting detail, so that what there is stands out—as do people; also you are more completely aware of the space and, especially, the larger forms within it and how the shifting sunlight plays across them. This alone would be enough to make the space alive and rich to experience. But it is made really magical by the understated yet unmistakable allusions to nature. In Aalto's sketch of the foyer the stairs cascade like water rapids hemmed in by galleries of stratified rock. Though as built, Aalto's tentative wavy line has been realised in precise pristine materials, this interpretation remains credible—especially because of the way the space focuses on the pulpit stair which holds the attention like a waterfall at the head of a valley.

Nordic Allusion

But the most particular and potent allusions arise from the way the light is handled. Untypically for Aalto, whose major spaces are usually lit from several sources including from above, this foyer is lit only from one side. (The only top-lights in the building are over the café. Though in plan they pun satisfyingly with the ground level auditorium columns, in reality they are functionally gratuitous Aaltoisms). Aalto's theatrical masterstroke with this foyer and confirmation of his poetic intentions was to face the windows west. The setting sun not only lends a lovely and lively warm glow to the foyer, but also through the tall windows becomes the low Nordic sun shafting through conifer forests – a familiar subject in Scandinavian art and literature – so lending a suitably mystic celebratory air to the

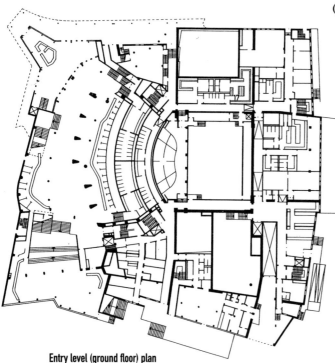

Entry level (ground floor) plan

drama of attending the opera. In such a context the inevitable tropical palms jollying up corners are an especially silly touch, marring a brilliant *coup de théâtre*.

Entering the auditorium is to move from enchanted evening to night itself. Walls, ceilings, seats and fire curtain are all bright royal blue (a colour approved by Elissa Aalto)—but they were originally intended as indigo, the colour of the night sky. Against this the curving timber slats, which stand free from the side walls to hide lights and television monitors for the stage, are like conifers bent by a breeze while the hovering white whiplashes of the balcony are floating clouds. If the abstracted trees wave attention towards the stage (and perhaps too much upwards) the 'clouds', in the way they lean over the stalls, tangibly force attention forward. Ravishingly beautiful, the space has all the hallmarks of an Aalto auditorium, both in the details described and in being wide and asymmetrical, so that everybody is close to the stage, and it feels comfortable with different sized audiences (capacity is 1125). Acoustics are excellent and never needed the anticipated fine tuning. For uses other than opera, such as concerts, theatre or speeches, acoustics are adjusted by altering the tilt of parts of the ceiling.

Certain details do raise some reservations. Standing on stage both the form and width of the auditorium places the audience in the palm of one's hand—just how effectively has to be experienced to be believed. But the price paid is some poor sight lines from the extreme left of the stalls—especially when the proscenium is closed down. (From 18 m it can close to 12 m and is usually played at about 16 m.)

Unfortunately the panels which close the proscenium do not continue the wood slatting of the wall and so mark a break between auditorium and stage. Nor are there the stepping side panels of Finlandia that link balcony and stage, embracing the audience and leading the eye down on to the action. Probably the shallow width of Essen makes any such linking-device unnecessary. In a way, the swinging line that extends from the side aisles around the front of the stage performs this role, but also results in an exceptionally wide and intrusive pit. (Nobody working in the theatre seems to mind nor even have any comment to make on this—they are pleased with auditorium and stage, technical and storage facilities but desperately lack adequate rehearsal space.) The fire curtain is most unusual, curving in front of the pit and being mainly raised from below with a smaller piece joining it from above. Finally, in the balconies, the delicacy and views through the wood slat fronted parts are a delightful touch, but from the rear seats you are very conscious of peering at the stage through a cinemascope slot constricted at top and bottom.

Back in the foyer, it is night here too. Without the slanting sun, the space is less magical than it was, though it is still immensely fine with the dashes of the lights now tracing the orbits of stars in the northern sky. Looking down from the gallery provokes thoughts about possibly problematic aspects of the foyer design. The far corner of the foyer catches attention: on one side are door-height windows on to a terrace but otherwise it is blankly muted, if not dead. Aalto it seems disliked or could be embarrassed by corners: he so frequently eliminated them by making entrances of them or sweeping wall-finishes around them, or as in vestibule and café here, counters before them, to play them down. Yet this one is a key part of the building where the main roof sweeps lowest and the whole thrust of the building juts at an acute angle into the park. It is difficult to imagine another architect not giving it more purpose and emphasis.

The funnel form that this prominent corner gives to the foyer suggests something that may also seem a little strange at first—that it is from here rather than from the entrance below that the real promenade begins. This was probably Aalto's intention: not until one has shed one's coat and started to climb into the foyer proper does the building dignify you as properly part of the audience. The funnel form also suggests that in summer, when no coats need be shed, Aalto imagined many arriving via the terrace from the park—a process recapitulated during intervals as the audience returns from terrace or café. The interpretation seems to be confirmed by the fact that though the sun is admitted from the west, the park can only be properly viewed across the terrace or sunken café. Through their wide windows the park is almost sucked – as if by hoover – into the building. (Or maybe Aalto is playing a game with Le Corbusier's notion of 'visual acoustics', and the allusion is to a horn or trumpet.)

In a way then, the building alludes to a traditional form of the theatre where the outdoors symbolically extends into the building to be embraced by external façades in foyer and auditorium. But here it is nature that is drawn in; there is no urban procession of street-like foyer and courtyard auditorium. Indeed the Essen auditorium is etherealised into night sky and cloud and the only allusion to the city is found in the external backstage fenestration. One could read this as the city reduced to a bureaucratic corset sadly necessary to support the natural creativity of art. Perhaps, though, latent in this design is an even more magnificent concept where the backstage area – now the usual disorientating rabbit warren of barely pleasant spaces – could have faced internal courts adjacent to and expressed in the walls of the auditorium and foyer. But of course this would have been very expensive. As it is, the built scheme both returns to the iconographic roots and *parti* of the Classical theatre yet subverts it by alluding directly to nature and not the lan-

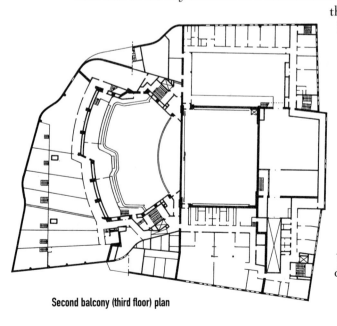

Second balcony (third floor) plan

guage and disciplines of Classicism that, though also derived from nature, now symbolise its antithesis: *civitas*.

It is on these terms, as being anti- or insufficiently urban that many architects and critics would nowadays reject the Essen Opera House (and perhaps why its completion has been so little celebrated). These people would prefer a building of more urban presence and connotations with impressive tall colonnaded entrances, rather than shy, low canopies, and so on. Yet the Aalto theatre is not only true to the early Modernists' belief that Classicism was played out and needed the reinvigoration of a return to its roots (which this building does in its iconography and metaphors if not in its planning and proportional disciplines) and their rejection of the congested city, it is also consistent with its time of conception and remains apt to its particular setting. It is after all set in a park and does, in turning its back, both acknowledge and give due deference to the drab streets beside. In stone cladding and upper roof it picks up the materials of its most prominent neighbour, the Saalbau.

Besides, Essen is not the most urban of cities. Typical of post-war Germany, overt trappings of *civitas* such as Classical columns have been shunned for their obvious unfortunate associations. Instead the public realm is decorated and dignified with the tamed nature of swirling cobbles, ground ivy, cascading streams and tubs of flowers. While much later in Stuttgart, Stirling expressed nostalgia for the lost city (rather absurdly considering the ringroad site), Aalto in the '50s optimistically celebrated the green city in a way that perfectly matches his site. And the pendulum may soon swing to where people again see Essen as a model of pleasant urban life. In the meantime, any but the most dogmatic anti-Modernist must hail the theatre as magnificent, rendering the new German museums to which people go on pilgrimages toy-like and childish in comparison.

Something though should be done about the landscaping around the opera house which tells more about the sculptor than of the architecture. Consistent with the building's main design themes, the trees already on site should be joined by others coming closer to the foyer windows and through the edges of this grouping should be woven an intricate lacework of paths—as shown on Aalto's site plan. These will do much to bed the building better in its setting so that it is not left so lumpishly alone.

213

Peter Buchanan

Pacific Rim and Planetary Culture

Peter Buchanan
April 1991

Throw away your atlases. They are all utterly obsolete. Familiar projections by Mercator and others are centered on the Greenwich meridian. Imprinted thousands of times over in our memories is the gestalt of continents framed by water and framing in turn between them the Atlantic and Indian Oceans. The Pacific Ocean is neither framed nor properly present. Nor too, often enough, is it evident how the USSR and Alaska lean towards and almost touch each other (like Michelangelo's God and Adam) across the Bering Strait. But, since the bombing of Pearl Harbor drew attention to the very centre of that ocean and its accessibility from both sides, the Pacific has progressively become not the edge of the world but its very centre. Perched precariously and opposite each other on its seismically unstable rim and locked in a symbiotic competitive interplay are Japan and California, the two key centres of the late twentieth century. Between them they invent and produce the crucial hard and software (of all sorts) that shape the work and leisure of all of us and our unfolding future too.

Richard Neutra, covered deck of Kaufmann House, Palm Springs 1946

This interplay is most obvious in electronics, in computers and canned entertainment, the latter best exemplified by Sony's ownership of Hollywood's Columbia Pictures as well as CBS. Plaything as well as workhorse, the computer was invented in the West and leading edge innovation in hard and software still comes mostly from California's Silicon Valley. But Western manufacturers not only face fierce competition from Japan, they are completely dependent on its microchips. And computer games and graphics introduce into the West a pictographic form of communication familiar to the Far East—which may also be, as William Irwin Thompson claims, a renewed appreciation and use of the most ancient of graphic modes, that of hieroglyphic thought.

Japan's symbiotic bond with California was first anticipated in the latter's architecture soon after the turn of the century in the houses of Greene & Greene and later in those of Harwell Hamilton Harris. Significantly the most characteristic architecture of both countries is domestic, specifically the single family house. And, unlike say Europe, basically the same type of house which varies only in size serves all strata of society whether from serf to emperor, or from labourer to megastar. Now, while the Japanese exemplify in their approach to nature a brutally exploitative frontier ethic like that which conquered the American West, the true inheritor of much of the essence of traditional Japanese architecture as well as of Zen's awe of nature and approach to gardening is the Californian home. Yet it is also almost the only Modern architecture in America that exemplifies the emancipatory social programme of its European equivalent. Even before Pearl Harbor, Rudolph Schindler and Richard Neutra had drawn on their Viennese background and the example of their mentor Frank Lloyd Wright to catalyse that mix of the Modern and the Japanese that has characterised the best Californian domestic architecture ever since—including the famous Case Study houses.

Parallels between traditional Japanese and Modern architecture (as excellently illustrated in California by the Case Study houses and others by Charles Eames and Craig Ellwood) are often noted. Both tend to the graphic and geometric, to gridded abstraction. Both tend to lightness and openness with space flowing between planar, often sliding, partitions. Both reveal materials and construction in a direct and unaffected manner to achieve a spare puritanic elegance as a quiet backdrop to life. Both separate structure from infill and use modular planning (in Japan based on the *tatami* mat). All these qualities are clearly seen in the architecture of Mies van der Rohe, particularly that of the Illinois Institute of Technology campus which some critics have seen as encapsulating the essence of Japanese architecture. But the stiff symmetry and rigidly repetitive modularity of Mies' Neo-Classical planning is utterly different to Japanese tradition where the *tatami* module allows for plans that are informal and irregular, sometimes almost meanderingly so. Instead of being, like a Miesian plan, abstractly self-contained in its very architectural order, the traditional Japanese plan resembles landscaping in its informality, and is perhaps itself a metaphor for

Richard Neutra, Nesbitt House, Brentwood 1942

the nature with which it is interwoven. Yet it is this very quality that the Modern California house often captures so well particularly those of Neutra.

Though all the qualities listed above are common in Californian architecture, perhaps the most persistent parallel between traditional Japanese and Modern Californian homes is that associated with the last of these qualities—the thorough integration of house and garden. In the most characteristic examples from both countries, the home is actually the whole plot: the boundary between grounds and building is blurred as garden and outdoor paving extend into and even through the house which in turn extends decks and overhanging roofs out into the garden. At night this integration is aided by lanterns that light the garden so as to be seen from the house. In Neutra's houses strip lights along the edge of wide overhanging eaves outside floor-to-ceiling windows brightly illuminate the garden so that it becomes part of the space of the house. And also with his houses, the pools that are so regular a feature of gardens in both damp Japan and dry California actually extend right inside past the full-height glass. Structural frames often reach out to rise from an outdoor pool, further tying together house and garden. Neutra also used reflecting pools set both close to and far from the house to echo and bring close distant mountains and sky (a device reminiscent of the borrowed landscape techniques of Japanese gardens), while simultaneously skipping the eye and spatial reach of the house outwards—usually, in a trick carried over from Wright, on a diagonal that eases the fluid slippage of space through house and garden.

The Neutra plan, and that of other Californian architects, is brilliant not just in its spatial fluidity and integration with its surroundings, but also for how fully and sensitively it serves its occupants. Such plans are deceptively simple yet precise and rich, achieving careful gradations of withdrawal and privacy from the open communal family areas to the separate specialised realms for parents, children and services—each with their appropriate relationship to a suitably sited and shaped, planted and paved part of the garden. One of the best syntheses of all this is the 'T' shaped prototypical house designed by Neutra (but sadly not built) for a large housing development. As a compact distillation of the needs and possibilities of twentieth century family life, it is on a par with Le Corbusier's brilliant set of apartment plans of 14 m² per person published in *La Ville Radieuse*. Also remarkable was Neutra's use of both advanced and standard industrial technology and his exploitation of ambient natural phenomena and landscaping to achieve comfort. His aesthetic of overlapping planes for instance not only achieves an interpenetration of house and garden, but also shades the large areas of glass and obviates cutting standard-sized frames and panels. And in some very

216

cheap houses, cooling was achieved by Venturi-effect aided ventilation with air humidified by evaporation from pools and regularly watered hedges.

In California the continuity of house and garden is encouraged by the balmy climate: in Japan it is possible only because the Japanese are prepared to endure even bitter cold for the sake of custom and aesthetics. Despite the striking similarities, and the undoubted influence of Japanese architecture on the Californian home, and some of its trendy rituals such as shared hot tubs. they each serve an utterly different life-style and ethos. Traditional Japanese domestic life is one of the most constricted and inhibited ever (by ritualised custom as well as by the *kimono*-restricted movement and quiet necessitated by the flimsy fabric of the houses). In contrast. the laid-back hedonistic life-style of California must be the most spontaneous and informal since Palaeolithic times. Similarly, Japanese culture's repression of individuality is the complete antithesis of California's glorification of the unique individual.

Consistent with its rampant individualism, California's domestic architecture includes far more forms (including much that is grossly vulgar or ephemerally trendy) than the classic Modern one described above. Japan's architecture is also increasingly heterogeneous, in places wildly so. Both countries exhibit the eclectic pluralism of our PostModern age that, in its play with historical forms and genres, is possibly a prelude to much deeper synthesis and cultural hybridisation — that of the coming Pacific Rim culture. But, in Japan's eclecticism there is a key strand, originating in a period after the heyday of the Californian house, which took a central idea from Western Modernism and transformed it into something peculiarly Japanese and in which they led and influenced the world.

Japan's Metabolists rationalised the Modernist notion of the building-as-machine. They made it more explicit and exaggerated in buildings that were to be slowly mutating assemblies of industrial components and machines of greater or lesser life span. Some Japanese architects and corporations still propose what are now to most of us in the West nightmare visions of the city as a megastructural, mechanically-serviced hive. Their enthusiasm for such buildings and cities reveals Japan's continuing suppression of the individual in favour of the corporate cypher of the 'salary man'. Ultimately such designs, like their British High-Tech equivalents (it is no coincidence that Foster Associates and Richard Rogers Partnership both have several commissions in Japan), are monuments to the preelectronic industrial age, and the primacy it accorded to productivity, that originally grew and then climaxed around the North Atlantic.

Private rooms, Temple of Nishi-Hongan-ji, Kyoto

In contrast to such an over-poweringly monumental and *macho* use of technology, the Modern Californian house (one of the original inspirations of British High-Tech before it was sidetracked by Brutalism and nostalgia) used equally advanced technology

Peter Buchanan

with the tact and delicacy that characterised the construction of the traditional Japanese home. This is all part of an extraordinary paradox. At the Western extreme of the Industrial West the spirit of Japanese architecture and Zen's reverence for nature inspired the Modern Californian home. Later the same underlying impetus became transmuted into the ecology movement and the endorsement of massive curbs against the excesses of industrial culture and its toxic pollutants. Japan though, in its rapid industrialisation and determined quest for market dominance and material wealth, cavalierly continues not just with massive pollution but also, for instance, in its ruthless slaughter of those intelligent sentient cetaceans, the whales and dolphins.

Japan is now the country that is probably most determined to commercialise our current frontier, outer space. And its pursuit of the building-as-machine together with the vast resources its construction companies are putting into research and development mean that it is likely to build, or at least collaborate on, the first big space stations and moon settlements. But as William Irwin Thompson writes 'in the world of space one is constrained to be on more intimate terms with one's waste. This, a knowledge that is brought back to earth, for aerospace technologies lead directly to new understandings of ecology. With satellites one sees the life of rivers and seas; with space capsules and shuttles one learns the placing of exhalation and excretion'. Such insights, brought home also by the tiny size and habitable area of Japan, will almost certainly ensure that its period as an environmental vandal will be relatively short-lived: it will soon regain the spiritual values now evident only in its traditions—and California.

What we are witnessing in these cross-overs of influence and inversions of ethos is the birth of a new cultural ecology, that of the Pacific Rim. If California and Japan are its leaders, they are by no means its only participants as the influence of the Californian (and Japanese) house right up the West Coast of the US and Canada and diagonally across the ocean in Australia testifies. If Japan has been threatening the economic supremacy of the US, it in turn is paranoid about eastern Asia's so called Four Tigers: Hong Kong, Singapore, Malaysia and Korea. And the impending development of China will unleash who knows what creative and economic energies. Seattle, Vancouver and Sydney will all no doubt be major players in this new culture, while Latin American writers contribute to its emergent sensibilities and some Chileans to its new view of science. Originally all the continents formed a single land mass and most of the globe was an enormous ocean—what is now the Pacific. As the continents drifted apart the other oceans formed between them. So the development and linking up of the Pacific Rim forms also the final interlocking of what will be a genuinely planetary culture, particularly as it is also a global electronic and aerospace culture with all the

Hio–en or covered open space in seventeenth century Japanese building

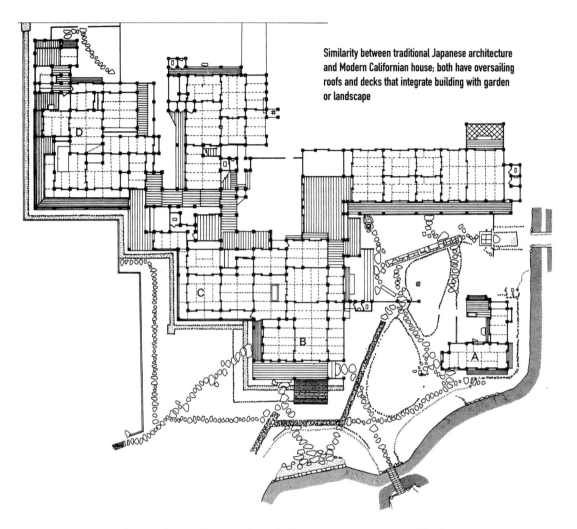

Similarity between traditional Japanese architecture and Modern Californian house; both have oversailing roofs and decks that integrate building with garden or landscape

new insights and experiences these bring to us. But to gain further perspective on the implications of this new cultural ecology it is instructive to briefly chart the evolution of our civilisation's three previous cultural ecologies.

Since its beginnings on the rivers of Mesopotamia, civilisation has progressed in gradual stages westwards, focused each time around increasingly large bodies of water. This process is noted in several of the books of historian and cultural commentator William Irwin Thompson and discussed in most detail in his *Pacific Shift*. In one of its chapters he charts how each cultural ecology arises and climaxes providing a core for its successor, and how each cultural ecology has its own characteristic political, economic and religious forms, as well as communication medium, literary and mathematical modes and so on. The first cultural ecology was Riverine and arose with the cities of Tigris and Euphrates. Its written medium was script; its mathematics, enumeration; and its polity the city-state. This last became the Greek *polis* of the early stage of the next cultural ecology,

Peter Buchanan

that of the Mediterranean. Here the written medium was alphabetic; the mathematics, the geometry that underpinned Classical and Medieval thought. The geopolitical form was empire, as with those of Rome and the Holy Roman, which carried over as those of Spain and Britain in the next cultural ecology, that of the Atlantic. Here the medium is print; the mathematics, the dynamic equations of motion; and the polity that of the industrial nation-state. The US climaxes the Atlantic cultural ecology, yet also launches the emergent fourth one of the Pacific and aerospace. In this the medium is electronic; its mathematics, the processual and multi-dimensional morphologies found for instance in catastrophe theory. And an optimistic assumption is that the emergent polity will be an ecology of nations, a complex mesh of interdependencies in which the unique contribution and character of each are cherished.

Thompson also shows in the same chapter how each cultural ecology is accompanied by its own form of pollution. Thus the Riverine cities failed because irrigation caused soil loss through erosion and salination. Mediterranean empires foundered when deforestation robbed them of timber for ships and rainfall for crops. Toxic pollution of earth, water and atmosphere is a curse of Atlantic culture. As well as the three previous kinds of pollution, our present and Pacific culture also faces a fourth kind, the psychic pollution of information and stimulus overload, and the resultant generalised paranoia. Pollution, it is now clear, is an inextricable accompaniment to civilisation as its other, its unconscious shadow. In facing up to this, in treating pollution as crucial information and unexploited resource, the cultural ecology of the Pacific might evolve into a post-civilisation one, the first that, even if it radically transforms the earth, will be benign if not gentle in its impact.

Being literary in orientation, Thompson has not speculated on the characteristic architecture of each cultural ecology. Yet this too might give us a relevant perspective. Harshly hierarchical, the pyramidal organisation of Riverine society under its priest-kings was explicitly expressed in the stepped pyramidal form of the ziggurats that raised temples above the marshes for gods to

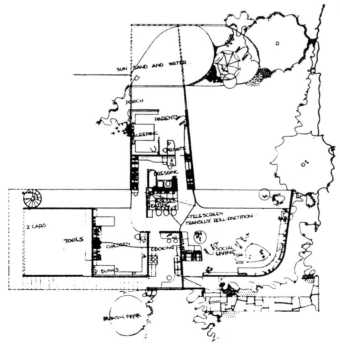

Richard Neutra, plan of standard house for Amity-Compton village development, California 1939

reside in. Mediterranean cultures emphasised the rights of the individual across their far-flung empires and their columnated edifices dignify the being of each citizen/column while representing the standardised order that they stand for wherever they are. Atlantic culture is perfectly expressed by the grid that provides the backdrop on which to plot the trajectories of calculus and physics; and in which nature is enmeshed by the grasp of technology (with its roads, rails and power lines) and abstracted into by the quantifications of science. The grid organised the columns of Neo-Classicism and itself became the prime expression of the repetitive banalities of corporate Modernism; it colonised the American landmass and is the frame on which its cities sprawl. The grid represents pure instrumentality, the diminishment of individuality and sensual experience, and alienation in its elimination of hierarchy and symbolic meaning. Yet the grid persists into the Pacific cultural ecology. But its lines are etherialising into intangible conduits of energy and information. Nature itself will no longer be suppressed by the grid, but will invade and flourish in it as the dominant sensual presence counterbalancing the intangibility of our electronic world in the high-tech/high-touch equation. And the grid will also fold into the non-orthogonal geometries of space frames and tensegrity structures,or crystalline configurations with their cosmic associations; and bend in accord with the new topological mathematics that only the computer can generate and as already exemplified by the Kansai airport that Renzo Piano is building for the Japanese city of Osaka. The grid then will evaporate or become less abstract, either cosmically, crystalline or biomorphically organic, both ultimately metaphors for nature and its inherent intelligence and transcendental spiritual values.

Though Osaka is on the Pacific Rim, Piano is European so endorsing that the Pacific cultural ecology is also a planetary one. The ethos of his practice too seems to look forward. It is not the normal productive business of a *homo-faber* professional (which of course may be highly creative and innovative) but a multi-national workshop geared to the playful creative experiment of *homo-ludens*. Hence there is a lightness and liveliness in Piano's work (both product and process) that contrasts with the overwrought and/or overwhelming ponderousness or lifeless perfection of much High-Tech. In this he not only continues its original '60s ethos but is also the only major architect who seems to still pick up from that fusion of West and East in the Californian home still built in that period. He does this with his inventive yet matter-of-fact and unmonumental use of advanced (and low) technology that recalls Neutra, Eames and Ellwood; with the way he beds his buildings in nature that penetrates, even permeates, them as with Neutra; and with the often biomorphically shaped components and joints that, unlike similarly shaped High-Tech ones, appear easily manipulable and dis-assembled. In this last quality it is Eames, as both product designer and architect, that Piano most closely resembles.

Some complain that Piano's work is unurban—just as the best Californian Modernism is suburban. Though some of Piano's recent buildings in Paris face up to and largely refute this charge, his light-weight architecture does avoid the *gravitas* associated with *civitas*. But then neither of the two key cities of the Pacific Rim, Tokyo and Los Angeles, are urban in the traditional European sense of forming an enveloping, continuous and coherent fabric. Instead, their very varied buildings are respectively packed in to and loosely dispersed in their movement networks. Exemplifying such '60s notions as the non-place-urban-realm, these cities were largely ignored by atavistic planning concerns of the '70s and '80s. Yet, because in its dissipation it is almost in the process of dissolving back into a lushly landscaped nature, Los Angeles is probably one model of the city of tomorrow. Certainly it is a model that is arguably consistent with our electronic future though still too dependent on polluting and energy profligate commuting and water hijacked from elsewhere. Renzo Piano's architecture then might not be so much unurban as post-urban.

Despite this, architectural theory's focus during the last decade on understanding the past and using this to criticise the inadequacies of the present (rather than trying to understand what is really happening now and what the future may bring) has not been irrelevant. For, as Thompson points out, each new cultural ecology is launched in part by distilling to essentials the previous ones. So at the core of the Greek culture that initiated that of the Mediterranean was Pythagoras' distillation of the teachings of Babylonian and Egyptian mystery schools into a system of geometry that maps the potentials of consciousness as much as the surface of the earth. Greek and Latin culture and ethics then formed the core of Atlantic culture, together with the artefacts hoarded in such places as the Louvre and the British Museum. Now it is English, the language of Britain and America with its vast recorded repertoire ranging from high literature to Pop lyrics, that is the universal language of Pacific/planetary culture. And it is into California's Getty Museum and Japan's galleries and department stores that the key artefacts of previous periods and cultures are being swept by the vortex of their purchasing power.

In these terms (as well as those of Marshall McLuhan's rear view mirror where we at last see clearly the culture we have just left), the retrospective focus of recent architectural and planning theory makes sense. And the key Californian architect/theorist of the last decades (certainly the only one other architects can learn much of real and lasting value from) is Christopher Alexander. His *Pattern Language* is a distillation of the architectural wisdom of all previous periods and, aptly enough, his major projects are for both developed and developing parts of the Pacific Rim – Japan, California and Oregon, Peru and Mexico – while followers of his are active in Papua-New Guinea. What all this represents is a necessary preliminary process of comprehension and synthesis before the urgent task of understanding, and developing a theory for an architecture and urbanism appropriate to our own times.

Just as Piano's work has close affinities with that of California up until the '60s, so Alexander seems to continue the Countercultural project of the late '60s.

Yet rather than making their work dated, this is precisely what makes it so apposite, for that optimistic and architecturally adventurous decade presaged so many of the concerns and aspirations that are returning to us in the '90s with the emergent Pacific culture. Instead of being concerned with style (no matter how distinctive the style of that period now looks in retrospect) and with merely advancing the fame of its designer, architecture then, and the technology it incorporated, was devised in the service of life—a full and enjoyable life at that, lived with a newly discovered spontaneity and sensual engagement with nature. It was

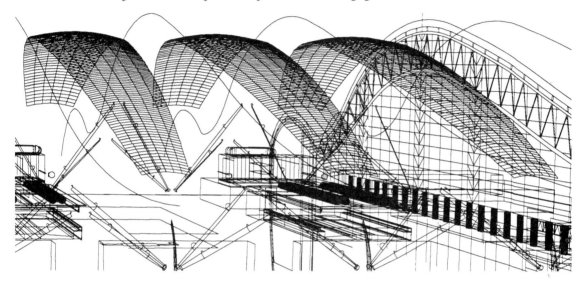

Renzo Piano Building Workshop, computer drawing of Kansai airport, Osaka 1991

also the period that saw the late masterworks of such Modern masters as Le Corbusier, Aalto and Kahn—works that in their density of synthesis, and in the depths of thought and psyche that they were drawn from, far eclipse anything that has come since. Though the '80s produced many exceptionally fine works, it was also a period of floundering and loss of faith, and a descent into superficial graphics and style. In contrast, the progressive clarification of the cultural ecology of the Pacific might provoke a return to a similarly ambitious yet humble architecture as that seen in its early prefiguring in the Modern Californian house —an architecture that might fully respect all the needs of people and planet. But this being the age of Gaia, it would transcend the hedonistically secular nature of the Californian house to include a sacred or spiritual dimension, that in intention at least inspired the best work by Neutra.

Peter Buchanan

Sunk in the Berg

BUILDING CRITIQUE
Museum project, Salzburg
by Hans Hollein

Michael Spens
January 1992

Hans Hollein has proposed a museum under the castle rock in Salzburg which will be, in effect, an architecture of space without external form, yet it will complement the historic core of the city and create a series of galleries which will allow curators much freedom.

Following a competition in 1989, two remarkable concepts came together. The Guggenheim Foundation was anxious to develop its involvement in Europe, beyond the existing yet idiosyncratic Peggy Guggenheim Collection in Venice. And Thomas Krens, the new director of the Guggenheim, was introduced to Hollein's competition-winning proposals, and became intrigued with the possibilities in Salzburg, a festival city of considerable cultural centrality where something of a vacuum had existed in the presentation of the visual arts. The idea of a sunken cave (the existing feature is known in German as '*der Sunk*') was generic in terms of museum topology here, and seems never to have been questioned as a concept.

There is an inherent conflict between the desire of museum curators to house art in architectural space that is itself distinctive, while seeking to minimise

Sectional model

the expression of architectural form to a point close to neutrality. This tension had in the 1980s created some of the best museum spaces, and some of the least satisfactorily resolved buildings. The controversy over the Guggenheim Museum in New York and its problematical spiral has long since yielded to the building's high rating as a key monument of that city: the Foundation's trustees remembered this at Salzburg. They, and the city of Salzburg, nonetheless rate such monumentality high, and became readily convinced about the workability of Hollein's vision.

A special characteristic of Hollein's work has always come from the urge to exploit unusual site conditions, even to confound what might initially appear as immutable circumstances whether of scale, or elevation, or conjunction, or typology. At Mönchengladbach (AR December 1982), for instance, the museum appeared as several buildings—certainly not the civic monument that Mönchengladbach's citizenry might have been led to expect would emblemise their growing regional centrality. Much earlier, at Eisenberg, the projected campanile to the new parish church for the lakeside village was to be commuted into a jetty at the far end of which a bell could toll and echo around the surrounding mountains. At the Haas-Haus (AR July 1991), mercantile prestige was celebrated with a baroque flourish yet did not detract from the Stefanskirche opposite. Even at Frankfurt, the triangular isosceles site accommodating the Museum of Modern Art there is reconciled consummately with the existing urban grain, the entrance made at the 'base' rather than the apex, as convention might have prescribed; the prow thereby achieves a symbolic importance marking a specific monumentality.

Mönchengladbach, Frankfurt, and Salzburg, if this project is to proceed, will create a uniquely formidable exploration by a single architect into the art museum type, conceived effectively in one decade. It is probable that Salzburg will prove to be the ultimate Late Modern masterpiece. The idea of establishing an art gallery in a sunken, rock-hewn cavern has inevitable atavistic references.

225

Competition section relating the castle, the catacumbal museum and the town

Michael Spens

To expand this concept to a series of caves and recesses lit spasmodically by shafts of sunlight or daylight involves delving which has profound implications for human sensibility. Hollein has put forward a schema so fundamental that its seemingly non-tectonic condition simply re-endorses basic timeless experiential codes in a way that utterly confounds the assumed precepts of PostModernists.

Hollein characteristically invokes first principles: a resolutely purifying immersion in space is prescribed, or rather a sequence of subterranean spaces to be experienced yet which cannot, *a priori*, be imagined. Viewed from above (as on the model) the roof lighting system barely intrudes over the surface of the rocky plateau. The *Sunk* to some extent dictates (or is allowed to dictate) the profile of the catacombed upper level galleries. The pronounced curvature of the periscopic light shaft projects above ground surface level to tree-top height, as an isolated clue to the true depth of the space below. The horizontal ramp reaching across past it to the lift shaft adds emphasis to this downward compulsion.

Model showing upper level galleries

The whole venture seems archaeological. but the object of discovery here is non-tectonic space, to be explored and revealed progressively. We are presented with void sculptured out of solid state — one absolute against another. So Hollein deploys these opposing conditions of raw material to play one against the other, without the intervention, still less mediation, of a constructional system. The built proportion of space, as opposed to excavated space, is purely marginal. The volume for the museum galleries and their circulation is obtained by excavation.

Hollein has wholly resisted the temptation for more gullible PostModernists, to elevate the new dome over the *Sunk*, in open competition with the castle. It is in this section that the clearest evidence of Hollein's appreciation of historical context is displayed. The proposal to *inter*, literally to entomb the museum complex, now seems wholly plausible: the Salzburg skyline simply could not accept any further insertions. The advantages of this symbolic and dramatic entombment of the objects on display in subterranean gallery spaces are substantial.

The Sunk, showing main circulation

Given that constraints existed on new development in the historic city, to offer in this way a feasible alternative bestows major advantages. The insertion under such controlled conditions of computerised lighting, micro-climate, security and monitored access allows the total integration of open floor-space of very substantial volume with the topography, offering clearly identifiable links at street-level to the existing urban pattern.

Spatially here too, there is the opportunity to explore fundamental criteria; as Hollein puts it: 'No longer is there a difference between plan and section, space is free to develop into all directions'. He has constantly sought in his working life a means of establishing the architectural basis for a dialectic by man between, first, his need for ritual and, second, his more sobering need of a preserved body temperature, since ultimate survival is deemed to require both. In this dialectic, Hollein explores the range of possibilities that lie between the natural and the artificial, the amorphous and the geometric. 'In sculpting space' Hollein avers, 'I offer myself as an architect and a free artist."

At Salzburg, the exhibition spaces vary between the strictly cellular (as in the lower level catacombs), the linear, and curvilinear (upper levels).

There are other, broader points in common with Mönchengladbach: the spatial ordering there was achieved by carving away space from a clear volumetric matrix (demonstrated in a particular drawing where a cubic grid overlays the site). So the elements of the complex are fragmented in such a way that their individual tectonic autonomy is enhanced without any infrastructural reduction nor diminishing of the practical museum functions. This reductivism operates too at Salzburg—here the rock facilitates such a process. The strata are carved out and down. The Mönchsberg mountain yields to the process. The rock surface is mostly left exposed within this rotunda open to daylight. The visitor experiences this as a climax, and yet a transitional space within the overall ordering.

Visitors can choose a variety of routes, some shorter, others more extensive. The foyer, approached from street level, provides an interchange through which all parts can be reached. But a second access is also possible at the upper level from the Mönchsberg plateau, likely to be particularly popular in summer.

Throughout, the disposition of exhibition spaces is defined by whatever museological preoccupations exist at any particular time; determined of course

227

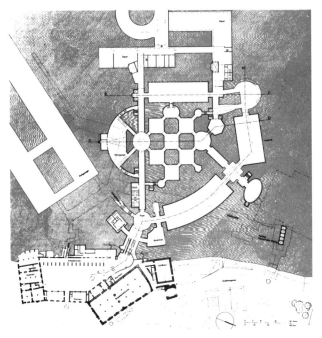

Lower level plan

by all the engineering requirements imposed by rock mechanics, as well as by routing and lighting factors. Conceivably there is an element of chance (as in sculpture) where the surface profile of the rock is most evidently to be displayed in the *Sunk* enhanced by the *chiaroscuro* of the rock strata via the daylight flooding through the domed rotunda.

At Salzburg, Hollein has proposed a museum which complements the historic core of the city upon which it literally abuts. Indeed the only immediate sign of anything as the visitor looks up the Getreidegasse at the Mönchsberg rock above the group of historical conversions to be effected below, will be (if Hollein has his way) the replacement of an asbestos-cement covered vertical water downpipe on the exterior of the rock by a golden metal sheath.

Hollein's negation of conventional structure by means of an atectonic solution, while continuing to offer the formal and appropriate arrangement of space provides a unique mechanism whereby curators can fulfil such challenges that arise over the presentation of objects (of art) whether individually, or in series. Distraction is kept to a minimum; presence (object impact) is maximised; discontinuity, where justifiable, occurs. Subconscious human reflexes to being underground are harnessed to advantage in optimising focus on objects and their timeless meaning. The whole is achieved reductively, via a minimisation of the conceptual framework of the museum and concentration upon the exhibits.

In 1996, the city of Salzburg will celebrate its millennial jubilee. Austria is being encouraged to celebrate the occasion by giving Salzburg a millennial birthday gift in the form of a timeless museum of art. This proposal would be nothing less than the appropriate architectural masterpiece. And for the Guggenheim Foundation, the spaces would make a superb corollary to their previous buildings, which would do full justice to the superb collection.

View over roof layout at upper ground level

Dissected axonometric of main spaces

A Sense of the Numinous

Peter Davey
July 1993

Galleries and museums cannot possibly take the place in our society of the temples of antiquity or medieval cathedrals as many have suggested. They are too exclusive, too cut off from daily life, the trouble with the Getty is that 'it is one thing to study and appreciate artefacts of the past, and quite another to fetishise them'. What the Getty does to some of the most sought-after works of art in the world happens to more mundane objects when they are wrenched from context and placed in even a small local museum.

Yet this process is almost inevitable, for the context of an artefact is temporal as well as spatial, and even were it possible to burn the museums and dissipate each item in the collections to where it came from, it would still not be resorted to its original authentic state because we can never recapture the time in which it was made, or see it through the eyes and with the values of its original makers and their public. Museums are necessarily artificial.

Ghirardo's argument is partly about location and the excessive honorific value that the Getty's geographical position and its approach give to the kind of art objects that it will contain. It is also about falsity of connoisseurship, that monstrous embrace between monetary and critical values which purports to access the merits of human artefacts.

Behnisch and Partners, Post Museum across river Main, Frankfurt 1993

Architecture can do something to counteract this ghastly prevailing attitude by reminding us of immemorial matters to oppose the values of the culture industry to Classical forms, as the proponents of PoMo or the officers of the Prince of Wales' own regiment of sycophants would want us to do.

I mean the loving care which Juan Navarro Baldeweg has used to show many moving aspects of light and water in his museum (for rather mundane objects) in Murcia; the delicacy with which the superb natural landscape of Nakagawa has been brought by Kiko Mozuna into juxtaposition with his highly artificial interior world; the way in which the great library of Alexandria will reflect on the Mediterranean and its cultures. Even poor Peter Eisenman, thrashing about among his clashing grids at the Wexner, is at least supposed to be indicating that reality may be a little deeper than the propositions offered by the mainstream commercial avantgarde works that the building houses.

In this context, it is not inappropriate to juxtapose such buildings for exhibition with the sequence of three churches by Lund & Slaatto, where light and space and form are used with great power and sensitivity to remind us of the glory of God's great creation.

None of these buildings would have been possible without Modernism. They all, as do the others shown in this issue show that Modernism is increasingly capable of capturing the numinous, as at exalted moments it has always been (Lewerentz at Klippan, Le Corbusier at Ronchamp).

231

The gallery will never replace the temple, but the buildings shown here indicate how the numinous can sometimes be brought into contact with the quotidian and how contemporary architects, through their art, can help counteract the prevailing tendency towards consumerism.

Peter Davey

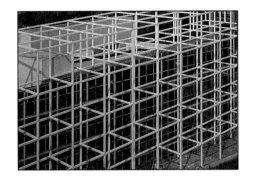

The Grid and the Grain

BUILDING CRITIQUE
Extension to university, Columbus
by Peter Eisenman

Diane Ghirado
March 1993

At a conference at the University of California, Irvine, in October 1989, Peter Eisenman firmly announced, 'Never believe what architects tell you about their work'. Despite this cautionary remark, Eisenman's *alter egos* and other students of his work have elaborated in considerable detail the design strategies which he adopted for the Wexner Center for the Ohio State University in Columbus, Ohio; the surveyor's grids for the state of Ohio, the city of Columbus, and the University; FAA flight paths into Columbus; and the University football stadium, among others. In perusing these indicators, I am reminded of a map published by the original *Domus* in 1933, which purported to chart examples of modern architecture in Rome. Concocted by the Milanese staff of *Domus*, the guide could only have frustrated the eager tourist, for they printed the city of Rome backwards. Such a misbegotten map reveals next to nothing about the subject, but a great deal about those who assembled it. So too with the plethora of grids Eisenman has laid out for the Wexner: it reveals much about its crafty cartographer, but gives only marginal information about the genesis of that building.

Eisenman has long employed a compositional strategy for which he is greatly indebted to Italian architect Giuseppe Terragni, in which cubes are rotated, pulled apart, gridded, transformed, and mathematical relationships are elaborated and calibrated in highly structured, regulated ways. Terragni too sited his Casa del Fascio with reference to Como's ancient Roman grid, but Eisenman's nimble manipulations of multifarious, highly abstracted grids are light years away from Terragni's elegantly straightforward ones.

After working with such tools for several house designs, Eisenman broke ground with the plane of the earth in House Eleven in a programme elaborated by Kurt Forster, now Director of the Getty Center in Santa Monica. Later, in the competitions for Cannaregio in Italy and the IBA in Berlin, again following cues from Forster, Eisenman excavated, in the case of Berlin, the various grids belonging to the city's complicated urban history for his own building. Most of Eisenman's subsequent projects have either fabricated or located grids of some sort to serve as the abstract field upon which to work out his compositional strategies; or, as Michael Graves wryly noted at the Wexner inaugural symposium, to play out the games which Eisenman invents and controls, with rules known only to him. As in that old con, the shell game, Eisenman directs attention to completely specious references while proceeding to manipulate the game at will.

Plan of Rome's modern buildings, with city plans reversed, *Domus* 1933

But the building does not depend upon the web of obfuscations spun around it, and quite unexpectedly, it is a fine building. Much credit goes to Richard Trott, Eisenman's partner, for the careful construction and high-quality detailing, work for which he is well known in Ohio, and which belies the standard complaints about the inevitability of shoddy workmanship. Eisenman knows he could not have chosen a better partner, for the team is also building the Columbus Convention Center and two other projects in the area.

Strength of Wexner

Resisting the temptation to produce a freestanding monument was both daring and wise, and is the source of much of the Wexner's strength. Most of the building consists of a threeblock slice between two older buildings, joining them and nearly doubling the floor area. It therefore appears deceptively small, even though it extends to three stories in places, and exceeds 100,000 sq ft of floor area. Most spaces are underground, which works well for the film theatre, studios, and gallery, but is not particularly felicitous for the fine arts library. Here natural light was sacrificed in order to preserve the integrity of the sandstone plinths for landscaping above—a questionable choice at best.

233

Diane Ghirado

Part basement level plan

234

The central arcade and passageway of scaffolding mark the central spine along which the various functions are deployed. Although a second axis complicates it, this straightforward scheme is deliberately blurred both within and without, for Eisenman/Trott defy conventional expectations at every turn, blocking vistas and introducing multiple complications such as dead ends and dangling columns. For example, they add perceptual puzzles with the shadows and reflections of the scaffolding on the translucent and tinted gridded curtain walls, not to mention locational puzzles for the visitor who struggles to tease order out of the complex spatial organisation. But it is not incomprehensible: diversity of spaces and materials ensures that one finally has enough clues to grasp and remember the building.

Having recognised the high quality of the Wexner project, three qualifications should be registered. The first concerns that element of the Wexner which stubbornly resists the artifice of the grids: the reconstructed armoury, the link between city and campus. These brick shells arose from the fabricated foundations of the old ROTC (Reserve Officers Training Center) and armoury building, a strange phenomenon to resurrect for any reason. Its forbidding, fortress-like brick towers explicitly resuscitate a highly problematical era in the life of American universities, when uniformed officer candidates marched about on the campuses and even carried arms. The original armoury dated from 1898 and, as in many other land-grant colleges, accommodated the National Guard, the state's strike force against its own citizens: striking workers in the nineteenth and twentieth centuries, civil rights marchers in the 1950s, antiwar demonstrators in the 1960s and 1970s. For Ohio, this building immediately summons memories of the slaughter of university students by the National Guard at Kent State University in Ohio in 1970.

American cities initiated massive armoury construction campaigns during the 1930s, when the fear of a revolution by the poor and unemployed prompted stern precautionary measures by frightened authorities. ROTC facilities became common in the 1950s during the McCarthy red-baiting and Communist hysteria, as symbols of government might, to be placed precisely where the far right has long believed that Communism and leftism are bred: the university. Government incursions into college campuses, covert operations to ferret out dangerous sorts who did things like supporting low-income public housing in the 1950s and opposing the war in Vietnam in the 1960s and 1970s, were conducted from offices that became local beach-heads of state authority, ROTC offices on university campuses. This is not, then, an innocent gesture.

History Repressed

The exhumation of this troubling symbol brings me to my second qualification. Much is made, in Derridean deconstruction and in Eisenman's version of it, of uncovering the hidden, of revealing the repressed, hence the conflation of multiple grids in the Wexner and of course, the armoury. The site's real political history is here repressed in favour of a decorative shell, perhaps the most compelling and powerful feature of the whole project. With its delicate craftsmanship and playful slices of tower, arch, and wall, in its Disneylandish caricature of the earlier structure, it effectively realises the gloomy prognosis of Walter Benjamin about the aestheticisation of politics. The fetishised structures are wittingly emptied of their history and rendered nothing more than cheerfully manipulable images which direct attention only to formal games. As Benjamin noted, such architecture, whatever other claims are made for it, serves as nothing more than elegant distraction.

Diane Ghirado

Gallery space and opening off ramp

Eisenman has used the theory of Derrida on deconstruction much as he now appears to be using Gianni Vattimo's 'weak thought' to legitimise the endless formal games with an intellectual gloss, and to foil criticism. When all reality is only textuality, when everything is a free play of signifiers, and when the architect's agenda consists of revealing the repressed, undermining, disclosing, summoning forth the fragmentation and alienation of today's society, all possible criticism is swallowed up in a black hole. Like total dogmatism, total relativism renders any discussion impossible. It is also a strait-jacket for the architecture itself, which leads on to the third point.

In more recent projects, such as at Carnegie Mellon, Eisenman has liberated the grid from its Cartesian limbo and adopted formal motifs clearly derived from Aldo Rossi. It is instructive to place the Wexner against the work of the two architects to whom Eisenman owes most, Giuseppe Terragni and Aldo Rossi. Perhaps it is unfair to measure the Wexner against their work, but the degree of hyperbole surrounding its inauguration demands some such comparison. The symposium – orchestrated by Eisenman himself – was a thinly disguised tribute to Eisenman, while the *potpourri* of *avant-garde* art which the Wexner claims to shelter turns out to be the product of mainstream glitterati whose work would never be subjected to *de facto* or *ex-post facto* censorship because their art is so profoundly inoffensive.

Terragni indeed struggled with grids, cubes, and transformations, but those manipulations neither remain concealed nor are overwhelmingly present in the built work; they are discovered rather than forced upon the viewer. In a project such as the Casa del Fascio in Como, these formal moves share centre stage with sensitively handled transparent, opaque, translucent, and reflective surfaces playing off one another, and with infusions of multiple light qualities—all of which are impossible to photograph or grasp in one

Section through ramped corridor looking west

image. Each material is handled with great subtlety, and the building is finally open-ended in its many possibilities. By contrast, the Wexner is flat and very nearly two-dimensional; its grids impose upon one another and at times verge on cacophony. It seems that this is Eisenman's intention, and, in line with suggestions from Vattimo, he seeks a 'weak image' which cannot be photographed or grasped in one view. In fact, the Casa del Fascio is far more elusive, far more difficult to capture on film, even if its exterior elevations apparently lend themselves to the 'strong image' which Eisenman now opposes. And surprisingly, although Eisenman's theories would appear to offer uncommon possibilities for rich spatial invention, he has not exploited them here.

Eisenman X-Ray

The gridded passageway also does not measure up to similar passageways in Aldo Rossi's work. In the arcades at the Gallaretese, the Broni school, and the Modena cemetery, Rossi also relied upon repetitive elements along one, two, or three sides of a passageway, but because of the materials and the dimensions and spacing of the elements, they extend with a measured, almost timeless dignity, an elegant and majestic backdrop to the promenade. Contrast this with Eisenman's scaffolding, which drives through the site with the relentless monotony of a picket fence. Without the roofs, parapets, or even vines of Rossi's arcades, the Wexner grid offers no prospect of transformation by different angles or degrees of light, no visual variety or delight. It is as if his vision is that of the x-ray, which registers only skeleton and the faintest trace of muscle, tissue, and flesh.

The difference between the Wexner and works by Terragni and Rossi lies in the absolutely controlled, if apparently arbitrary, surprises that the Wexner offers, which skirt dangerously close to one-liners. The other two architects do not rely upon such complicated artifice to entice the viewer, but allow their buildings to yield up their treasures, many of which are unanticipated, slowly and over time. With his highly diagrammatic structures (some interiors seem not unlike a dentist's waiting room), Eisenman apparently deliberately seeks out the 'depthlessness' which some commentators believe is characteristic of PostModernism.

Unfortunately, he has succeeded. But he has failed in another objective: he claims to advocate an alienating architecture, but this building is profoundly ingratiating, and has been warmly received by a wide range of precisely those people Eisenman sees as complacent and deceived by contemporary consumer culture. The fact that it is still a fine building is testimony to the resilience of materials and construction to the artifice of theory.

North-east view of the Wexner Centre slicing between two existing buildings

Diane Ghirado

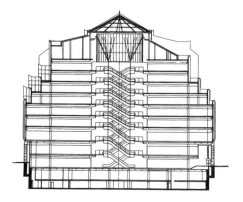

Suspended Animation

BUILDING CRITIQUE
Escalator System
by YRM Architects

Penny Mcguire
November 1993

Within 3 Minster Court, the Gothic horror that was designed by GMW and fashioned by the cold hand of corporate finance to loom over the City of London, a YRM team had installed what is claimed to be the world's tallest assembly of escalators. The building was originally intended as offices for the Prudential. In 1989, YRM was appointed as architects, structural engineers and interior designers for fitting-out the building. In August 1991, the place caught fire, and was subsequently stripped out. The new scheme was made to the requirements of the London Underwriting Centre.

The building had originally been designed as open-plan offices for dealers on three lower floors, with the remaining floors for normal office use. In contrast, the London Underwriting Centre had to be able to accommodate up to 90 companies with as many as 1500 underwriters occupying the building and up to another 1500 brokers visiting them at any one time. The existing provision for circulation and access was inadequate.

YRM decided to enlarge the main entrance to the building, nearly doubling its size and extending the existing atrium. This, intended to be the exhilarating heart of the City centre, has a bank of 16 escalators stacked in scissor formation across its centre. The escalators carry traffic between floors, leaving existing lifts in the cross to deal with longer journeys.

The escalators, with glass bridges leading to and from the surrounding galleries, are suspended on a structure of four vertical steel rods. The entire structure, which weighs 152 tons, is hung from four clusters of six steel rods connected to a meter-high ring beam around the top of the atrium. This welded plate girder is supported by 12 pairs of steel columns, added around the circumference of the atrium as part of the fit-out.

The glass bridges of the escalators, which are cantilevered from floor slabs, would normally take no vertical load from the structure of the escalator. But they are designed to support the vertical load of an escalator in the event of failure of any of the steel rods from which it is suspended.

Escalators are immaculately detailed; with an aluminium-clad steel casing, acid-etched glass side panels and frosted glass on the bridges, lit from beneath. The Thyssen mechanism is known for its quiet performance and the atrium itself is acoustically damped with perforated steel cladding panels at high level, backed with mineral wool quilting. There is a mixture of daylight from the glazed atrium roof and artificial lighting from within the skylight, and from spot lights mounted on the galleries at each level.

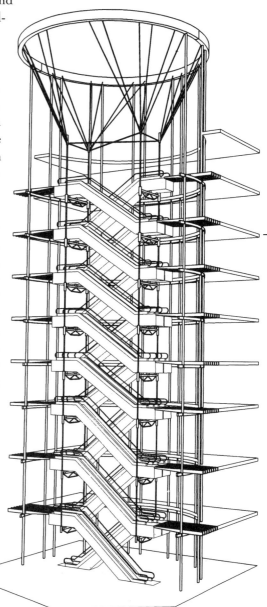

Axonometric of tower and bridges

Suburbs

240

THEORY

Peter Davey
July 1992

One of the troubles with suburbs is that they are so popular, much to the chagrin of all properly minded critics. For all the millions of words spilled by commentators as diverse as the Prince of Wales and ourselves in favour of the virtues of communal life offered by the pattern of the Great European City, very large numbers of people want to move out of the centre of town as soon as they can afford to do so. While we rave about the beauties of Siena or Seville, they want a house with a garden where they can bring up the kids with dignity and a degree of privacy that life in tenement or tower block simply cannot provide. Hence the huge explosion of suburbia round the city centres that we adore: the sprawl of haphazard development that surrounds almost everywhere but Venice, which for topographic reasons has to separate suburbs from its ancient heart.

Yet the problems that beset suburbanites are very great. Suburbs deconstruct life. If you live in California or New South Wales, you may have a third of an acre, but you have to travel at least half an hour to work, as much again in a different direction to get to the shopping mall, or to the baseball or cricket pitch. Leisure, consumption, production and dwelling are totally divorced. There is none of that haphazard conjunction of different parts of existence that living in cities offers: the casual meeting in the street, the fizz, the overlap of work and the things we do when we are not working into a creative continuum from which

Richard Norman Shaw, Bedford Park, London (photographed in 1881)

civilisation itself has emerged. In mediaeval times it was said that 'city air makes men free'. It still can. Then the contrast was between citizenship and serfdom. Now, it is between urban variety and the often highly restrictive set of values which is more or less imposed by social and environmental pressures when you buy a house in the suburbs. (Though since the emergence of the urban under-class as part of the Industrial Revolution, the city does not offer many of its inhabitants the freedoms that its upper-middle class and Royal protagonists extol so lovingly, and for many, suburban living, with all its drawbacks, is a better deal than a rundown inner urban housing estate).

How Green?

For all their trees and lawns, suburbs are not particularly green. Though suburban living as we now understand it was first made possible by the out reaching tentacles of London's railway system between 1850 and 1930, this relatively ecologically economical means of transport was replaced in the cities of the New Worlds by the automobile, even to the extent of making the rail lines into freeways. So the great suburbs are to a very large extent made possible by a hugely polluting and selfish transport system. City centres have been wrecked to make commuter parking space, and countryside is eaten up by motorways. No wonder that the inhabitants of the suburban democracies use such a disproportionate amount of the world's resources.

241

In the last two or three decades, a new phenomenon has emerged which makes suburban living even less green. As companies have located workplaces outside cities to escape urban decay and high local taxes, or to find cheap land on which to develop, more and more people are compelled to make circumferential journeys from one suburb to another, rather than the radial ones which were traditional since the creation of railways. These circumferential journeys are usually greater in distance than radial ones, and must almost always be made by car (or by double rail journeys, because circumferential public transport either does not exist, or is very inefficient). For most, the only way of avoiding excessive travel in these circumstances is to move house, which is wasteful of resources and disruptive of family and communal life. And, like an old tree, the core of the organism rots while the ruin retains a semblance of life.

The Case

But however wasteful and disruptive suburbs may be, at their best, they have had nobility. In their earliest appearance outside mediaeval cities, they offered a healthy way of life compared to insanitary conditions within the walls. The nineteenth century explosion of suburbs was driven by a similar desire to escape from unpleasant urban conditions—the very people whose capital funded industrialisation were the first to use their dividends to avail themselves of the opportunity of escaping from its malign and polluting effects. Early Picturesque derived experiments in the 1840s and '50s evolved such enduring types as the tree-lined domestic street, the front garden and the semi-detached house. They were large-ly created (as suburbs almost always have been) by almost unknown developers.

But architects and planners have had a powerful influence. Norman Shaw's work for Jonathan Carr at Bedford Park in west London between 1875 and 1880 set a pattern for suburban building that has lasted to this day. The ver-nacular derived houses laid out on irregular streets surrounded by lawns, flow-ers and trees is repeated all over the world. It certainly inspired the expression of turn-of-the-century experiments by people like Parker and Unwin at Letchworth and Hampstead Garden Suburb which were intended to bring the benefits of suburban living to the industrial poor. Unwin's geometrical analyses attempted to demonstrate how economies could be made by developing suburbs as rectangles defined by semi-detached houses with private gardens front and back, and com-munal facilities in the middle of each block, rather than as strips of terrace hous-ing with gardens only at the back. (The savings were in the reduced costs of road and infrastructure development.) [1] As Mervyn Miller has shown,[2] Unwin's rea-soning was fallacious, but the pattern he suggested was immensely powerful between the Wars in Britain and in the US where Clarence Stein developed the Radburn Plan, which Lewis Mumford called 'the first major departure in city planning since Venice'.[3]

242

Radburn, with its block perimeters penetrated by *culs-de-sac*, and separat-ed traffic and pedestrian systems (which linked the communal centres of the blocks) was specifically designed to cope with the motor car in the most humane possible way. It failed because of the Depression,[4] but it helped to inspire some of the most decent post-war planning, in contrast to the high-density blocks set in parkland which came from the thinking of Le Corbusier and *Charte d'Athènes*, where even the problem of parking was ignored. The disastrous results of these Continental theories can be seen in the rings of '60s concrete *banlieues* round all French cities.

The last innovative instance of Radburn-inspired development in Britain was the evolution of perimeter planning in the late '70s with corrugated walls of terraced housing round large open spaces that contained communal facilities.[5] Since the collapse of the new public housing programme in the '80s, suburban development in Britain, as elsewhere in Europe, has been left to the private mar-ket. This, with the fall in agricultural land prices in developed countries caused by overproductive (and fundamentally ecologically unsound) forms of cultiva-tion, has led to yet more sprawling development, overextended infrastructure, and waste.

In the developed world, if land cannot be used for agriculture, there should be a general supposition that it ought to be turned into forest, in an attempt, however small, to counterbalance the horrendous destructions of the last few decades. More compact suburbs are desperately needed for the sake of the planet and human sanity. And so is a means of knitting together the essential suburban activity-dwelling with other aspects of human existence. Legislation is needed, but workable alternative suburban models must be invented before it can be enacted.

It must be admitted that even the most heroic experiments were partial failures. The town centre of Letchworth was never built because of the First World War; Hampstead's communal facilities were puritanically primitive; Radburn came to grief in the '30s before it could develop into a community. The post-war English New Towns, descendants of the Garden City ideal, were so divided up by well-meaning strips of greenery that they have become breeding grounds of boredom.

The Hope

Leon Krier's attempt to make a suburb of Dorchester for the Prince of Wales[6] is a much vaunted attempt to invest new development in the countryside with civilised qualities. It may well fail because it does not come to terms with the car, and by creating a relatively large number of local centres which have picturesque rather than social or economic functions.

Other models which might be more fruitful are the best business parks like Stockley,[7] where work, leisure, transport and parking are woven together with and by nature. If housing could be incorporated into the mix, and perhaps some of the perimeter planning theory of the '70s, ecologically and humanly rewarding settlements might begin to emerge. Or some of the Danish and Dutch communal housing experiments[8] might be tried on a larger scale. Or we could start to look again at some of the best achievements of the '60s and '70s in developing low rise high-density housing—Atelier 5's Siedlung Halen in Berne, for instance, which has scarcely been bettered in more than 30 years. And we have to re-think workplace and leisure in relation to suburban living, evolving local centres like The Ark, by Ralph Erskine, that can combine them both.

In a free society, anyone who wants should be able to cultivate his own garden literally and metaphorically. But, to allow this, invention in both planning and architecture are desperately needed.

1 The key argument is in Raymond Unwin, *Nothing Gained by Overcrowding. How the Garden City Type of Development may Benefit both the Owner and Occupier*. Garden Cities and Town Planning Association, London 1912.

2 Mervyn Miller, *Raymond Unwin: Garden Cities and Town Planning*. Leicester University Press, Leicester 1992, pp126–138.

3 Lewis Mumford, *The City in History*, Secker & Warburg, London 1961.

4 See Clarence S. Stein, *New Towns for America*, New York 1961.

5 *AR* April 1980, pp205–214.

6 *AR* August 1989, pp4–9.

7 *AR* September 1989, pp42–48.

8 *AR* April 1985, pp62–71.

Peter Davey

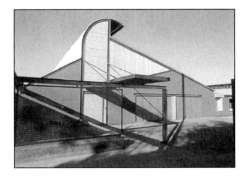

South African Sensibility

BUILDING CRITIQUE
Educational and Community Centres
by Jo Noero

Catherine Slessor
July 1994

More than 15 years have passed since work from South Africa was published in the AR. Now that a form of political consensus has been achieved, it seems appropriate to include some examples of current South African architecture in this issue devoted to building in hot dry climates. This is a very modest and understandably tentative first step; we hope to explore the country more thoroughly next year. Here we present two schemes by Jo Noero, awarded the 1993 Erskine Scholarship for the projects shown here. Compared with the fashionable excesses of much current American and European architecture, the strong, socially minded work of Noero brings us back to our senses. His approach combines placemaking and purpose in an enlightened response to climate, context and technology. Above all, buildings must engage the enthusiasm and creativity of their occupants—in many cases those at the bottom of South Africa's monstrously skewed social system, the marginalised and dispossessed township populations. Noero's pragmatic, yet refined functionalism is a timely reminder of the power of architecture to heal division and improve the lot of humankind—qualities that will be greatly in demand during the coming years, as South Africa

Curving corrugated metal roofs of the Soweto Centre

struggles to transform itself into a multi-racial democracy, with equality and prosperity for all its citizens.

Soweto Careers Centre

The Centre was established in 1978 as a response to the crisis in education precipitated by the 1976 student uprisings in Soweto, the sprawling black township on the edge of Johannesburg. Since its inception, the Centre's basic aim has been to provide professional career guidance to school

The simple construction methods resemble those of squatter camps

Main community hall

leavers, but its remit has gradually expanded to encompass other, related, community needs. By the early '90s it had become clear that the existing accommodation could no longer house the Centre's continuing diversification of activities, so an alternative strategy was sought. The existing complex consisted of a prefabricated asbestos cement component system, arranged in a plan symbolically resembling a spent lightning bolt. In view of the scarcity of resources it was decided to retain the original buildings, which formed a framework for a series of new additions. The client body was opposed to any form of gratuitous, paternalistic reference to black culture and required that the form of the new complex should be free of any obvious cultural association. As a result, the form of new building is a direct consequence of addressing such basic determinants as space, climate, materials and structure.

245

The site adjoins the main road which passes through Soweto, nestling into the dry, dusty, plastic-strewn veld near a busy local hospital. While identifying the need to impart some kind of civic presence, it was also recognised that environmental problems of pollution and noise should be minimised. To this end, a valley section set at an oblique angle to the road was developed. The valley section was derived from the decision to scoop light and air through curving, funnel-like rooflights down into the hall and classrooms below, so helping to acoustically insulate the spaces and creating some sense of interior drama.

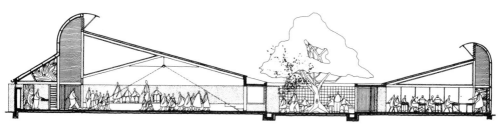

Cross-section through the main hall and classrooms

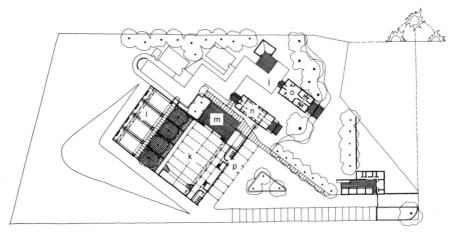

Ground floor plan (approx. 1:1500)

The new additions dock into the old zig-zag plan at strategic points. The hierarchy of volumes is dominated by a large rectangular hall that can be used for local functions such as wedding receptions. One wall slides away to connect with an internal courtyard, revealing glimpses of the veld beyond through the courtyard's open grille block wall. In a setting where resources are so limited, spaces must be capable of adapting to a range of uses. Hence the computer centre, which was principally intended to encourage computer literacy among students by enabling them to access career guidance, is also used during the evening by a business consultant to train local people in how to use computers and enhance their prospects. Similarly, the classrooms are lined with study carrels which are leased to mature and other students for use in the evening.

Noero's abstraction of form and materials into a culturally neutral yet architecturally engaging functionalism, is reminiscent of Glenn Murcutt's tectonic experiments in similar climes. The technology is deliberately simple, owing much to the ad-hoc component construction of squatter camps, with infill panels of plywood and glass slotted into standard steel window frames. Undulating corrugated metal roofs and flashes of raw colour provide welcome visual texture and help to distinguish the new building amid the harsh surroundings. Internally, teaching spaces are intended to transcend the notion of conventional classrooms, since they are used as forums to discuss issues which impinge upon shifting the consciousness of disaffected Sowetan youths from apathy and anger to hope. Individual teaching spaces are designed to alter the students' perception of the iniquitous educational system by convincing them

Duduza's linear street

that they are not simply attending classes, but rather being inducted into a new understanding of how to take control of their lives. To this end, classrooms are brightly and optimistically coloured, with natural light scooped from above and

246

reflected into the classroom, creating a back-drop for the course leader. The sense that Noero has responded aptly and imaginatively to the context of place, social life and resources is confirmed by the reaction of the building's users, who have responded enthusiastically to the new facilities in their midst.

Duduza's community hall and internal courtyard

Duduza Resource Centre

Like the Soweto Careers Centre, the new Resource Centre in the township of Duduza has a dual educational and community function. The initiative behind the new building came from a group of local community members who managed to enlist the support of industrialists in the adjoining district of Nigel. The original aim was to provide accommodation for a series of informal education projects initiated in response to the crisis in black education. When it was realised that any constructive political change would eventually make this kind of piecemeal system redundant, the Centre was designed to encompass a variety of uses and be capable of future adaptation as a community college.

The Centre is accessible to all members of the 45,000 strong community 24 hours a day. The facilities are arranged on a linear circulation spine, intended to replicate the scale and ambience of a street, but the adjoining glass-fronted 'shops' house various community projects and teaching spaces. Covered seating, out of the sun's glare, is provided for those waiting for assistance. Responses to climate are also expressed in other ways—shadow casting integrated grilles and pergolas articulate the main access-way and covered walkways defining routes lend further shade. As at Soweto, the walls of the classrooms are lined with study carrels for evening use. For a nominal sum, individuals can rent a workspace, locker and a light (for the majority, there is no proper electricity supply, which makes evening home study impossible).

247

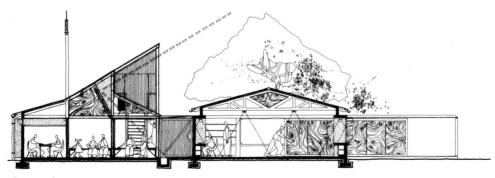

Cross-section

Half-way along the main spine, the intimate rhythm of the street gives way to an open courtyard, defined on one side by a two storey administration building which acts as the civic heart and spatial focus of the scheme. It also provides an anchor for future expansion.

With the exception of this great focal hall, the buildings that make up the Centre are generally single storey, spreading across the site forming a succession of courtyards, the smaller of which are used for semi-public gatherings. Landscaping completes and the integrates the new civic microcosm with the wider world, as do the facilities located along the community edge of the complex, such as an informal market, and bus and taxi ranks. In some ways, although created in Third World circumstances, the Centre is a pertinent example of Richard MacCormac's First World notion of local, as opposed to foreign transactions (AR March 1994). In MacCormac's hypothesis of urban development and renewal, buildings act as a framework for diverse activities, or transactions, appropriate to the community they serve. Like a coral reef, the building stock is continually re-colonised over time. Similarly, in Duduza, the basis of a framework has been established, but with the necessary potential to be adapted and altered as required. The luxury of demolishing a building deemed to have outlived its usefulness and starting from scratch, is currently not a viable option in South African townships. Resources must be conserved, although as the political and economic balance shifts, such attitudes may eventually change. For the present, the Centre continues to impart a sense of dignity and delight to community affairs and it was for both this building and the Soweto Community Centre that Jo Noero was awarded the 1993 Erskine Scholarship.

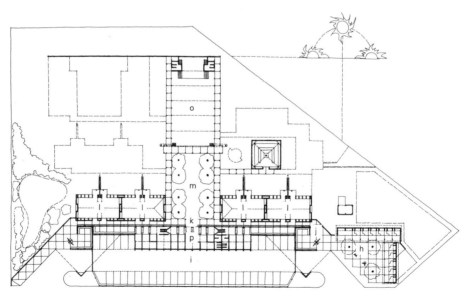

Ground floor plan (approx. 1:1000)

Big Blue

BUILDING CRITIQUE
Regional Government headquarters, Marseilles
by William Alsop

Colin Davies

December 1994

Will Alsop likes to make out that his design method is completely irrational; that the strange forms of his buildings, all those cigar-shaped objects on legs, arise directly from his imagination rather than from the problems posed by brief, site and available technology. This is true, up to point. His first instinct when starting work on a project is not to set about collecting and analysing data but to paint a painting, or a sketchbook full of paintings. The paintings are then translated into buildable form and adapted to accommodate the brief. The method is radically subjective. Alsop paints what pleases him on the principle that if at least one person is satisfied there is a chance that others will be too. There is no attempt to derive form from function in the time-honoured Modernist manner, no appeal to an imagined objective realm in order to justify design decisions.

For Alsop, the idea that architectural form can arise naturally from the solving of practical problems is a myth. Architects conspire to keep the myth alive by a series of elaborate post-rationalisations, but they know in their hearts that the basis of creativity is ultimately irrational. Alsop simply ignores the myth and accepts the reality.

The method has now been put to the test in a really big building for the first time. The Hôtel du Département in Marseilles is the headquarters of the local authority for the area—Bouches du Rhône. Occupying a site to the north of the city centre, next to an elevated motorway junction and served by a *metro* station, the building is a startling presence in an otherwise shabby and characterless district. Two features scream for attention. First, its colour a deep, vibrant ultramarine like a distilled concentrate of the Mediterranean sky. Second, its shape, or at least one of its shapes—a long, thin, curved and tapered object, not so much a cigar as a half eaten fish, lifted above the parapet of the motorway on seven splayed pairs of legs. This shape obviously doesn't have much to do with traditional upright, rectilinear architecture. It is a pure sculptural invention.

Or is it? The separation of this object from the rest of the building is actually justified in straightforward functional terms. The object has a name – the *Délibératif* – which denotes not its shape or its colour or its resemblance to any other object but simply its intended use. A basic analysis of the brief has already taken place. Two main functional categories have been identified: political and administrative. The *Délibératif* accommodates the political functions – two council chambers, a function room and a club – while administrative functions are housed in the rest of the building, known, appropriately enough, as the *Administratif*.

Atrium looking south

This has a much more conventional form—two parallel, upright, rectilinear office blocks on either side of a big top-lit atrium.

One other main formal element completes the ensemble, an object like a squashed Swiss roll with an outer crust of profiled metal, hovering over the taller of the two office blocks. Once again the separation of this form is justified in functional, or at least territorial terms: it houses the offices reserved for the politicians and an apartment for the president of the council.

Despite all the apparent irrationality then, at a strategic level the building actually articulates its functions in a fairly straightforward manner. There is also a time dimension to this functional analysis. The *Délibératif* is intended to be a permanent setting for the political functions of the building, assembling, debating and making decisions—whereas the *Administratif* is conceived as functionally flexible and changeable. The *Administratif* is basically just an office building, after all, and there is no guarantee that the decision to centralise the administration of Bouches du Rhône which is the *raison d'être* of the building, will not be reversed at some time in the not too distant future.

But there seems to be a contradiction here. If the *Délibératif* is intended to be permanent, one would expect the form to be tailor-made to fit the function. In fact the fit is very loose. The main interior spaces were not even designed by Alsop himself but by Andrée Putman (the Council chambers) and Charles Bové (the Members' club). Putman's interiors especially seem determined to ignore the shape of the object they inhabit, hiding the wrap around section behind flat suspended ceilings and stepped auditorium floors. Conversely there is nothing about the fish-on-a-plate external form that gives any clue to the nature of the spaces within. The clear implication is that the interiors might one day be ripped out and replaced and that the function of the building might easily change.

But this is a rational, Modernist way of thinking and it simply doesn't interest Alsop. For him the precise relationship between form and function is irrelevant, provided the form does not impede the function. The *Délibératif* is not meant to display or symbolise its function by referring to a conventional repertoire of forms. Rather it is the very strangeness of the form, its weird animal quality, that is important, marking the site as a special place like a tribal totem.

251

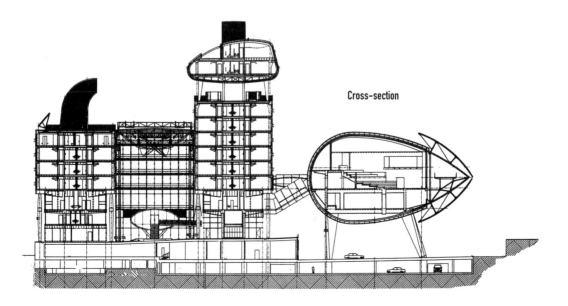

Cross-section

Appropriately, the cladding of the *Délibératif* is a scaly skin of triangular colour-coated steel panels, though its full extent is only visible from the upper floors of the adjoining office block. On the side facing the motorway, the skin has been peeled back to reveal the curved ribs of the tubular steel structure supporting open walkways and fire escape staircases. Another kind of skin, in the form of a stretched fabric awning, shades the walkways and reduces solar heat gain in the debating chambers. Viewed from this side, the character of the *Délibératif* is ambiguous, the animal image giving way to an industrial quality that might almost be described as High-Tech. The difference is that no card-carrying High-Tech architect would ever propose such an irrational structure. Structural ratio-

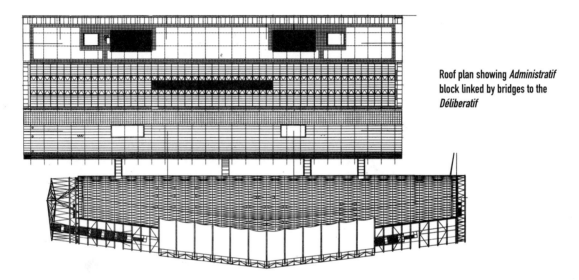

Roof plan showing *Administratif* block linked by bridges to the *Déliberatif*

nality is of no more interest to Alsop than functional rationality. What appears to be a single, integrated steel structure is actually made up of several components, separately attached to a massive concrete platform. This is a shape that has been made to work structurally, not the logical expression of an engineering solution.

The image of a tribal gathering place marked by an animal totem may seem inappropriate for a piece of no man's land by a motorway in a big city, but the building is intended to change all that. Apart from the motorway, there is not much in the way of built context for it to respond to. Confident of its status as an important public institution, it is free to dictate its own terms. This may not have been a special place before, but it is now. Already there are signs of a revival of commercial activity in the area, and the city (as opposed to the regional) government has reinforced the importance of the site by building a domed concert hall for Rock music next door.

Conventional responses to built context are as irrelevant to Alsop's method as conventional expressions of function and structure. The buildings around the site are much less important to him than the larger context of land, sea, sky and,

The 'médiathèque' in the atrium

especially, climate. But once again the apparently irrational forms of the building turn out to be at least partly justifiable in functional terms.

Wind is to Marseilles what rain is to London. The typical citizen of Marseilles is acutely aware of the direction of the wind – the cold Mistral from the north or the hot, humid Sirocco from the south – and its likely effect on his or her physical and psychological well-being. Alsop therefore makes some attempt to justify the design in aerodynamic terms. The justification is not very convincing, however. If the basic forms were generated by wind tunnel tests, why was it necessary to bolt on a variety of baffles and deflectors? In any case the analysis seems to contradict Alsop's basic principle of irrationality. Isn't this precisely the kind of post-rationalisation that he seeks to undermine? To be fair, it seems that the climate-modifying features of the original competition-winning design have been watered down as the scheme has developed through about 17 different versions. The changes have been radical. In the original design there were three parallel office blocks, the *Délibératif* was enclosed in its own atrium and there were sophisticated proposals for passive heating and cooling elegant, painterly V and X-shaped *pilotis*, the latter extending over two floors, conform to a regular rhythm and have clear conventional precedents in the Modernist tradition.

Stained glass artist Brian Clarke has been let loose on the vast blue expanse of the building's main façade, but his freehand stripes and scrawls are so subtly contrasted that they look more like protective tape left over by the cladding sub-contractor. Somewhere along the development process, Alsop's design for this part of the building seems to have been straightened out and lamed.

Not that the final result is disappointing. On the contrary, the arrangement is eminently legible and easy to use, with the bridges marking the position of the lifts and the escalator link to the *Délibératif* placed right in the middle of the space. The forms and spaces are well proportioned on the basis of the golden section, Alsop's favourite. The detailing of the textured glass walls is simple and refined, and the daylight that floods the atrium is pleasantly diffused, without any uncomfortable glare. It all works beautifully, but it is not much like an Alsop painting.

Bridges and escalators link the *Administratif* block to the *Déliberatif*

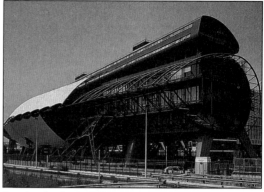

East view showing the *Déliberatif*

Surprisingly, the architect has no regrets about the compromises that have been made. He is not, he says, unduly protective of his concepts and he accepts that the design of a big building is a collaborative effort. His first design proposals are, he says, merely 'a platform for a conversation'. Generally, the client has been supportive and has only said no to those features of the design that might have pushed it over the boundary between the bizarre and the absurd. The proposal to attach an aviary to the south end of the *Délibératif* was one such feature, though, as Alsop says, if he had called it a garden or a terrace rather than an aviary he might have got away with it.

Architecture and politics are always closely allied in France. The building was always meant to be a landmark and a symbol, a symbol of openness and democracy but also of the power and importance of the regional government. Public reaction has generally been positive. 'Bravo' was the headline in one of the local papers. Alsop reckons that if the clients have one regret, it is not that they have been made a laughing stock, but that in the end the building has turned out too safe.